THE CHILD AND THE STATE IN INDIA

Frontispiece. Madiga, age 12, bonded laborer in a village near Hyderabad

THE CHILD AND THE STATE IN INDIA

CHILD LABOR AND EDUCATION POLICY IN COMPARATIVE PERSPECTIVE

Myron Weiner

PRINCETON UNIVERSITY PRESS   PRINCETON, NEW JERSEY

Copyright © 1991 by Princeton University Press
Published by Princeton University Press, 41 William Street,
Princeton, New Jersey 08540
In the United Kingdom: Princeton University Press, Oxford
All Rights Reserved

Library of Congress Cataloging-in-Publication Data
Weiner, Myron.
The child and the state in India : child labor and education policy in
comparative perspective / Myron Weiner.
p.   cm.
Includes index.
ISBN 0-691-07868-8 (cl. : acid-free paper) — ISBN 0-691-01898-7
(pbk. : acid-free paper)
1. Children—Employment—Government policy—India. 2. Children—
Employment—Government policy. 3. Education, Compulsory—India.
4. Education, Compulsory. I. Title.
HD6250.I42W45   1991
331.3′4′0954—dc20   90-37869   CIP

This book has been composed in Linotron Caledonia

Princeton University Press books are printed
on acid-free paper, and meet the guidelines
for permanence and durability of the Committee
on Production Guidelines for Book Longevity
of the Council on Library Resources

Printed in the United States of America by
Princeton University Press, Princeton, New Jersey

10 9 8 7 6 5 4 3 2 1

(Pbk.)
10 9 8 7 6 5 4 3 2 1

To Miriam and Chana

Contents

Tables _____

Preface

WITHOUT financial support from the Smithsonian Institution and the Ford Foundation in New Delhi this study would not have been possible. I am most grateful to them.

My grateful thanks also to those who read and commented on an earlier draft of this manuscript: Rukhun Advani, Ajit Bhattacharjea, Neera Burra, S. N. Eisenstadt, Meena Gupta, Ronald Herring, Ramesh Kanbargi, Atul Kohli, Dharma Kumar, R. Sudarshan, Michael Tharakan, Lucian W. Pye, Saul J. Weiner, Sheila L. Weiner, and Martha Zuber.

I also wish to acknowledge the assistance of Smitu Kothari, Usha S. Naidu, C. A. Perumal, Prayag Mehta, John Kurrien, Chitra Naik, P. Lakshmanan, Girija Eswaran, Nasir Tyabji, Kartikeya Sarabhai, T. S. Papola, Susan Shirk, P. M. Shah, William Cousins, Assefa Bequele, K. Satyanaryana, Swarna Jayaweera, C. R. de Silva, P. R. Gopinathan Nair, Devaki Jain, Pai Panandikar, Chanchal Sarkar, Pran Chopra, G. V. Mohan, Suma Chitnis, Bhabani Sen Gupta, Lincoln Chen, Harbans Singh, Paul Chowdhuri, Andrea Menefee Singh, B. G. Deshmukh, Ela Bhatt, Jayshree Mehta, S. M. Mukherjee, Ram Joshi, V. G. Kulkarni, C. T. Kurien, G.V.K. Rao, Bidyut Sarkar, Lakshmi Jain, K. G. Rastogi, B. B. Patel, V. K. Kulkarni, Leela Gulati, Pushpati John, J. N. Rao, A. Padmanaban, Surajit Sinha, K. N. George, Michael Hsiao, S. Ramanathan, James Melchior, Anand Swarup, Anil Bordia, Sunand Bhattacharjee, Tom Kessinger, Nathan Glazer, Robert Levine, Mrinal Datta-Chaudhuri, Lois Malone, and Beth Datskovsky. I am also indebted to numerous Indian government officials in the state and central ministries of education and labor and to many social activists, educators, trade unionists, and employers who consented to be interviewed.

For research assistance I thank Richard Deeg, Jennifer Nupp, Richard Locke, Narendra Subramanian, and Ketaki Bhagwati.

Numerous institutions permitted me to use their library, make use of their records, and in other ways facilitate my research. These include the International Labor Organization in Geneva and UNESCO in Paris, which provided me with materials for the comparative portions of this study. I also benefited from materials and assistance provided by the International Commission of Jurists (Geneva), the World Health Organization (Geneva), UNICEF (New York), the Indian Institute of Education (Pune), Defense of Children International (Geneva), the United Nations Center of Human Rights (Geneva), the Indian Ministry of Labour and Ministry of Education (New Delhi), the Tata Institute of Social Sciences (Bombay), the Ford Foundation, the National Institute of Public Cooperation and Child Development (New Delhi), the Ministry of Small Scale and Cottage Industries (New Delhi), the International Labor Organization (New Delhi), the Mahatma Gandhi Labour Institute (Ahmedabad), the Nehru Foundation for Development (Ahmedabad), the Sardar Patel Institute (Ahmedabad), the Indian Institute of Management (Ahmedabad), the National Council of Educational Research and Training (New Delhi), the Indian Council of Social Science Research (New Delhi), the Homi Bhabha Science Education Center (Bombay), the Nana Chowk Municipal School (Bombay), the Ahmedabad Science Center, CHETNA (Ahmedabad), the Center for Development Studies (Madras), the Madras Institute of Development Studies, the Madras Institute of Management, the Administrative Staff College (Hyderabad), the Institute for Social and Economic Change (Bangalore), the Giri Institute of Social Sciences (Lucknow), the Indian Tea Board (Calcutta), and the Indian Cultural Development Centre (Madras).

Finally, I wish to thank those who listened to and commented upon my presentations at seminars in New Delhi at the Center for Policy Research, the India International Centre, and the Ford Foundation; in Pune at the Indian Institute of Education; in Madras at the Madras Institute for Development Studies; and in Cambridge at the Boston University-Harvard-MIT South Asia seminar and the MIT Center for International Studies MacArthur Seminar on Institutional Perspectives on the State and Third World Development.

January 1990

THE CHILD AND THE STATE IN INDIA

1

The Argument

The Problem Explained

THE governments of all developed countries and many developing countries have removed children from the labor force and required that they attend school. They believe that employers should not be permitted to employ child labor and that parents, no matter how poor, should not be allowed to keep their children out of school. Modern states regard education as a legal duty, not merely a right: parents are required to send their children to school, children are required to attend school, and the state is obligated to enforce compulsory education. Compulsory primary education is the policy instrument by which the state effectively removes children from the labor force. The state thus stands as the ultimate guardian of children, protecting them against both parents and would-be employers.

This is not the view held in India. Primary education in India is not compulsory, nor is child labor illegal. The result is that less than half of India's children between ages six and fourteen—82.2 million—are not in school. They stay at home to care for cattle, tend younger children, collect firewood, and work in the fields. They find employment in cottage industries, tea stalls, restaurants, or as household workers in middle-class homes. They become prostitutes or live as street children, begging or picking rags and bottles from trash for resale. Many are bonded laborers, tending cattle and working as agricultural laborers for local landowners. "The government," a senior education official told me, "should not force poor parents to send their children to school when it cannot provide employment for all adults. Children are an economic asset to the poor. The income they bring in and the work they do may be small, but parents close to subsistence need their help."

Most children who start school drop out. Of those who enter first grade, only four out of ten complete four years of school. Depending upon how one defines "work" (employment for wages, or full-time work whether or not for wages), child laborers in India number from 13.6 million to 44 million, or more.

Indian law prohibits the employment of children in factories, but not in cottage industries, family households, restaurants, or in agriculture.

Indeed, government officials do not regard the employment of children in cottage industries as child labor, though working conditions in these shops are often inferior to those of the large factories. Said the director of the Ministry of Labour: "In Sivakasi [the site of India's match and fire-cracker industries where 45,000 children are employed], we understand that child labour in factories has gone down. They have in fact gone to the smaller units, the cottage type small units, which are not covered by the Factories Act. This is bound to happen. This is a positive sign. It is a move towards reduction and abolishment of child labour."[1]

India is a significant exception to the global trend toward the removal of children from the labor force and the establishment of compulsory, universal primary-school education. Poverty has not prevented govern ments of other developing countries from expanding mass education or making primary education compulsory. Many countries of Africa with in-come levels lower than India have expanded mass education with im-pressive increases in literacy. Botswana, Cameroons, Equatorial Guinea, Gabon, Gambia, Ghana, Ivory Coast, Lesotho, Libya, Madagascar, Mauritius, Réunion, Rwanda, Swaziland, Zambia, and Zimbabwe have literacy rates in the 50 percent to 75 percent range. China, which had an illiteracy rate comparable to that of India forty years ago, now has half the illiteracy rate of India. South Korea and Taiwan, both poor countries with high illiteracy rates a generation ago, moved toward universal and compulsory education while their per capita incomes were close to that of India. Adult literacy rates in both countries are now over 90 percent. In contrast, India's adult literacy rate in 1981 was 40.8 percent. Between 1961 and 1981 the total number of adult illiterates in India increased by 5 million per year, from 333 million to 437 million. India is the largest single producer of the world's illiterates.

The historical evidence delinking mass education from the level of na-tional and per capita income is also persuasive. In many countries the diffusion of mass literacy preceded the Industrial Revolution, and gov-ernments often introduced compulsory education when levels of poverty were high: German municipalities in 1524; Massachusetts in 1647; Scot-land, Austria, and Sweden in the late eighteenth and early nineteenth centuries; Japan in 1872; newly independent South Korea and Taiwan shortly after the World War II.

This study attempts to provide an explanation for why India's policies toward children in education and employment are different from those of so many other countries. Why is the Indian state unable—or unwilling—

[1] Interview with Ms. Meena Gupta, director of the Ministry of Labour, published in *The Lawyers* (New Delhi) 3, no. 7 (August 1988), p. 33. Ms. Gupta helped frame the Child Labour (Prohibition and Regulation) Act of 1986.

to deal with the high and increasing illiteracy, low school enrollments, high dropout rates, and rampant child labor? Why did government commissions reviewing child labor and education policies as recently as 1985–1986 not call for compulsory education or for legislation to abolish child labor? How are we to understand these policies in a country whose governing elites profess to be socialist and many of whose bureaucrats, politicians, and intellectuals are advocates of an intrusive state? Why has the state not taken legislative action when the Indian Constitution calls for a ban on child labor and for compulsory primary-school education, positions frequently reiterated in government reports as a long-term objective? Between official rhetoric and policy there is a vast gap, and it is puzzling why the Indian government does not do what it says it wants to do.

The central proposition of this study is that India's low per capita income and economic situation is less relevant as an explanation than the belief systems of the state bureaucracy, a set of beliefs that are widely shared by educators, social activists, trade unionists, academic researchers, and, more broadly, by members of the Indian middle class. These beliefs are held by those outside as well as those within government, by observant Hindus and by those who regard themselves as secular, and by leftists as well as by centrists and rightists.

At the core of these beliefs are the Indian view of the social order, notions concerning the respective roles of upper and lower social strata, the role of education as a means of maintaining differentiations among social classes, and concerns that "excessive" and "inappropriate" education for the poor would disrupt existing social arrangements.

Indians reject compulsory education, arguing that primary schools do not properly train the children of the poor to work, that the children of the poor should work rather than attend schools that prepare them for "service" or white-collar occupations, that the education of the poor would lead to increased unemployment and social and political disorder, that the children of the lower classes should learn to work with their hands rather than with their heads (skills more readily acquired by early entry into the labor force than by attending schools), that school dropouts and child labor are a consequence, not a cause, of poverty, and that parents, not the state, should be the ultimate guardians of children. Rhetoric notwithstanding, India's policy makers have not regarded mass education as essential to India's modernization. They have instead put resources into elite government schools, state-aided private schools, and higher education in an effort to create an educated class that is equal to educated classes in the West and that is capable of creating and managing a modern enclave economy.

The Indian position rests on deeply held beliefs that there is a division between people who work with their minds and rule and people who work with their hands and are ruled, and that education should reinforce rather than break down this division. These beliefs are closely tied to religious notions and to the premises that underlie India's hierarchical caste system. It is not merely that India's social organization is inegalitarian and that caste implies a system of social ranking, neither of which is unique to India. What is distinctive is a particular kind of social mobility, the mobility of groups rather than individuals. While there is considerable group mobility in India, powerful forces of both institutions and beliefs resist changes in group status. Even those who profess to be secular and who reject the caste system are imbued with values of status that are deeply imbedded in Indian culture. One does not readily escape from the core values of one's society. In much of the world, religious institutions and beliefs (including secular beliefs derived from religion) played a role in the diffusion of mass education and in state intervention, but in India Hinduism (and Islam as well) has not been a force for mass education. While in many countries theologies or secular ideologies have stood for a system of national education aimed at social equality, in India education has been largely an instrument for differentiation by separating children according to social class. For this reason, those who control the education system are remarkably indifferent to the low enrollment and high dropout rate among the lowest social classes. The result is one of the highest rates of child labor in the world, one of the lowest rates in school attendance, and a literacy rate that has fallen behind most of the third world.

These views are not readily apparent in official statements of government policy or in the speeches of public officials, but through a close scrutiny of official documents and through extensive interviews with officials we can discover these beliefs. Policies and programs that otherwise appear irrational, hypocritical, or inefficient can be rendered comprehensible. To understand these policies we must first identify the beliefs and premises upon which they are based. By comparing Indian policies toward child labor and compulsory education with those of other countries we can demonstrate that a study of belief systems provides us with a more consistent, theoretically satisfactory, and empirically based explanation for what we observe than do other explanations. And to demonstrate that policies are constrained neither by resources nor merely by pressures from affected interest groups, we shall show how widely these beliefs are held in Indian society. The explanation for policy lies not in interest group politics nor state interests, but in the beliefs and values of elites that shape their political actions, that is, in India's political culture.

The Rhetoric

Since independence the government of India, every commission appointed by the government, the ruling Congress party, all opposition parties, and all state governments have advocated ending child labor and establishing compulsory, universal, primary education for all children up to the age of fourteen. This commitment dates to the turn of the century when Gopal Krishna Gokhale, then president of the Indian National Congress, unsuccessfully urged the British to establish free and compulsory elementary education. In the 1930s provincial governments under the control of the Indian National Congress passed legislation authorizing local bodies to introduce compulsory education. The Indian Constitution of 1950 declared that "the State shall endeavor to provide, within a period of ten years from the commencement of this Constitution, for free and compulsory education for all children until they complete the age of fourteen years."[2] The goal was reconfirmed by successive central governments, by the Planning Commission, Parliament, and state governments. What are called compulsory primary education acts were passed by most of the state governments, while the number of primary schools leaped from 210,000 in 1950 to 529,000 by 1986.

Legislation restricting the employment of children in mines and factories was introduced by the British early in the century. More extensive legislation was passed following the recommendations of the Royal Commission on Labour in 1932. The Indian Constitution contains a number of provisions intended to protect children, including a categorical ban that declares that "no child below the age of fourteen years shall be employed to work in any factory or mine or engaged in any other hazardous employment."[3] In the 1950s Parliament passed several acts prohibiting the employment of children in plantations, mines, merchant shipping, and in the bidi (indigenous cigarettes) and cigar industries. The use of apprentices below the age of fourteen was prohibited. As with so-called compulsory education legislation, these measures had widespread support.

Both goals were reconfirmed in 1979, the International Year of the Child, when the Indian government appointed a commission to inquire into the state of India's children and to make recommendations for their improved well-being. The Ministry of Labour established a sixteen-member committee, including members of Parliament, representatives of various institutions dealing with children, and representatives of depart-

[2] *Constitution of India*, article 45.
[3] Ibid., article 24.

ments of the central and state governments, to examine the problems arising out of the employment of children. The commission was unequivocal in its support for both universal primary education and for bringing an end to child labor.

The Reality

Though forty years have passed since the Indian Constitution went into effect, most observers would agree with the late J. P. Naik, India's foremost scholar of education, that "the goal of universal primary education remains as elusive as ever before."[4] According to the government of India, in 1979 there were 42 million children between the ages of six and fourteen—or 32 percent of the age group—who were not in school, but according to Indian census data and academic studies of dropouts, nonattendance is nearly twice as large. Official government estimates are that 60 percent of children drop out of school by class five and only 23 percent reach class eight. The Education Ministry reports that 62 percent of the eleven-to-fourteen age group is not enrolled. Moreover, the number of children in this age group not attending school actually increased from 25.3 million in 1970 to 28.3 million in 1979.

In 1981 the Indian census asked for the first time whether a person was attending school or college. The result gives us a measure of school attendance that is independent of the enrollment figures provided by India's educational system (see tables 1.1 and 1.2). The 1981 census reported that 82.2 million of India's 158.8 million children ages six to fourteen did not attend school. Only 52.2 million of India's 123.7 million rural children ages six to fourteen were in school (34.4 million boys, 17.8 million girls). In urban India 24.4 million of 35.1 million attended school (13.5 million boys, 10.9 million girls).[5] The highest attendance is among urban males in the ten-to-fourteen age group (77 percent) and the lowest is among rural females in the six-to-nine age group (31.3 percent). (These figures, it should be noted, are substantially at variance with official ministry figures on school enrollments. Since the census figures are consistent with many independent field studies conducted by independent research organizations, I will use them throughout this study.)

The school attendance figures account for India's low literacy rate. In 1981 only 41.4 percent of India's population above the age of five was

[4] J. P. Naik, *Elementary Education in India: A Promise to Keep* (New Delhi: Allied Publishers, 1975).

[5] *Census of India 1981. Series 1, Part II-Special. Report and Tables Based on 5 Per Cent Sample Data*, Table C-4 (New Delhi: Registrar General and Census Commissioner, 1983), p. 208.

TABLE 1.1
School Attendance, 1981 (millions)

	Age Group	Total Population			Total Attending School		
		Persons	Male	Female	Persons	Male	Female
urban	6–9	15.8	8.1	7.7	10.6	5.7	4.9
	10–14	19.3	10.1	9.2	13.8	7.8	6.0
rural	6–9	57.4	29.6	27.8	22.9	14.2	8.7
	10–14	66.3	35.0	31.3	29.3	20.2	9.1
total		158.8	82.8	76.0	76.6	47.9	28.7

Source: Census of India 1981. Series 1, India, Part II-Special. Report and Tables Based on 5 Per Cent Sample Data (New Delhi, 1983), p. 200 (urban), p. 205 (rural). India's children, including those under six, number 263 million, of whom 135.8 are male and 127.2 are female. They constitute 39.5 percent of India's total population.

TABLE 1.2
School and College Attendance, 1981 (percent)

	Age Group	Persons	Male	Female
rural	6–9	39.9	48.0	31.3
	10–14	44.2	57.8	29.2
	15–19	20.5	30.9	8.9
	20–24	4.7	8.2	1.3
urban	6–9	67.1	70.4	63.6
	10–14	71.5	77.0	65.2
	15–19	42.9	50.2	34.5
	20–24	13.4	18.5	7.5
total	6–9	45.8	52.8	38.3
	10–14	50.5	62.1	37.5
	15–19	26.4	36.0	15.5
	20–24	7.2	11.3	3.0

Source: Census of India, 1981. Series 1, India, Part II-Special. Report and Tables Based on 5 Per Cent Sample Data (New Delhi, 1983), p. 92. Since many children do not start primary school until they are above the minimum school age, the proportion of attendance in school is higher in the age group ten to fourteen than in the younger age group.

literate (53.5 percent male, 28.5 percent female) with the highest literacy rates among urban males (74 percent) and the lowest among rural females (20.7 percent). In 1981, 56.6 percent of the ten-to-fourteen age group, 55.4 percent of the fifteen-to-nineteen age group, 52 percent of the twenty-to-twenty-four age group and 45.1 percent of the twenty-five-to-thirty-four age group were literate (see table 1.3).

One measure of the limited effectiveness of India's primary-school education system and its inability to expand enrollments fast enough to
keep pace with population growth is the increase in the number of illiterates: 333 million in 1961, 386 million in 1971, and 437 million in 1981.
The percentage of literates in the entire population has risen, however,
from 24 percent in 1961 to 29.5 percent in 1971 to 36.2 percent in 1981
(see tables 1.4 and 1.5).[6] The low school-attendance figures are reflected
in the high illiteracy rate among young people.

Official figures on child labor are also indicative of the government's
failure to deal with the problem. The government reports that in 1983,
17.4 million Indian children below the age of fifteen were in the labor
force, constituting 6.8 percent of the rural labor force and 2.4 percent of
the urban labor force. While the vast proportion of India's working children are employed in agriculture, many are engaged in industrial employment: in carpet making 9 percent of the labor force is children; in
brassware, 25 percent; in bidi, glass, and bangles, 33 percent; and in
matches, 42 percent. Of those employed on plantations, 8 percent are
children. Other studies put the number of child workers higher. By including children who do not receive wages but work full-time, the Operations Research Group, a respected research organization in Baroda,

TABLE 1.3
Literacy Rates by Age, 1961–1981

Age	1961	1971	1981
5–9	19.6	23.2	30.6
10–14	42.2	49.8	56.6
15–19	38.4	51.4	55.4
20–24	33.5	44.7	52.0
25–34	28.4	34.8	45.1
35 +	22.2	25.2	30.2

Source: O. P. Sharma and Robert D. Retherford, *Recent Literacy Trends in India, Occasional Paper No. 1 of 1987* (New Delhi: Registrar General and Census Commissioner,
1987), p. 11.

[6] O. P. Sharma and Robert D. Retherford, *Recent Literacy Trends in India* (New Delhi:
Office of the Registrar General and Census Commissioner, Occasional Paper No. 1 of 1987,
1987), p. 6. The total number of illiterates grew from 222.5 million in 1901 to 294.2 million
in 1951. The growth in the number of illiterates is the result of a continued high rate of
illiteracy among young people. In 1981, 43.5 percent of the ten-to-fourteen age group and
44.6 percent of the fifteen-to-nineteen age group, were illiterate. In the latter age group,
56.7 percent of the females and 34 percent of the males were illiterate (*ibid.*, pp. 30–31).

TABLE 1.4
Population, Literacy, and Illiteracy, 1901–1981 (in millions)

Year	Population	Literates	Illiterates	Increase in Illiterates	Literacy Rate (percent)
1901	235.1	12.6	222.5		5.4
1911	248.2	14.7	233.5	+ 11.0	5.9
1921	246.7	17.7	229.0	− 4.5	7.2
1931	273.4	26.0	247.4	+ 18.4	9.5
1941	312.0	50.2	261.8	+ 14.4	16.1
1951	353.1	58.9	294.2	+ 32.4	16.7
1961	428.0	102.6	325.5	+ 31.3	24.0
1971	533.5	157.3	376.2	+ 50.7	29.5
1981	665.3	241.0	424.3	+ 48.1	36.2

Source: *Recent Literacy Trends in India, Occasional Paper No. 1 of 1987* (New Delhi: Registrar General and Census Commisioner, 1987), p. 6. These figures for all years exclude Assam, where the census was not taken in 1981. Including Assam (with estimates for 1981), the number of illiterates was 333 million in 1961, 386 million in 1971, and 437 million in 1981.

TABLE 1.5
Rural vs. Urban Literacy Rates (percent of literates to total population)

	1961			1971			1981		
	Persons	Male	Female	Persons	Male	Female	Persons	Male	Female
Total	23.9	34.4	12.9	29.5	39.5	18.7	36.2	46.9	24.8
Rural	18.8	28.9	8.4	23.7	33.8	13.1	29.7	40.8	18.0
Urban	46.9	57.4	34.4	53.4	61.2	42.1	57.4	65.9	47.8

Source: *Census of India, 1981, Series 1, India, Part II-Special. Report and Tables Based on 5 per cent Sample Data, Series 1* (New Delhi, 1983), p. 82.

estimates that 44 million children in the five-to-fifteen age group are in the labor force.

The Indian government has not hidden its inability to end child labor and to establish compulsory primary-school education. Indeed, few governments have been as open about their difficulties in this area, or have been as forthcoming in producing studies and providing data on the magnitude of child employment and truancy. The *Report of the Committee on Child Labour* (1979), for example, provides detailed data on the employment of children by sector of the economy, by industry, and by state, derived from the census, the National Sample Survey, and from data collected by the Labour Bureau.[7] Similarly, the Ministry of Education has published detailed data on primary and secondary school enrollments and dropout rates by state, with detailed data on scheduled castes and tribes. The government of India has also provided funds to research institutions to collect and publish studies dealing with the magnitude and determinants of child labor and nonenrollments in schools.

Recently the government of India has moved away from its earlier objective of establishing compulsory elementary education and removing all children from the labor force. The Labour Ministry has indicated that "despite the provisions of restrictive labor laws, the practice (of child labor) continues unabated because exploitation of children is of financial advantage to employers and an economic compulsion to parents."[8] The government, therefore, accepts child labor as a "harsh reality" and proposes that measures be taken to improve the working conditions of children rather than to remove them from the work force. Under new legislation the government proposes to give attention to eliminating the employment of children in hazardous occupations, improving conditions of work, regulating the hours of work and wages paid, and providing nonformal supplementary education programs for working children. These new policies, long advocated by a number of government officials, represent a significant modification of the policies recommended by the Committee on Child Labour that primary attention be given to the enforcement of child-labor laws.

The new policies were initially put forth by the minister of labour and by the development commissioner of small-scale industries in presentations to the Committee on Child Labour. "The type of education that is now being imparted in schools," said the development commissioner, "makes it completely unattractive to the parents of children, particularly in the rural areas, where children are considered an economic asset. In the circumstances prevailing in our country, it would be unrealistic not to expect that children who are capable of working would be put to work. It is also a matter for consideration whether such work would not, in fact, provide a good input to the healthy growth of these children provided it is conducted under well regulated and healthy conditions."[9]

A similar position was taken by India's Education Ministry, which concluded that in lieu of compulsion, alternative voluntary, nonformal education should be provided working children. Substantial funding was provided for part-time education in the sixth and seventh five-year plans. The National Council of Educational Research and Training (NCERT), the

[7] Ministry of Labour, *Report of the Committee on Child Labour* (New Delhi: Government of India, 1979).

[8] Ministry of Labour, *Annual Report 1983–84* (New Delhi: Government of India, 1985).

[9] Ibid., p. 54.

paramount institution in its field, funded by the Ministry of Education, recommended the creation of more all-girl schools, the greater use of women teachers, and the initiation of campaigns by social workers to persuade parents to keep their daughters in school. Educators called for free textbooks, free uniforms for poor children, and free lunches. The emphasis is thus on the expansion of educational facilities, the use of persuasion, and the establishment of nonformal part-time programs, rather than on compulsory education. The key notion in child-labor policy in India became "amelioration," not abolition; and in education; "incentives," not compulsion.

Government officials assert that they have not given up the long-term goals of ending child labor and implementing compulsory primary education. The new policies, they argue, simply reflect their judgment that existing legislation cannot be implemented at this time because of prevailing social and economic conditions. Legislation is weak, they say, because of the impediments that lie within society: chronic poverty forces poor parents to put their children into the labor force; parents do not believe that they or their children would benefit economically if their children were in school; and children acquire skills through employment not through formal education. They also point to opposition by employers to the enforcement of child-labor legislation: employers prefer children to adults because they are more pliable, work for lower wages, are not unionized, have supple fingers that enable them to work in many crafts more effectively than adults, and the low wages paid to children enable some industries to survive that might otherwise not be able to compete either in domestic or international markets.

There is a normative dimension to these arguments: the state, it is argued, ought not to intervene since poor parents need the income of their children. It is thus a matter of social justice that the children of the poor be allowed to work. And there is a political element to these arguments: powerful employer interests impede the implementation of child-labor legislation or any measures that would remove children from the labor force. Thus the state ought not to act, and it cannot act. Nonaction has both a moral and a practical rationale.

It follows from these arguments that the abolition of child labor and the establishment of compulsory education must await a significant improvement in the well-being of the poor. As employment and income increase, so the argument goes, it will no longer be necessary for the poor to send their children to work and the benefits of education will become more apparent. A related argument is that changes in technology will eventually reduce the demand for unskilled child labor and place a premium on education. Only then will parents send their children to school to acquire the education they need to find employment. It is also argued that, with an improvement in the national budget, government will be in a better position to increase expenditures in primary education.

These societal-centered explanations do not stand up against historical and comparative evidence. As we have already briefly suggested, the notion that mass education depends upon the level of per capita income is contradicted by historical and contemporary comparative evidence. In Sweden, Scotland, colonial New England, and Prussia high levels of literacy were achieved in the eighteenth century when incomes were low and prior to the development of modern, industrial, urban societies.

Among contemporary developing countries there is also no clear relationship between literacy and per capita income. India has an adult (over age fifteen) literacy rate of 40.8 percent, while in China it is 72.6 percent; Burma, 78.5 percent; Indonesia, 74.1 percent; Tanzania, 85 percent; Sri Lanka, 86.1 percent; and the Philippines, 88.7 percent (see table 7.2). And while literacy for India as a whole is low, the state of Kerala, with a per capita income no different than that of the rest of the country, has a literacy rate (of those over five) of 85 percent.

A number of Asian countries experienced spectacular primary-school attendance rates prior to their rapid economic growth. In the short space of thirty years, between 1873 and 1903, the Japanese government increased elementary-school attendance from 28 percent to 94 percent.[10] By 1913, 98 percent of the age group was attending school. South Korea, with only a third of its children in primary schools in 1941, universalized primary education by the early 1970s. Its literacy rate increased from 55 percent in 1944 to 90 percent. In China, primary-school education expanded rapidly after 1949. In 1979, China enrolled close to 147 million children in 920,000 formal schools, an enrollment ratio of 93 percent, compared with 25 percent in 1949. The literacy rate among the population aged fifteen and above is 72.6 percent, an increase of 52 percentage points since 1949.

Nor do resource constraints explain the differences in educational performance between India and other countries. India spends 3.6 percent of its GNP on education—less than Kenya (6.7 percent), Tanzania (4.3 percent), or Malaysia (7.8 percent), but more than Burma (1.6 percent), China (2.7 percent), Sri Lanka (3.5 percent) and Indonesia (2.0 percent) (see table 7.2).[11] Compared to these other countries, moreover, a larger proportion of India's education budget is spent on higher education. While the percentage of the college-age group in higher education was only 1 percent in China, 4 percent in Sri Lanka, 1 percent in Burma, and

[10] Herbert Passin, "Japan," in James S. Coleman, ed., *Education and Political Development* (Princeton: Princeton University Press, 1965), p. 272.

[11] World Bank, *World Development Report 1985* (New York: Oxford University Press, 1985).

4 percent in Indonesia, it was 9 percent in India, the highest among the low income countries in the third world.[12]

Thus there is historical and comparative evidence to suggest that the major obstacles to the achievement of universal primary education and the abolition of child labor are not the level of industrialization, per capita income and the socioeconomic conditions of families, the level of overall government expenditures in education, nor the demographic consequences of a rapid expansion in the number of school age children, four widely suggested explanations. India has made less of an effort to move children out of the labor force and out of their homes into the school system than many other countries not for economic or demographic reasons but because of the attitudes of government officials, politicians, trade union leaders, workers in voluntary agencies, religious figures, intellectuals, and the influential middle class toward child labor and compulsory primary-school education. Of particular importance, I will argue, are the attitudes of officialdom itself, especially officials of the state and central education and labor departments and ministries. The desires of low-income parents to send their children to work or to employ them at home, and of employers who seek low wage, pliable, nonunionized labor, is of secondary importance because elsewhere in the world a large proportion of parents and employers have also supported child labor and opposed compulsory education. It is the absence of strong support for governmental intervention from within the state apparatus itself and the absence of a political coalition outside the state apparatus pressing for government intervention that explains Indian policy. Official declarations from government and statements by politicians, officials, educators, and social activists notwithstanding, there is very little political support in India for compulsory education or for the enforcement of laws banning the employment of children.

The Design

To demonstrate my argument that the primary difficulties in the achievement of the stated goals of the Indian government lie in the beliefs of those who make and implement policies rather than in what are called the "social realities" of India, I shall proceed at several levels. In chapter 2 I shall provide the reader with a brief picture of the situation of India's children: their place in the labor force and in the school system. For this chapter I have drawn from my visits to places in which children work, to

[12] World Bank, *World Development Report 1987* (New York: Oxford University Press, 1987).

Indian schools, and from my conversations with Indian children in match factories in the south Indian town of Sivakasi, in rural areas outside of Hyderabad, in the city market of Bangalore, in rural Karnataka, in the bustees (slums) and bazaars of Bombay, in schools in Pune, and in rural Maharashtra. Many of the children were extraordinarily articulate about why they left school, the circumstances of their parents, and whether they saw any way out of their situation. The stories were similar. Parents removed them from school either to enter the work force or to help at home. In no cases did local school teachers, social activists, religious leaders, party workers, or government officials try to persuade or prevent the parents. Some of these children voluntarily attend nonformal education classes, usually at night after a full day of hard work, in the hope that they can become literate or reenter the formal school system. While I cannot claim to have conducted a systematic study of the views of Indian children and their work experiences, I did come to understand that these were often at variance with the impressions about them held by many adults.

With the assistance of officials of education departments and of activists in nongovernmental organizations, I visited primary schools, vocational and technical training schools, and nonformal education programs. I have also drawn heavily from various government reports and from numerous excellent studies by Indian academics of the situation of Indian children in various industries.

In chapters 3 and 4 I turn to a description of the attitudes of government officials, educators, and activists. This material is drawn from 112 interviews I conducted in Delhi, Ahmedabad, Bangalore, Bombay, Trivandrum, Madras, Calcutta, Pune, Hyderabad, and Lucknow. Chapter 3 deals with attitudes toward child labor, and chapter 4 with education. These findings are given in the form of dialogues between myself and those I interviewed. I have tried not to intrude my own views, but to use my questions and comments as a way of stimulating and provoking a fuller expression of views from my respondents. Since it would be tedious to report all of my interviews, I have chosen those that effectively articulate what I found were the most frequently expressed attitudes. In both chapters I have also presented interviews with those who take issue with the prevailing sentiments. These interviews, though exceptions to the mainstream, suggest that Indian thinking is by no means monolithic.

The opposition by most officials, including educational officials, to compulsory education, and the low level of concern with school dropouts is one of the surprising findings. Even in Calcutta, Marxist politicians and administrators took the position that nothing could or should be done to remove children from the labor force and require that they attend school. Everywhere the arguments were the same: children should work to support themselves and their families; children would not earn any more as adults if they went to school; the schools fail to teach skills that make children employable; by entering the labor force as apprentices at an early age children acquire usable skills; educating peasant children only leads them to seek employment in the urban labor market, creating more unemployment, pressure on urban services, and urban unrest. Officials regarded education for the masses not as liberating but as destabilizing. Educators and officials also questioned the value of compulsion. The state, they said, has no right to force children to attend school and thereby deny parents of their income. Some pointed to the economic benefits to the country of child labor, especially in export industries such as carpet weaving where the manual dexterity of children and their low wages enhances the industry's capacity to compete in world markets.

Chapter 5 shows how these attitudes shape Indian policies toward compulsory education and child-labor laws. Policies in these areas are not simply the result of pressures from affected interest groups but are an expression of the values and beliefs of policymakers and influential citizens. Policies adopted in the mid-1980s to revise child-labor laws to legalize some types of child labor and to create a system of part-time nonformal education for children who either have never entered or have dropped out of the primary-school system are examined. The new National Policy on Education introduced by the Rajiv Gandhi government is also described. Both sets of policies, it will be shown, arise from within the state apparatus and reflect the kinds of views articulated in chapters 3 and 4. They tell us a great deal about how people in positions of authority and influence in India think about the development of human resources and the nature of the social order.

A historical comparative perspective is introduced in chapter 6. I heard so many arguments in India for accepting what officials called the "harsh reality" of the situation of children, and for the acceptance of the existing situation by so many educators, social activists, trade unionists, and others who might be expected to be forces for change, that I began to wonder how it happened elsewhere that decisions were made that the state should legally remove children from the labor force to place them in schools. That led me to turn to the historic experiences of the United States, the United Kingdom and other European countries, and Japan in the nineteenth century. Chapter 6 reviews the historical debates in these countries over the introduction of compulsory education and child-labor laws and examines the composition of the political coalitions that led to state intervention. My concern here is with identifying the circumstances—particularly the beliefs—that made state interventions possible and to explore their relevance for the Indian situation.

Chapter 7 examines the experiences of South Korea, Taiwan, the People's Republic of China, Sri Lanka, and several other contemporary instances in the third world where states have successfully intervened to enforce compulsory education and markedly brought down the incidence of child labor. I will also examine differences within India, focusing on the success that the Indian state of Kerala has had in spite of a per capita income not noticeably different than that of other Indian states. By holding the mirror up to these developing countries and to the historical experiences of what are now advanced industrial countries we better understand the role that beliefs play in shaping policies in India.

Chapter 8 considers why countries so different from one another in their levels of economic development, forms of government, and cultures have, in contrast with India, made education compulsory and child labor illegal. Why were coalitions for reforms created elsewhere, but not in India? This concluding chapter reviews the policy interventions of other countries, then considers what comparable measures could be adopted in India were the appropriate leadership available.

The positive side to this analysis is that India need not wait until income levels of the poor have risen, population growth rates have slowed, employers have need for a more skilled labor force, or government has greater resources. Indeed, such changes in the country's economic and demographic conditions would not result in the voluntary end of child labor and in universal primary-school education. The experiences of other countries also suggests that it is within the power of the Indian government to make education compulsory. Otherwise, child labor will not be ended and literacy will not become universal.

The negative side of this analysis is that deeply and widely shared attitudes, not simply of a handful of policymakers but of educators, social activists, and trade unionists who elsewhere have been in the forefront of reform movements for the abolition of child labor and the establishment of compulsory education, stand in the way of effective policies. Political change in the central or state governments will not necessarily result in policy changes since on these issues there are no differences among India's political parties. Non-Congress state governments have taken no more initiative than have Congress governments, though the states share responsibility for elementary education and for the enforcement of child-labor laws. If the impediment to change comes because of the attitudes of those who make, implement, and influence policy, and if these attitudes are based on deeply held beliefs that are not easily shaken, is reform likely? Yes, but only if there is first a change in the way in which policymakers and those who influence them think about the problem.

2

India's Working Children

MADIGA, age twelve, was the most educated of the half dozen boys that I met tending cattle outside a village twenty kilometers from Hyderabad. Madiga spent four years in the village primary school. A year and a half ago Madiga was taken out of school by his parents to work for Mr. Reddi, the owner of a local dairy. Madiga's parents had borrowed 2,000 rupees from Mr. Reddi to cover the costs of their eldest son's marriage. To pay for the interest on the loan, and as a form of security, Madiga was put to work for Mr. Reddi. The landlord pays Madiga a pot of rice (sixteen kilos) and twenty rupees a month. If he had a chance, Madiga said, he would return to school, but he could not leave Mr. Reddi until his parents repaid the loan. Since his parents are agricultural workers, it seems unlikely that they could ever save enough to pay Mr. Reddi. "Why did your parents borrow for your brother's wedding?" I asked. "It was a matter of family prestige," Madiga explained.

The other boys I met had at most a year or two of school. One of the boys tending cattle, age eight, had never attended school. Like Madiga, they were ex-untouchables and they were all bonded laborers. The local village, Pratab Singaram, has a primary school, but only about half the children are enrolled. While the boys care for the cattle, the girls help at home so their mothers can work. The school headmaster was not very precise as to how many children actually attended school and how many who entered first grade continued through primary school, but an unpublished study conducted in 1980 at the prestigious Administrative Staff College in Hyderabad reported that while 900,000 boys and 646,000 girls were enrolled in grade 1 in rural Andhra, only 230,000 boys and 126,000 girls were enrolled in grade 5.[1] In other words only 23 percent as many children were in grade 5 as in grade 1. Since grade 1 enrollments had not significantly increased, it seems reasonable to assume that only a quarter of the boys and a fifth of the girls completed four standards, the minimum years of school most experts regard as necessary to ensure retention of effective literacy in later life.

[1] *School Enrollments in Andhra*, Administrative Staff College, Hyderabad, 1980.

How Many Working Children?

How many of India's 82 million children not in school are in the work force? One difficulty in estimating how many children work is that many work without wages in the fields or in cottages alongside their parents, unreported by the census. Large numbers of children work in cottage industries producing carpets, matches, firecrackers, bidis, brassware, diamonds, glass, hosiery, hand-loomed cloth, embroidery, bangles, and traditional handicrafts, often for wages, but sometimes without wages alongside their parents. On tea plantations, children pluck leaves that they add to their mothers' baskets, and only when they reach the age of twelve or thirteen are they given a basket of their own. Children who tend their parent's cattle, fetch water and wood, and prepare meals are not classified as working children, although they are if they do the same work for pay for others.

Even those who are paid wages are not easily counted. The number of children employed in cottage industries is not reflected in census data. Nor are many children employed as domestic servants for the middle class. Nor are children working in restaurants, tea stalls, and in wayside shops. Children are hawkers, newspapers vendors, ragpickers, shoeshine boys, and helpers on construction sites. They break stones in quarries and load and unload goods. Many children work as "apprentices"—some in government workshops—and are presumably not reported as employed. And there are the street children, especially beggers and prostitutes, who are underreported.

Given the uncertainties of definition and the complexities of enumeration, it is no wonder that estimates of child labor vary so greatly in India. India's 1981 census reports only 13.6 million children in the work force, 8.1 million males and 5.5 million females, or 7.6 percent of all children between the ages of five and fourteen.[2] Of these, 11.6 million were in agricultural work. A little over a million work in manufacturing, processing, repairs, trade and commerce, transport, construction, and other services. Many are employed in household industries and small workshops: in the carpet industry, where children work in their own cottages or in the homes of master weavers and loom owners; in the glass and bangle industries, mainly in factory sheds; in diamond cutting, brassware, bidi manufacturing, zari making, and as ragpickers.

Other studies put the number of child workers higher. The official National Sample Survey of 1983 reports 17.4 million child laborers, while a study by the Operations Research Group of Baroda, sponsored by the

[2] *Census of India 1981. Series 1, India, Part II-Special*, tables, p. 2.

Labour Ministry, concluded that the child-labor force was 44 million, including children paid in kind as well as in cash.

With estimates varying so greatly, it is particularly difficult to assess whether child labor has increased or declined. The government's Labour Bureau reports a significant decline in factory employment since 1948, but a change in the law may have led to the appearance of a decline. The Factories Act of 1948 provides that units employing ten or more workers and using power, and twenty or more workers not using power, cannot employ children. The result is that children work in the smaller shops not covered by the act while factory owners ask children to leave the factory when factory inspectors make their rare visits. A comparison of the 1971 and 1981 censuses suggests that child labor has increased: the 1971 census reported 10.7 million children in the work force (4.6 percent of all children) and in 1981 the census reported 13.6 million working children (5.2 percent of all children). These census figures are consistent with the National Sample Survey data, which reported 16.3 million child laborers in 1972–1973 and 17.4 million in 1983.

A comparison of child labor and school attendance data among the states is revealing. All studies agree that Andhra Pradesh has the highest incidence of child labor, Kerala the lowest. Andhra is well below the mean on literacy rates and on primary- and middle-school enrollment, while Kerala is the highest.

Children's Work

What kinds of work do non-school-going children do? What are the conditions under which they work? What do they earn? What skills, if any, do they acquire? How dependent is the household upon them for income? Do children voluntarily leave school or are they asked to by their parents? A number of reports on conditions in particular sectors of the economy provide us with some answers.

The Bangalore City Market

Walking through the Bangalore city market is a slender fourteen-year-old Muslim boy, Muhammed, carrying a sign advertising rat poison. He started work at age seven in a shop where he boiled cocoons to remove their silk. He left after a bad scalding on his arm ("without compensation," he said ruefully) and took on various jobs until a friend showed him how to mix chemicals to make rat poison. Now he peddles his own wares, sign in hand, in the city market.

Some children in the market work in shops owned by their parents and relatives. One fifteen-year-old boy, also a Muslim, sells ornaments for cattle. He has never attended school and for many years has worked in his father's shop. He says that someday the shop will belong to him. Nearby, two boys work in the spice and nut shop of a relative, each earning ten rupees a day.[3]

Numerous children work as shop assistants. A few are in school and work part-time, but most are full-time employees. Some of the stalls are workshops with small boys helping out, doing metal work, carrying out repairs. In one stall at the edge of the market an eleven-year-old Muslim boy who never attended school has worked for five years alongside his father, an autorickshaw mechanic. He is paid five rupees a day.

The manager of the Globe Engineering Works, a grand name for a small 20 foot by 20 foot workshop across the road from the central city market, said he began work as a helper in the workshop sixteen years ago, when he was only seven. He was uneducated and was paid four annas a day (a quarter of a rupee). Today, he said with pride, he earns 1,500 rupees a month, and has a printed card with his name as manager. He taught himself to read and write and to do numbers. The shop is clean and the machinery used for threading pipes (marked Nottingham, 1894) is well-polished. He employs two boys, both Muslims like himself. The older boy, Said, age thirteen, is paid 200 rupees per month and is being taught how to use the equipment. The younger boy, age eleven, is paid five rupees a day to keep the shop clean and run errands. Neither boy has been to school. Until he was twelve, Said stayed at home helping his mother care for his three younger sisters. The manager is particularly keen on helping Said learn the trade.

Near the Globe Engineering Works are numerous restaurants and tea stalls. They are staffed by children washing dishes and cleaning tables. A twelve-year-old boy cleaned the table in the outdoor restaurant where I stopped for lunch. At the age of ten he was sent by his parents, agricultural laborers in a district in Tamilnadu, to Bangalore to find work. Completely uneducated and illiterate, he came to the city ("I came alone!" he said with pride) and found employment in the restaurant. His wages are 160 rupees a month and he sleeps and eats in the restaurant. When he is older he hopes to work as a waiter, earning 600 to 700 rupees a month.

Street Children of Secunderabad

As in Calcutta, Bombay, Madras, and all other large and medium-size cities of India, Secunderabad has numerous children working in the

[3] One rupee equals approximately 7 U.S. cents.

streets as beggars, ragpickers, prostitutes, and vendors. Some are engaged in petty crime and some are addicted to drugs. They are often harassed by the police.[4] Though most live with their parents, some are orphans or runaways. In Secunderabad, I visited Prema Seva Sadan, a Catholic-run home for street children. The center feeds and houses 140 boys, many of whom fled to the streets after having been abused by parents and relatives. One boy explained that he fled his home in a village in Kurnool district after he was beaten by his parents. He became a ragpicker in nearby Hyderabad. The man he sold rags to gave him drugs until he became addicted. Another boy had been beaten so hard by his stepfather that he became crippled in one leg, and he took to begging. Still another was an orphan whose uncle sent him to Hyderabad to find work. All the boys have been picked up from the street by the priest and his co-workers. Some of the boys are disturbed and from time to time there have been suicide attempts.

Poor families will sometimes come to the Prema Seva Sadan to ask that their children be admitted, but the center will not accept them. Whenever possible the staff tries to find the parents and close relatives of the boys to arrange for their return. The center runs two workshops, one to teach carpentry, another sewing. The boys in the carpentry shop make stools for sale, though the emphasis is on training rather than marketing. The boys in the sewing class also earn money by tailoring. About a dozen boys are taught reading and writing by a teacher who comes to the school daily. A few of the boys go to a neighborhood school. They are free to leave the home at any time. Some leave when they find jobs, a few go back to their family, and some return to the streets.

The Match Industry of Sivakasi

Working children are to be seen everywhere in the town of Sivakasi, several hours' drive from the well-known south Indian temple city of Madurai. Devi, a girl of ten, sits on the veranda of her house making match boxes. With extraordinary dexterity, her little fingers fold small pieces of wood into a box. Then, with her forefinger she spreads paste on a piece of paper that she then wraps around the box. The box is thrown into a pile and she begins again. The youngest member of the family, she has done this work for two years. Both her parents and her three older brothers work as agricultural laborers.

---

[4] The award-winning film *Salaam Bombay*, produced and directed by Meera Nair, effectively captures the plight of street children in Bombay and their harassment by officials.

Sivakasi is perhaps the most publicized center of child labor in India.[5] Children are employed in the match, fireworks, and printing industries. Children are brought to Sivakasi by bus from neighboring villages within a radius of about twenty miles. They are loaded into buses and vans from three to five in the morning to get to the factories at six or seven, and they return home between six and nine in the evening. As many as 150 to 200 children are packed in a vehicle. The children work for about twelve hours, but they are away from home for over fifteen hours. Forty-five thousand children below fifteen years of age work in Sivakasi or in nearby workshops or cottages within their own village, perhaps the largest single concentration of child labor in the world. Three-quarters of the child workers are girls. Each village has an agent who enrolls the children and ensures that they are awake when the transport arrives. The agents receive a monthly salary of 150 rupees. They may pay parents an advance of up to 200 rupees for each child laborer enrolled. The advance is then deducted from the child's salary.

There are many small workshops just outside the town employing children, mostly from nearby villages. The children fill slotted frames with a pile of splints the length of matchsticks. The full frames are locked and the tips are dipped into a hot solution of gum and chemicals and then put to dry. When dry, the frame is opened and the matchsticks are put into matchboxes. Each matchbox is handmade. With a brush or roller, the striking surface of the matchbox is coated with chemicals. Brand labels are placed on the boxes, which are then packed together into cases. Children are paid on a piece-rate basis. Younger children, those between four and ten, earn from seven to ten rupees a day, while older children earn ten to fifteen rupees. While the children are usually eight or older, in one workshop on the tamarind tree–lined road between Madurai and Sivakasi I found a three-year-old girl helping her eight-year-old sister stack matchboxes. Child labor is legally permitted in the small "family-owned" workshops, but not in the factories.

Kamala, who says she is sixteen, works in one of the match factories in the town. The "factory" is little more than a large shed where several hundred girls spend their day putting splints into slotted frames. Kamala comes from a village outside of Sivakasi, where her father works as an agricultural laborer. When Kamala was six she cared for a younger sister and a younger brother while her mother went off to work in the match factory. At eight Kamala was earning several rupees a day squatting on the veranda of her home making matchboxes. A year later she found work

[5] A major, widely discussed analysis is Smitu Kothari, "There's Blood on Those Matchsticks: Child Labour in Sivakasi," *Economic and Political Weekly* (2 July 1983). See also Manu N. Kulkarni, "Match-Making Children in Sivakasi," *Economic and Political Weekly* (22 October 1983).

in a small match-making shop on the main road just outside her village. At fourteen, the legal age for working in a factory, she went to work in the factory in Sivakasi. Factory conditions are better than in the small workshops, which lack toilet facilities, have poor lighting, and often lack adequate drinking water. Kamala is small and thin, looking several years younger than she claims, but then so do many of the other girls in the factory. I asked Kamala if she could read or write. No, she said, she had never been to school.

The situation at Sivakasi came to public attention in 1976 when a bus full of children turned over and many of the children were fatally injured. When it was reported that the children were employed in the Sivakasi match industry, the state government of Tamil Nadu appointed a one-man commission to investigate. At the time, Harbans Singh, a soft-spoken, bearded turbaned Sikh, was a senior officer in the state Board of Revenue who had previously been an official of the state government's industry department. As a one-man commission, Singh toured the area, visited factories in Sivakasi, and talked with employers, local government officials, union representatives, and parents. He found widespread violation of the Factories Act and the Employment of Children Act, which prohibit the employment of children under fourteen. He found children as young as five and six working in the match factories. Most of the children in the factories had never been to school. They were exposed to dangerous chemicals and there were frequent accidents. They worked long hours under harrowing work conditions with little opportunity to rest or play. He founded collusion between factory owners and doctors who were supposed to certify the ages and health of children. He also reported that the Minimum Wages Act was violated and that government officials responsible for the enforcement of the acts did nothing.

Harbans Singh did not recommend the abolition of child labor in the industry. He agreed with the member of Parliament from Sivakasi who said that "child labour is an economic problem and should be tackled accordingly without causing hardship to the families of the child labourers and also without upsetting the industries which have created employment." Abolishing child labor, he wrote, "will upset their industries which are the major source of income in the area not only for the children but also for the adults."[6] When I spoke with Singh some years later at his home in New Delhi, where he had retired, I asked him why he thought child labor in the match industry should not be prohibited. He said that the entire district is poor since there is little rainfall. Agricultural pro-

[6] Report of T. Harbans Singh on the Problems of Child Labour in Various Factories and Industries in Ramanathapuram District. Reprinted in A Documentation on Law Relating to Employment of Children (New Delhi: National Centre for Human Settlement and Environment, 1986), pp. 137, 139.

ductivity is low and there is considerable unemployment. By working in the factories the children, he said, are able to contribute income to the family. The industry has employed children ever since the factories were built in the 1920s. The industry had been started by two Nadar businessmen. The Nadars are a low-caste community, traditionally toddy tappers, who became prosperous through trading in palm products. Some settled in Sivakasi, a market town that had become a substantial trading center by the end of the nineteenth century. In 1922 two Nadar businessmen, after hearing that there was profit to be made in the production of matches, imported machinery from Germany and jointly set up a factory in Sivakasi. Because labor in the area was cheap, they subsequently decided to switch to hand production. Shortly thereafter, other Nadar entrepreneurs started their own factories. With credit given by the State Bank of India in the 1950s, the Nadars were able to expand their factories. The producers organized the All India Chamber of Match Industries in Sivakasi, representing 115 units, to handle country-wide marketing.

WIMCO, a Swedish-owned mechanized company formed in 1927 in India, is the major competitor. WIMCO and other mechanized units employing only 6,000 workers produced 4.3 billion matchboxes in 1978, or 30 percent of total production, at a lower cost than the nonmechanized sectors, which employed 250,000. In an effort to protect the nonmechanized sector, the government imposed an excise duty on WIMCO and created a Khadi and Village Industries Commission to help develop the cottage match manufacturers and to aid in marketing.

The factory owners and managers told Singh that their profits were low and that if they could not hire children and had to hire adults at higher wages they could not compete with WIMCO. The factory owners thus used the widespread opposition to multinationals as a way of protecting their own interests in the employment of child labor. Though he did not examine their financial accounts, Singh was persuaded that the abolition of child labor would result in the closure of many of the factories and that this would worsen the economic situation for the community. "If they didn't hire children they could hire adults from the surrounding areas," said Singh, "but the industry has been built on the exploitation of child labor. The managers told me that if they had to pay higher wages they could not compete with WIMCO even with the high excise tax the government has put on the multinational. Unemployment is relieved by the match industry. If you banned the employment of children many families would lose the contribution that the children make."

Rather than ban child labor, Singh called for remedial measures. Wages for children should be raised, and if that created a hardship for the employers then the government should impose a higher excise tax on WIMCO. He wanted factory owners to move work to the villages and set up sheds so the children would not have to travel long distances for so many hours. "Let the buses carry the goods instead of carrying the children," he said. Since many of the children would still continue to work in Sivakasi, he urged that the buses be improved. He also recommended that a system of nonformal job-oriented education be provided to the children at the factories from eight to ten in the morning so that they could have some education even as they worked.

In 1988 the government initiated a program in Sivakasi for providing nonformal education, free health care, and free lunches for children working in the factories. The costs were met by the Union Labour Ministry. Critics of the program noted that the provision of lunches meant that employers were now ensured of child labor since children would be given the meal only if they showed up for work. Employers would also no longer have to worry about government labor inspectors since child labor was thereby legalized by the state.[7] The government, however, insisted that only children fourteen or older would be permitted to work in the factories.

The Glass Factories of Firozabad

Two types of furnaces are used for making glass in Firozabad, a town in Agra district where 99 percent of India's glass bangles are made and that is the center of India's glass-blowing industry.[8] The pot furnaces are smaller. The temperatures in these furnaces range between 700°C and 800°C. Tank furnaces are much larger, with temperatures as high as 1,800°C. Glass bangles are made illegally in the tank furnaces, which have a larger capacity and can run round the clock, though the bangles are of slightly inferior quality as the color is added after the molten glass is removed. Bangles are arranged on the trays by small boys for the *pakai-wala*—the man who places the trays of bangles into the furnace. Child workers also carry burning loams of glass stuck on the tips of four-foot-long iron rods without handles, known as *labias*. The workers are constantly on the move with the blazing materials. The *labias*, with the ball of blazing glass on their tips, are given to the glass blowers. The blown

[7] See "Scheme for Sivakasi Child Labour," *Hindu International Edition* (16 April 1988). For a critical assessment of the government's program to ameliorate the child-labor situation in Sivakasi, see Walter Fernandes, Neera Burra, and Tara Anand, *A Critique of the National Child Labour Program, Sivakasi* (New Delhi: Indian Social Institute, July 1987).

[8] Neera Burra, "Glass Factories of Firozabad," *Economic and Political Weekly* (15 November and 22 November 1986). See also Sheela Barse, "Glass Factories of Firozabad," *Indian Express* (5 April, 6 April, and 7 April, 1986); and Debasish Chatterji, "Child Labour in Glass Industry," *Surya India* (June 1986).

glass is then put into a mold and carried by the children to another worker, who cuts it. The children work close to the heated furnaces and sometimes draw molten glass from the furnace. The air is full of chemical fumes, soot, and coal dust. The floor is littered with broken glass.

In the larger factories all the workers are paid by the hour or day. In small units where bangles are joined, workers are paid on a piece-rate basis. These small units employ about twenty workers, including three or four children each. In poorly ventilated rooms acetylene flames are used to join the ends of the bangle to form a ring, a process called *judai*. Other processes include creating grooves (*katai*), baking (*pakai*), and painting the grooves with minute portions of liquid gold before it is again baked to remove impurities. Some of these processes are hazardous, particularly when the bangles are placed against whirling wheels that generate glass dust and high heat. Children are employed in all these processes.

The factories of Firozabad process a great variety of glass products: bangles, bulbs, tumblers, jugs, chandeliers, cut-glass utility items. Factory owners do well by selling these products and by reselling unutilized coal that had been allocated to them by the government at prices well below market prices. Skilled workers are paid sixty or sixty-five rupees per day, but work lives are short. Few workers are able to continue past the age of thirty-five. Children are paid ten rupees per twelve-hour shift and when they are old enough to move into glass-blowing positions, they can double their daily wages.

According to the Labour Department of the Government of Uttar Pradesh, 13 percent of the 65,000 to 70,000 workers employed in these glass units are children. The Labour Department at Firozabad has recommended that child labor should not be banned because unless a child starts working at a very young age he will not get acclimatized to the intense heat. Children are also valuable because they can move at a great enough speed so that the molten glass does not harden before it can be fashioned by the adult workers. The Labour Department has suggested that hostels be constructed so that children who are on the night shift will have a place to stay nearby. Though night work for children is forbidden under the 1948 Factories Act, children as young as seven and eight work on the night shift. Factories run all night to avoid the expense of having to shut down the furnaces every evening.

Neera Burra, who visited the glass factories at Firozabad, puts the number of workers and child workers higher than those reported by the Labour Department. Interviews with factory owners, workers, and local politicians lead her to estimate that the labor force is between 150,000 to

200,000 and the number of children below the age of fourteen who are employed is between 40,000 and 50,000.[9]

The Pottery Industry of Khurja

Most of the five thousand or so children employed in the pottery industry of Khurja in Uttar Pradesh are *phantiwalas*. The boys pick up the empty molds from the *phanti*, or piece of wood on which five or six molds are kept, and bring them to the potter. The boys then carry the filled molds out into the sun to dry. The work is described locally as *uthai rakhai*, literally "pick up and put down." The *phanti*, with its molds, weighs from eight to eleven kilograms. According to the sociologist Neera Burra, who spent nineteen days in Khurja interviewing workers, factory owners, *thekedars* (contractors), master craftsmen, traders, doctors, and government officials, children made a thousand return trips in an eight-hour working day, covering a distance of six or seven kilometers.[10] The children also carried the half-dry pots to the workers for finishing. The children stack mugs, unload the containers that contain the unbaked clay goods before being fired in the kilns, scrape rough edges from mugs and other crockery pieces, clean the power-driven machines used by the potters, remove pebbles from the clay, clean the premises, and run errands.

Many of the children working in the potteries of Khurja are the children of local workers. Most are illiterate, though some have studied up to the fourth standard. The children earn up to 150 rupees a month for an eight-hour day. Unskilled workers are paid 200 rupees a month, and skilled workers 400 rupees. Burra notes that workers who started young—many of the children are eight or nine—and worked for fifteen or twenty years earned exactly the same as new adult entrants. Burra's findings are confirmed elsewhere in a longitudinal survey conducted in 26 villages near Hyderabad from 1965 to 1976, which found that those who began work as agricultural workers as children without having attended school actually earned less than those who had deferred entering the labor force until they were older and had been in school for several years. Those who began work at a young age proved to have lower body weights when they became older, and were therefore paid less by the landowners who employed them, than those who attended school. There

---

[9] Burra, "Glass Factories of Firozabad."

[10] For this review I have drawn from Neera Burra, *A Report on Child Labour in the Pottery Industry of Khurja, Uttar Pradesh* (New Delhi: DANIDA, November 1987, mimeo).

is thus a relationship between early entrance into the labor force, nutritional status, and life-time wage-earning capacity.[11])

Since silica is one of the raw materials used in the clay, pulmonary fibrosis caused by the inhalation of dust is a health hazard. Many workers develop asthmatic bronchitis and tuberculosis. Dr. Saxsena, the hospital superintendent at the local Khurja hospital, reports that many potters come to the hospital with tuberculosis. Twenty-five or thirty adult potters and an equal number of children visit the local clinic in town each day, with most of the complaints being pulmonary related.

Though pottery is a traditional industry in Khurja—blue pottery with Persian designs and colors and hookahs (smoking pipes) were among the traditional products—the present industry is relatively new. A Pottery Development Center was opened by the state government in 1946 with eight potters. Students were recruited and helped to become entrepreneurs. An industrial estate with eighteen pottery units was constructed. The pottery industry in Khurja produces for a wide market, unlike the local traditional village potters, who continue to produce for the local community. There are now 250 functioning pottery units producing 15,000 tons, or more than 20 percent of all the crockery produced in the small-scale sector in India.

Nearly 20,000 workers are employed in the pottery industry, of whom 5,000 are children below the age of fourteen. While a few units have less then ten workers, most of the units employ more than twenty-five workers and some as many as eighty or ninety. In order to evade the Factories Act, however, many of the units are listed as having less than ten workers. There is a ban on the employment of children under the age of fourteen in factories, but the ban does not apply to smaller units. In smaller units employers are also not required to provide drinking-water facilities, toilets, employees' medical insurance, and bonuses. There is also no job security in small units. "Everyone in Khurja—workers, employers, contractors and traders," writes Burra "were aware that under the Factories Act, child labour is expressly forbidden. When I first visited Khurja and talked to people, everyone denied that child labour existed. But when I showed them photographs of working children, then they said that the reason for their denial was because there was a ban on the employment of children under the Factories Act."[12]

Neither the workers nor the children are traditional potters. Most come from families of agricultural laborers. Often, agricultural families will send their children to work in the potteries. Children usually sup-

[11] K. Satyanarayana, A. Nadamuni Naidu, and B. S. Narasinga Rao, "Agricultural Employment, Wage Earnings, and Nutritional Status of Teenage, Rural Hyderabad Boys," *Indian Journal of Nutrition* 17 (1980), pp. 281–286.

[12] Burra, *A Report on Child Labour in the Pottery Industry*, p. 22.

plement family income, though a few are primary supporters. "Laxman Das is 12 years old," writes Burra, "and is a local Khurja boy. He and his younger brother, age 9, are the sole earning members of their family. Laxman Das was embarrassed at being asked what his father did and said: 'he has retired.' He and his brother support a seven-member family. The contractor, who was standing nearby when I was interviewing Laxman Das, said 'The man's a drunkard. The mother is lazy. They do no work because they have children to support them.' "[13]

. Another boy, Opal, started working when he failed the sixth-standard exam. He was thirteen. "My parents needed money for the marriage of my sister so my brother and I started working in the potteries. I thought that after a while I would go back to school but once you leave school there is no going back. We still have sisters to settle. My parents have very little land."[14]

Some adults bring their children to work. "Our wages are so low," explained one parent, "that often we have no choice but to take our children to work to supplement the family income."[15] Most of the children come from scheduled-caste or Muslim families. It should be emphasized, however, that these are not family-run units. Most of the Khurja factories are privately owned and are engaged in the mass production of low-cost goods. The working children are not traditional apprentices and are acquiring no skills that enhance their opportunities for higher wages.

Burra reports that the factory owners expressed a preference for child labor. "If an adult is asked to do this work of fetching and carrying he would take too long. Adults can't move with the speed that children can. It is not work meant for adults." Adult workers in factories where children were not employed said, "We don't like this work because it is tiring. The body of the child is supple and he can run fast, bend down and get up quickly without any problem. When you are older, it is difficult to do this work."[16]

A Village Near Pune

Our last account of working children is drawn from a visit to a village thirty kilometers from Pune. Strictly speaking these are not working children, for almost none are paid for the work they do. They are the daughters of ex-untouchable and low-caste families who are kept at home to help in the household. I spent an evening with twenty-five of these girls,

[13] Ibid.
[14] Ibid.
[15] Ibid., p. 23.
[16] Ibid.

ages nine to thirteen, who meet every evening in the one-room village schoolhouse for a nonformal education program. In this program there are no formal hours or curriculum and no examinations. The children come from seven to nine in the evening. They play and sing, are taught reading and numeracy, and are given some instruction in basic health and science. The children showed me a simple scientific experiment they had learned and answered my question about germs. The teacher, a local woman, is paid by the Institute of Education in Pune, a nongovernmental research and training organization. Rudimentary teaching materials are also provided by the Institute. This program is one of several experimental programs run by the Institute headed by Mrs. Chitra Naik, a well-known educationist.

One by one each of the girls answered my questions. What was their name and age? What do they do during the day? What do their parents do? Had they ever been to school and for how long? The children were remarkably articulate. Half of the children had been to school for one year or less, a few had completed two years of school. Only one girl had completed the third standard. None were literate before coming to the program, including the girl who had completed the third standard. A few of the children work for wages but most were at home helping their mothers. They look after their younger siblings. (Almost all were the eldest daughters). They fetch water and firewood and care for the cattle. Since their mothers often work, many of the children prepare the main meals for the entire family.

I asked the class whether they would have liked to remain in school. All but two girls raised their hands. The two explained that they had done so badly learning to read that they didn't want to remain in school, but the others said they left school at the request of their mothers. I asked the children if they would keep their own daughters in school. All of them raised their hands. "But what would you do," I asked, "if you had to work and needed your eldest daughter to take care of your younger children?" "I would send my babies to my mother-in-law," said one girl. "We could have a crèche," said another, "and we could have someone watch over all the children." "Who would take care of the cattle?" I asked. "We could bring the cattle together," another girl replied, "and hire someone to look after them." The children clearly did not regard their parents' decision about their schooling as choiceless.

Observations

This review of the child-labor situation in the Bangalore city market; in Secunderabad; in the match, glass, and pottery industries; among bonded laborers in Andhra; and in a village near Pune suggests a number of observations:

1. Child labor in India is largely a preindustrial, precapitalist labor force. Almost none of India's children work in mines or in large factories, as was the case in England and the United States in the nineteenth century. India's children are mainly in the unorganized informal sector, including cottage industries and the tertiary service sector, or in agriculture. Child labor in India is not the product of industrialism and capitalism, but represents the persistence of the traditional role of the child as a worker.

2. Child workers in India are largely illiterate. Most have never been to school and those who attend school drop out before completing four standards. Among Western countries in the nineteenth and early twentieth centuries, children in the labor force had completed six to nine years of compulsory education and most could read and write.

3. Since education is not compulsory, children begin work at very young ages. Even children of pre-primary-school age can be seen working in cottage industries.

4. Few children outside of agriculture can be said to be apprentices learning traditional family skills. The urban working children described here are in relatively new occupations and few are following in the footsteps of their parents. The image of the child as an apprentice to a master craftsman is a romantic one unrelated to reality.

5. The "skills" acquired by the children are rarely those that could not be acquired at an older age. Indeed, the skills are typically of a low level: simple, routinized, manual tasks or carting.

6. Employers and government officials have a notion of children's work, involving speed, patience, manual dexterity, suppleness, and so forth, which is of benefit to employers. Since some of these attributes diminish with age, their early use does not necessarily enhance the employability of children as they grow older. To the contrary, the high risk associated with this work can reduce the subsequent opportunities for employment.

7. Early entrance into the labor force is no assurance of a higher wage later. Wages paid to adults are not determined by whether or not they worked as children. Where the growth of children is stunted as a result of premature employment, their wages as adults may be less than those who enter the labor force at an older age.

8. The ban on factory employment of children combined with fewer restrictions on child employment in cottage industries is an inducement for employers to subcontract to smaller shops where wages are lower and working conditions are inferior.

9. While parents gain from the employment of their children—or by using the labor of children at home—it remains unclear how much worse off the

family would be if the children were in school. Financial contributions by children to household income are often small. Children sometimes work to pay debts incurred by the family related to the marriage of their children, and household labor, though valuable and valued, is not necessarily indispensable. As children in the nonformal village school near Pune argued, their parents' decisions to remove them from school was not the only available choice.

It is important to keep these elements in mind as we turn to a descriptive report on the attitudes of government officials and others toward child labor, its causes and consequences, and the factors that influence their thinking about the desirability and feasibility of ending child labor.

1. Muslim boy in his father's shop selling ornaments for cattle, Bangalore city market

2. Boy in sewing workshop in a Catholic home for street children, Secunderabad

3. Muhammad, age 14, peddler, Bangalore city market

4. Boy employed in metalworking shop, Bangalore city market

5. Match factory employing women and young girls, Sivakasi

6. Boys filling slotted frames to make matchsticks in workshop outside of Sivakasi

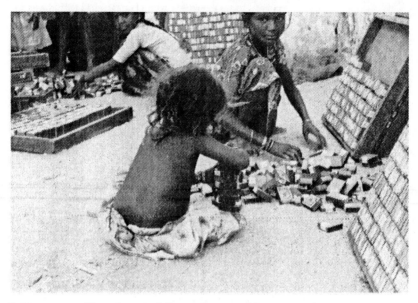

7. Three-year-old working with her eight-year-old sister

8. Three-year-old stacking matchboxes in workshop outside of Sivakasi

9. Devi, age 10, making matchboxes on the veranda of her home in Sivakasi

10. Girl stacking matchboxes in workshop outside of Sivakasi

11. Boy selling condiments, Bangalore

12. Boys carting papers of printing workshop, Sivakasi

3

Dialogues on Child Labor

The Harbans Singh Report

THE reaction to the Harbans Singh report on the condition of working children in the match industry in the south Indian town of Sivakasi provides us with a microcosm for understanding the entire range of responses toward child labor by government officials, social activists, and trade unionists. We begin this review of attitudes toward child labor with an interview with the official who was secretary of the Tamilnadu Labour Department at the time Harbans Singh submitted his report to the government.

I asked the official, Mr. Padmanaban, to describe to me his reaction and that of other officials to the Harbans Singh report and whether any of its recommendations were implemented. Mr. Padmanaban first commented on the overall situation in Sivakasi.

"Sivakasi is a very backward agricultural area. The main industries are matchsticks, firecrackers, and litho printing. A few enterprising entrepreneurs set up these factories in the 1920s. It's a backward area and the people in it are backward. First the parents started to work in these factories and they said let the children work too. The sticks are given to the peasants and they take them to their houses to make the matches. The whole family does the work at home."

Don't children also work in the factories?

"Yes, there are some ten-to-fourteen year olds. They are the ones who don't have earning members in their family. Sometimes the father is too old to work, or if the father is working he says why not the son too. Here every man wants his son to take on the same job. If the father works in the factory he wants his son to do the same work.

"The employers also want the children. It is easy to handle the child in the factory. There are no discipline problems, no unions. Another factor is that the children have nimble fingers. They are deft. The children can do more work than the adults. And the children only get one-third or one-half of the wages adults get.

"But you have to ask," he continued, "why is the boy working in the factory? You see, it is a question of survival. In agriculture you must work three months at least before you can get any money from what you sell, but in the factory you can get quick money. Child labor has been there for a long time. It has to be regulated. There must be proper transportation, proper facilities, and most important, proper wages. The children should not be treated as sweat labor. There must be a proper study area for the children who leave the school to go for these jobs. And the legis- .lation is not adequate to give them protection."

What would happen if child labor were banned?

"There are hundreds of factories there with children under fourteen. Are we going to close down these factories? The parents say 'We want our children in these factories.' The children must work to support their parents, especially the old parents who do not have any income. The adults do not want to work there since they can get work elsewhere, so they say send their children."

If wages were higher wouldn't adults take these jobs?

"The economic status of the factory requires that the children must work there. You must look at the problem from an economic and from a sociological point of view. It should not be viewed in isolation. We say that where the children are employed, then you organize some education for them. You make a child skilled in the factory. The child working in the factory learns how to make firecrackers and maybe something else. You see, the factory owners have picked up this young material. The material has to be molded, isn't it? You have to give him some skills. Let the child have his meal in the factory. Provide toilet facilities. You enrich this boy or girl to become a really skilled worker in the factory. If you take the child out of the factory, the factory would close and no one would have work.

"A father is working there, so he will want his son to work there too. It is the same in agriculture. The father brings his son to work in the field and to help with the animals. So the father thinks that if there is unemployment on the land, why not take his ten or eleven year old to the factory? Why not train him so that his future is assured? If I am helpless and have no land, no patronage, no political claim, and I am working in the factory, I would like my son to come to the factory so that when I retire my son can work and support the family. It is like an apprenticeship. The typical man in a backward village, he says that a ten-year-old boy is no longer a child. You may say he is a child, but the villager says that if he can walk a distance of one kilometer, go to the cinema, talk to people, and can work, he is not a child."

Why not wait until the child is older before putting him to work, I asked?

"Unemployment is so high. If I wait until my boy is eighteen, will he be assured of a job? Who will give him a job after eighteen? This does not apply to people with power or to people with some land. Then the son can get some adult to help him take up a job. But in our state fifty or sixty percent of the people are below poverty. They earn maybe two hundred fifty rupees a month. This is the compelling reason for children to work. If you put twenty thousand children in Sivakasi out of work, what will happen to their families and who will give them employment when they become eighteen and the factories are closed?"

Was the Harbans Singh report ever released to the public?

"No, it was intended as a confidential report to the government. When the government commissions a report, normally it does not make it public. The labor minister asked us what to do about Sivakasi. I told him how can we end twenty thousand jobs. A government official has to be practical. And the minister knows that there would be a political problem if we abolished these jobs. So I should be practical, not theoretical, when I speak to the minister."

A Social Activist's Perspective

Though the Harbans Singh report was never released, its contents were widely discussed in the press as a result of the efforts of a young activist, Smitu Kothari, who obtained access to the report and publicized its findings. Kothari went to Sivakasi, met the children and their parents, owners, managers, foremen, distributors, government officials, and leaders of the local political organizations. He photographed the children at work and in a number of articles in the popular press reported his findings. His reports confirmed and amplified what appeared in the Harbans Singh report.

"The general working environment in most of these cottage industries," he wrote, "was appalling. Cramped spaces, practically no ventilation and filthy floors were evident in about every unit we visited. Puddles of chemicals around the vats of chemicals were also evident in most units."[1]

Though Kothari visited Sivakasi six years after Harbans Singh had submitted his report to the government, he found no indication that safety conditions had improved. An accident, he reported, took place in September 1981. There was a massive explosion at the Arunchalam Fireworks on the outskirts of Sivakasi, killing thirty-two, persons including six children. A few months later, in February 1982, in a nearby village, a firecracker factory went up in flames killing six more children. The children had been stuffing explosive powder into the firecrackers when the accident occurred.

[1] Smitu Kothari, "There's Blood on Those Matchsticks: Child Labour in Sivakasi," *Economic and Political Weekly* (2 July 1983), p. 1193.

Writing about why there was child labor at Sivakasi, Kothari blamed the government's development program. "The underdeveloped drought-prone conditions of the district have made possible the recruitment of children in a growing cottage and small scale match sector that competes with a multinational match industry," he wrote.[2] When I spoke to Kothari in his office in Delhi, where he edits a monthly magazine for activists in voluntary organizations, he went on to say that "child labor is the result of development. We have a policy that makes it impossible for people to be absorbed in the labor force. Government neglected to develop irrigation in the Sivakasi area, so it remains poor and the children inevitably become laborers." According to Kothari, various proposals to create irrigation schemes in the district were turned down by the government. He is convinced that the proposals were killed "because employers do not want to develop the region since they want to be able to employ local people at low wages." When Kamaraj Nadar became chief minister of the state, he said, the government supported the Nadar factory owners who opposed the development projects. Tamil Nadu, said Kothari, has implemented a number of irrigation projects efficiently, but per capita expenditures for irrigation in Ramanathapuram district, where Sivakasi is located, is very low. "I think that the only way you can deal with the problem of child labor is to develop the land. If there is enough employment for adults they will not need to send their children to work in the factories."

Kothari is opposed to banning child labor. "When considering intervention," he wrote, "we are faced with a grim reality where we have to accept that in this situation we can, at best, humanize this development. . . . Displacing the 45,000 children in Sivakasi . . . raises another serious dilemma. The displacement will not only affect the livelihood of their parents but will give a boost to the multinational WIMCO as the small and cottage sectors will definitely be hit by this step. An alternative could be for these sectors to semi-mechanise their operations. Ironically, the small-scale sector has refused to use these on the plea that it would displace employment." Kothari also opposes replacing children with adults. "If . . . displacement takes place, can their parents who because of economic compulsion send their children to work, work in their place? This will, of course, mean a final step in their alienation from their lands."[3]

"The only really significant change that can reduce child labour," he continued, "is to launch a massive irrigation programme in the area. Not only will substantial land be made productive, parents of working children who own this land will experience economic recovery. But as was

[2] Ibid., p. 1194.
[3] Ibid.

pointed out earlier, there will be tremendous resistance to this from the
owners of industry." Kothari concluded on a militant note. "We can
therefore conclude that there is only a political solution to the problem.
Solutions have to be conceived and activised outside the present framework. Meanwhile only a major involvement by action groups and/or trade
unions, which agitate for the children's rights, can change the plight of
child labour not only in Sivakasi but all over the country."[4]

What is the attitude of trade unions toward child labor in Sivakasi? In
the West, unions were in the forefront of the movement to abolish child
labor on the grounds that adult workers were displaced by poorly paid
children. I put the question to Kothari. "There are four trade unions in
Sivakasi," he replied, "but none of them are interested in enforcing the
child labor laws. In fact I cannot think of a single union that has taken up
the cause of child labor. I think the unions don't take up the issue because there is a shortage of work in Sivakasi and the children come from
the same families as the union members. Moreover, employers make the
argument that the work done by children is suited for them and could
not be done as well by adults. The same argument is used in the carpet
industry. The firms want more children. They say there is a shortage of
children in Sivakasi!"

An Industrial Relations Official

I raised the same question with Dr. P. Lakshmanan, director of the Tamil
Nadu Institute of Labour Studies in Madras, a center devoted to the
teaching and training of trade-union workers and factory inspectors. For
many years Dr. Lakshmanan has worked closely with trade union leaders
as well as with government officials and managers. His institute is under
the state Department of Labour. "The unions at Sivakasi," he said, "mainly
want better wages and amenities for their members, they don't really
care about child labor."

Why?

"Well, they would be unpopular with the parents of the children. The
parents support the employers. Besides, the unions are not there in the
cottage industries where the children work. One reason employers prefer
child labor is that the children don't join unions and agitate! Children are
obedient. Any type of work can be extracted from the children. You can
tell a child to clean the table or go for coffee, but not an adult. Adults
will be conscious of hours of work, but children will work until the em-

[4] Ibid., p. 1199, 1200.

ployer releases them. And they are nimble. They can do some work better than adults."

I asked Dr. Lakshmanan if he thought the labor inspectors in Tamil Nadu could enforce the child-labor laws.

"If you look at the employment registers in the factories you will not see any children listed. The employers pay them cash, they do not pay any benefits, and the wages are lower than what they pay adults. So it is difficult to enforce the minimum-wage laws or get any benefits for the children. The employers send the children out when they hear that inspectors are coming. We could send the police with the inspector to surround a factory, fine the employer, and make him put the children on the register. But if we catch him, he will list the children, but then strike them off the register the next day. And if we go to court, he will only have to pay fifty or a hundred rupees. The law says there can be a fine or imprisonment, but judges will not imprison an employer. So the employer only needs to pay the fine and then he can break the law again. And if he is caught breaking the law again and we went to the court, it would take the court another six months to find him guilty and he would just pay the fine again! In Tamil Nadu last year there were three thousand seven hundred prosecutions under the provisions of the factory acts, and about three thousand five hundred convictions. The total fines came to about six hundred forty-three thousand rupees, an average of less than two hundred rupees per fine.[5] That includes all violations. There are no separate figures on child labor. Most of our labor laws are not enforced. To do that you need to change the attitudes of the employers and you must make workers aware of their statutory rights.

"The various committees appointed by the government," he pointed out, "have not recommended banning child labor. What would the children do? Poor people say that their children are an asset, that they need to employ their children. If you go to parents and tell them that they should send their children to school, the parents will say that they need to send their children to work."

I asked him if anything had came of the recommendations of the Harbans Singh report a decade earlier. Had there been any improvement in the condition of the children? He said that the report called for the raising of wages for the children, setting up sheds in the villages so the children need not travel to the factories, and the establishment of nonformal education. The only improvement so far, he said, was that there was now a nonformal education program for about 900 children.

[5] Most of the earlier acts pertaining to the illegal employment of children provided for fines of up to 500 rupees. The Child Labour (Prohibition and Regulation) Act of 1986 lays down a minimum penalty of 10,000 rupees. No data are available as to the enforcement of the new act.

Matches, he said, is not the only industry in Tamil Nadu with child labor. "There are children here working on the plantations, making bidis at home, and working in the hotels and small shops. So many retail and wholesale shops employ children. There are more hotels coming up here so there are now more children working."

Do you think there has been an increase in child labor in Tamil Nadu?

"The percentage of children as workers is declining, but the number of children working is going up. That is because of the population increase. As the labor force grows, the number of child laborers increases. Take Sivakasi. If I am a parent, then last year I may have sent two children to work there, but now I have another child so I send him to the factory too. There are more children now in Sivakasi than there used to be."

Do you think, I asked, the government will ever release the Harbans Singh report to the public?

"The report says the law is not enforced, so it would create a bad impression with the public if it were issued. Then why should the government publish the report until action is taken? And after action is taken, then the report is out of date so it is too late to publish it."

A Catholic View

Father K. N. George, director of the Madras School of Social Work, is a Catholic priest known for his strong opinions, especially on matters affecting the poor. A small, bouncy, loquacious man, Father George characterized child labor as a "necessary evil." "The wages you get in agriculture are very low. Agricultural workers are paid fourteen rupees a day. The husband and wife work, and they may have, say, three children. So they take the children to work with them. Sometimes the children get two rupees for looking after the cattle. Then there are children working in mechanic shops, in tea stalls, in hotels and garages. They work twelve hours a day or more. They don't get proper food, their clothing is inadequate and they just sleep on the ground. But at least when they work in a garage, they learn a job. Sometimes their parents work on construction projects and the children help. If we stop the children from working, they will have an empty stomach. So my view is that it is a necessary evil until the parents have enough income to support the family.

"Here in Madras there are about one thousand boys doing ragpicking, earning about four rupees a day. They get paid for the rags and the employers then sell those rags for ten rupees. We have a project to give the boys gloves and some hot food. But, I say, let the boys be a source of income for their family. I think we need to think about second-best solutions. I don't think we can enforce the legislation without hurting the families."

A Labour Ministry Official

The view that regulation and amelioration rather than abolition are what is called for was echoed by a high official in the Ministry of Labour in New Delhi, a one-time member of the International Labor Organization (ILO) governing board and a highly influential person in the field of labor policy in India. Given the dependence of the poor upon child labor, he explained, it is unrealistic to try to end child labor at this time. But, he went on to say, the government should end child labor in dangerous industries such as firecrackers and diamond cutting. "We should also put more effort into improving conditions in the other industries where children work. We should shift the match industry to the villages so children would not have to travel and the work would be safer. We should improve ventilation where the children work. We should provide benches for the children working on the hand looms. And we should give the working children at least one hour of education a day. The education should be provided by the employer with the help of voluntary agencies."

It would be a mistake, he explained, to have a uniform minimum-age law for employment since it couldn't be enforced. For the same reason he was opposed to making child labor in the cottage-industries sector illegal, especially since that sector hires so many children from poor families. "But we shouldn't make child labor legal either! Let us keep it this way, but we should do more to improve the education and condition of children in small-scale industries and in the cottage-industries sector."

Another View from the Labour Ministry

I asked Mrs. Girija Eswaran, the ranking official in the Labour Ministry concerned with child-labor laws and their enforcement whether she had any evidence that the enforcement of child-labor laws in Sivakasi would hurt the poor because employers would close down factories, or whether the employers would then simply hire adults. "I met with the employers at Sivakasi," she said. "They are quite brazen about the use of child labor. They said that they would show me their books so I can see how little profit they make. They said that if the government ended child labor they would cut costs by mechanizing rather than hire more adults. The employers know that the politicians and the parents would be in an uproar if we tried to end child labor. So they feel quite strong in dealing with the government. You know, the children are exploited by employers, parents, the unions, the politicians—they are all in collusion with the government, which does not enforce the law."

Mrs. Eswaran said that her ministry was trying to get some studies on the economics of child labor. "We need to know if companies would fail if they could not employ children." The Commerce Ministry, she said, is concerned with encouraging the growth of small-scale and cottage-industries to expand employment, and they insist that many small shops would close if they could not employ children. The carpet industry, bangles, matches, and other cottage industries would be badly hurt. The ministry also points out, she added, that some of these are important export industries. "They tell me that the carpet industry would collapse if children were not employed! Other countries, they say, like Pakistan, employ child labor and how could we then compete with Pakistan? The Commerce Ministry says we must look at the economics of it." In the mid-1970s, she said, India was able to expand substantially its carpet exports after the Shah of Iran had banned the employment of children in the carpet industry, pushing the price up and reducing their exports.

The Commerce Ministry, she added, was itself an employer of child labor. The Development Commissioner of Handicrafts under the Ministry of Commerce runs apprenticeship programs to teach children to be carpet weavers. There are government training centers in Kashmir, Uttar Pradesh, and other parts of northern India. The children—they are supposed to be twelve, but many are younger—are given nominal wages (200 to 300 rupees per month) while they learn to weave, and then they are given positions in small weaving workshops and in factories. Often, she said, they work on pit looms within their own home in rooms that are damp, dimly lit, and ill-ventilated.

I asked Mrs. Eswaran if she thought that the officials I had spoken to were right in thinking that it was possible to improve the working conditions for the children. "We have tried to improve conditions for children working on pit looms. The carpet is nine feet long so they put the loom into a large pit and the child sits on the cold ground. It is so wet and cold sometimes that the children get cramps in their feet. But there is nothing you can do about it since the village houses are too low to put the loom at ground level. We suggested that the employers build a loom shed, but the parents say they don't want it. They say that each hut should have its own loom since the whole family works the loom, and they each take turns. It is literally a cottage industry.

"In Firozabad," she continued, "I saw bangles made in the cottages. Little children work alongside the women. The glass is molded in the factories, and in the houses the bangles are joined with a candle. There are other parts to the process of bangle making and some of it is done in the village houses. I have been to these houses. The squalor is sometimes unbelievable."

What about enforcing minimum wages?

"In the tea plantations," she said, "the unions objected to proposals to raise the minimum wage. They think that then the employers wouldn't hire the children! If the children were not hired, the tea-plantation owners would go outside the plantation to find workers and when the children grew up they would not be able to find jobs. In the plantations it is the custom that employers hire the children of the tea-plantation workers and if a worker dies then her children are hired."

An Economist

Nasir Tyabji, an able young economist at the Madras Institute for Development Studies, examined the contribution of child labor to household income and the contribution of labor to the costs of production in the match industry. The idea of the study, he said, was to find out whether child labor was essential to the household and to the industry. "The amount added by the child to household income seems to be small," he reported, "but it is often stable. So it can be important, especially when the parents are in agriculture. We don't have any data on the second question yet, but we think that the labor costs are not as important as people think. We don't have any evidence that the match industry in Sivakasi would go under if they couldn't hire children and had to pay higher wages to adults. But if that were the case then the excise taxes on WIMCO could be raised to protect the small-scale industries. They are protected already," he pointed out.

"When all is said and done we need to ban child labor. If children were removed from the work force there would be more jobs for adults. Sivakasi has to be attacked. The problem is that the government has not been willing to deal with it."

Why? I asked.

"There are about eighteen families who control the industry and they are all tied to the politicians. When there was that bus crash and so many children were killed the government minister said he would take firm steps to end child labor. But nothing happened. It is because there is a nexus of the employers, the politicians, and the families."

Mr. Tyabji's views were exceptional. Of the dozen people I interviewed in Madras, he was one of two (the other an exgovernment official also working at the Madras Institute of Development Studies) who believed that child labor should be banned at Sivakasi and elsewhere in the state. All the others said that the government should try to ameliorate the conditions of work. Though they agreed that child labor should be prohibited in dangerous occupations, they did not think child labor should be prohibited in the match industry.

A Tea-Plantation Official

"The workers," said the former chairman of the Tea Board in West Bengal, "are as attached to the land as the tea bushes. They were born in the tea estates. They live there all their lives. They die there. The mother who works in the tea gardens has no place to leave her children. She puts her child on her back and brings the child with her when she works. What is more natural then that the child wants to know what the mother is doing and wants to help her pluck the tea. That is how the child becomes a worker. It is easy for children to pluck. Their fingers are nimble and the bushes are at their height. The child plucks the leaves and puts them into her mother's basket. Whatever the child plucks increases the pay of the mother. I would not say that the children are employed. They are helping their parents. Then, when the child is twelve, she is given a basket of her own and earns her own wages. She is paid half of what an adult is given."

The tea plantations of West Bengal and Assam employ 21,000 children between the ages of twelve and fifteen, 14,000 adolescents from fifteen to eighteen, and 203,000 adult males and 224,000 adult females. No figures are kept on how many children under twelve—the minimum age for employment in the tea plantations—"help" their parents. Adults are paid 9.70 rupees a day, children 4.95 rupees. Workers are also given cereals at reduced rates, 20 percent lower than the market price, and each family is given living quarters, a single living room, a kitchen space, and a common bathroom.

Until a few years ago, I was told, the owners of the plantations were responsible for providing education to the children of plantation workers. Then the government passed the responsibility onto the district boards, but the tea plantation owners must still pay for all costs at the primary school except for the teacher's salaries. Primary school, standards one through five, is, I was told, "compulsory." "Yes, it is compulsory," said the former chairman of the Tea Board, "but it is not enforced in a God-forsaken place like that. By class four, most of the children drop out. When they are nine or ten years old they are actually working and do plucking with their mothers. During the plucking season, from June through September, the mothers get additional wages on a piece basis. When it is off season the workers prune the bushes and do other work.

In the harvest season the whole family is working. In the plantations there is both recognized and unrecognized child labor, since some children are below and some above twelve years of age. During these four months there is also some additional contract labor and these workers also bring their children. Minimum wage laws do not apply to contract laborers, who are all paid by piece work. During the harvest season as much as forty percent of the labor force may be contract labor.

"The workers call themselves coolies. That mental attitude is there, so they say, of what use is an educated child. As it is the tea industry cannot absorb all the children into the labor force. Except during the harvest season there is not enough work. About half the children in the plantations enter the labor force there, while the other half have to go outside the plantations to find work."

The secretary of the West Bengal Labour Department explained to me that the minimum age for working on the plantations was twelve, compared with fourteen in industry, because plantation work was not considered hazardous. "We in the department are willing to raise the minimum age to fourteen, but the basic problem is that the parents want to send the children to work. The plantation unions also say that the work isn't hazardous and it adds to the income of the family."

But, I asked, don't the unions understand that if there were no child labor, more adults would be employed?

"No, they say that all the members of their families are working in the plantations now, so they would lose income if their children could not work. The practice in the tea plantations is that if a worker dies his child is then employed. If the children were not hired, the unions say, then the owners would go outside the plantation to bring in workers, and then when the children grew up they would not be able to find jobs on the plantations. They also say there is no point in educating the children since the only jobs are in the plantations. If the children were educated where would they go to find work?"

Do all the children remain to work on the plantations?

"No, some young hill people get education and join the army—particularly the Nepalis—and some come down to the plains for employment. They take jobs in shops, become drivers, or work in repair shops. The hill people are more interested in education than the plains people. There are some good schools run by the missionaries in the hills, and a few run by the government. There are fewer schools in the plantations in the plains and most of the children there drop out of school by the third grade."

What happens to them? What kind of jobs do they get?

"Those who don't find work in the plantations go to the cities to find jobs. They work in shops serving tea and cleaning tables. There are no restrictions on the employment of children in domestic work and the middle class here hires children. There must be tens of thousands of children doing that kind of work in Calcutta. The boys or girls usually work in two or three houses during the week. They don't go to school, they only do domestic work."

A Labor Secretary on the Carpet Industry

The carpet industry is a major employer of children. In Uttar Pradesh and in Kashmir the Government of India Handicraft Board has set up apprenticeship programs to enable children to learn to do carpet weaving at an early age. Private establishments prefer to hire children. "The employers," explained the secretary of labor in Uttar Pradesh, "say that the children's fingers are small. They have nimble little fingers, and they can move them faster. The children can make more knots in the carpets than adults because of their little fingers."

The secretary described the conditions under which the children work, in rooms that are crowded and have poor ventilation and bad lighting. "I complained to one manufacturer," the secretary explained, "but he said it would cost more for them to put in better lighting and windows and benches. I said that the bad lighting was hurting the eyesight of the children so he should provide better lighting. And he said that the ministry should provide eyeglasses for adults!"

Can't you do anything about it? I asked. Couldn't you prosecute him? "No, the Factory Act does not apply to these small establishments. It only covers places employing more than ten persons. So there is no statutory protection for children in factories that employ under ten people. We think the act should be amended to cover these small establishments. We can inspect factories but under the law the labor department does not have machinery to deal with the unorganized sector at all. And even in the case of factories, if an employer is found in violation, the fine is only two hundred to five hundred rupees. The case can take two years, and once the inspectors have made the "mistake" of bringing a case for prosecution then the inspector will have to go to court many, many times to win the case. The act says there can be imprisonment for one month or a fine for violating the labor laws, but the court always makes it a fine. No one ever goes to jail for violating the labor acts.

"In the carpet industry the owners say that the costs will go up if we abolish child labor. The owners say they will not employ the adults if they cannot hire children."

Why?

"Oh, just to teach them a lesson! The carpet owners are usually high-caste Hindus or well-off Muslims. They are not bothered about poor people. Now the Commerce Ministry has set up a program for children in the carpet industry. They are taught how to improve their carpet work, how to join the threads together and to finish off the carpets by scissors. These things are taught by the industries department. And the children are given a certificate! But these children are not made literate. They are not getting a general education. That is because the parents are greedy. So an awakening has to be brought to the parents. They need to know that an investment in the child is more important than the little income they can get from their children."

Is it true, I asked, that the Commerce Ministry supports the use of child labor in the carpet industry? I was told by an official in Delhi that the ministry is concerned that if children were not employed in the carpet industry, India could not effectively compete with Pakistan and Iran in the sale of carpets and exports would fall. They also argue, I was told, that you must start teaching carpet weaving at an early age and not wait until the children are fifteen.

"Yes, that is the view in the Commerce Ministry, especially in the Handicraft Board, but I don't share those views. The other problem, perhaps the greatest problem, is the demand of the people. There were reports of poor conditions in the carpet factories in Mirzapur, and some employers were prosecuted. There was talk of closing down the factories. People in the area were scared that they would not be able to get employment for their children. There were cries in the Congress party that without work these people would not have food. But we said we should prohibit the employment of children. When we arrived in Mirzapur, the children started running away from the factory saying that the antichild labor people have come! There is now a committee under the central Ministry of Labour with labor ministers from four states looking into the question of how working conditions for children can be improved. But we should prohibit the employment of children! If the laws were enforced then employers would have to hire adults and pay fixed wages. Now we cannot get employers to pay even the minimum wages to children. The problem is that we have no field agency in this department that can enforce child-labor or minimum-wage laws. In all of U.P. we have only forty inspectors under the Factory Act to inspect ten thousand factories. These labor inspectors deal with child labor too, but they cannot deal with the unorganized sector. Our laws are outdated.

"In rural areas employers do not even know that the employment of children is an offense. It is with the same with bonded labor. There is no enforcement agency. We found that some members of the U.P. legislative assembly had children working for them as bonded laborers under old contracts."

How does bonded labor come about?

"Suppose I borrowed one hundred rupees some years ago from a land-lord in the village. Then I work for the landlord to repay the debt. I get some payment as livelihood, and the rest of the work is for repaying the loan. And if I die before paying off the debt, then my children or grand-children must work for the landlord! Often children are sent as bonded laborers to pay off the loan. If we enforce these laws on bonded labor and child labor, there is bound to be some class conflict."

I have met many government officials in state and central government labor departments, I told the secretary, but he was the only official I had spoken to who was so strongly opposed to child labor. How, I asked, did he come to develop such strong views on this issue?

"I belong to a scheduled-caste community in the Punjab. We had no land. We were agricultural laborers. We had no money to spend on fes-tivals. At nine my father took me out of school and sent me to work. I rebelled and wanted to stay in school. I even threatened suicide! So my parents agreed to let me stay in school. I was at the top of my class, so I stayed on in school and went to college. Ultimately, I entered the Indian Administrative Service. I was the oldest child and other members of my family, my younger brothers and sisters, followed me to school. I don't think my father was so poor that he had to send me to work, but it was not the custom in his family to send children to school. Many parents do not think, but just send their children out to work. If we in the govern-ment emphasize that children should not be sent to work, then they will go to school.

"Now all my children are in college. If I had listened to my father I would still be working in the village."

4

Dialogues on Education

A Ministry of Education Official

"DID you and other officials," I asked a senior official in the Ministry of Education, "who had been working with Rajiv Gandhi on the government's new National Policy on Education consider making education compulsory? If you did, what were the arguments for and against, and why was a decision made *not* to make it compulsory?"

"The question didn't arise," came the reply, "because we already have compulsory-education laws in sixteen of our twenty-two states, though given the social conditions in the country it has not been possible to enforce the laws."

I know, I continued, that you have numerous state laws called "Compulsory Education," but what you have is enabling legislation that permits local authorities to make education compulsory, but does not compel them.

"That's not so," the official contradicted me. "These laws may not be enforced, but they do provide for compulsory education. The question was raised in Parliament when the prime minister introduced the new education policy and my assistant researched the matter for us."

Once again I challenged him. I explained that my understanding was that the state legislation is modeled after the British parliamentary act of 1870, which says that local authorities are *permitted* to write rules requiring parents to send their children to school and setting penalties for those who fail to do so. A decade later, in 1880, the British Parliament passed legislation *requiring* local authorities to make education mandatory. I hadn't seen all the state legislation in India, but none that I had seen made it mandatory upon local authorities to establish compulsory education.

You're wrong," said the official, and he called his assistant and instructed him to bring in the state legislation. After the assistant entered with a large folder in hand, I suggested we look at the legislation for Tamil Nadu since I had just been there, had read the legislation, and had discussed the matter with the former finance secretary of the government, who told me that none of the local authorities had ever made education compulsory. The assistant handed me the Tamil Nadu legislation and I recited excerpts from the relevant section (article 44): "any local authority *may* [my emphasis], by a resolution passed at a meeting specially convened for the purpose and supported by the votes of not less than two-thirds of the members present, resolve that elementary education shall be compulsory within the whole or a specified part of the local area under its jurisdiction."[1]

The official looked surprised. We then turned to other state laws. The Punjab law also said that local authorities "may" make education compulsory.[2] I noted that in my travels I had found few local authorities that had made education compulsory and that state governments were not pressing local authorities to write bylaws to set up enforcement machinery.

"That's just as well," said the official. "I was once posted in a union territory which had a compulsory education act. I found poor people were subject to penalties for not sending their children to school. Some teachers were charging parents ten rupees a month for *not* reporting that their children were *not* in school! How could a poor man send his son to school when he needs him to care for his cattle? Villages have no system of stall feeding. According to the Operations Research Group study there are forty-four million children working. If these children can't be prevented from working, then to impose compulsory education would be to deal with the problem in an ostrich-like fashion. There's a double problem. We have an educational system that is not adequate for our children, and a social system that obligates poor people not to send their children to school. So how can we punish poor parents if their children are not in school? In 1995 the government will take a fresh look at child labor and then we can look at the compulsory education question. There is no point in saying things that you cannot do.

"I think," he continued, "that by and large the people of India want their children to be educated, so we do not need coercive power to send their children to school. Besides, what right do we have to compel parents to send children to schools that are not worth much. The teachers aren't any good. Often they don't even appear at the school. We must first provide the country with schools that are worth something. Right now our schools are trash!"

I explained that I now understood why government officials had developed a system of nonformal education for working children. It provides education for children who are working and it is seen as more useful for

[1] *Tamil Nadu Elementary Education Act, 1920*, with amendments to 1973 (Madras: Government of Tamil Nadu, 1973), article 44.

[2] This is a standard feature of state education acts. Initiative for the establishment of compulsory education is given to local authorities subject to the approval of the state government. However, several state laws do permit the state government to take the initiative. I have not found any communities, however, where compulsory education has been instituted.

the children of the poor than the primary schools. "Many parents and children," he interrupted, "also prefer a system of part-time education." Then why not make nonformal part-time education compulsory for children who do not attend primary schools? He avoided the question and, saying that people were waiting to see him, terminated the interview.

I left his office surprised that a high government official was unaware that state governments had not made education compulsory, but on second thought I realized that we had disagreed on a technical matter. Whether the legislation says "may" or "shall," all government officials agree that in fact virtually no authority in India makes education compulsory. There are no enforcement authorities, no provisions for the compulsory registration of names and birthdates of children, no enumeration registers, no procedures for issuing notices to parents and guardians whose children are not attending school, and no penalties for failing to send children to school. No cases against parents or guardians are brought before administrative agencies or courts. Nor have elected or appointed officials in the state or central governments pressed for the enforcement of compulsory-education legislation.

What was more interesting in our discussion was to hear the view that education should not be made compulsory not only because parents need the income of their working children but because the educational system is itself worthless. It was a view I had heard before, but not from a high-ranking education official within the central government.

An Ahmedabad Social Activist

The most articulate and severe critic of India's educational system that I encountered was Mrs. Ela Bhatt. Mrs. Bhatt is a well-known social activist in Ahmedabad and a member of Parliament. She is the founder and organizer of the Self-Employed Women's Association. SEWA has organized thousands of women and children, including workers in the bidi industry, garment makers, and ragpickers. Many of the women and children collect scrap and junk from middle-class families, such as bags, bottles, and rags, which they recycle for sale. About a third of the members, she said, are ex-untouchables, another third Muslims, and the remainder belong to lower castes. SEWA was initially affiliated with the Textile Labour Association, one of the powerful unions in Ahmedabad, but it was expelled when, according to Bhatt, she and the union split over the issue of employment reservations (or quotas) for Harijans ("I supported the Harijans"). Ela Bhatt is regarded as the doyen of social activists in Ahmedabad. She has successfully brought together people in the unorganized sector, people not easily organized. She has created self-help projects and attracted attention and financial support from outside agencies. She is widely regarded as an articulate spokesperson for poor women.

"Our present education system is good for nothing," she said as we began our conversation on the small patio of her modest home in Ahmedabad. "The schools do not build character nor are they able to prepare the children for self-employment. Teachers should be sympathetic to children and teach them what is relevant. But what is the situation? The teaching is poor. Sometimes the teachers are not even present, especially in the farming season. For the development of the country, social values should be given to the children in school, and that is not done."

What social values?

"Work, discipline. Not to cut trees. Communal harmony. Equality. Bringing an end to untouchability.

"If I am a poor family," she continued, "but I am paid enough, then I will not want to send my child to work. I would send the child to school. If workers had more income child labor would decrease. But one point is left out. Schools do not prepare for careers. There are vendors whose sons have degrees, but their sons do not have jobs. The educational system has educated them to become clerks. We think that if we go to school we should have white-collar jobs. There is no regard for manual labor in our educational system. So these educated sons have become an antisocial element now.

"Our primary schools are worthless. The children do not learn. I see children in the municipal schools up to fourth standard and still they do not know how to write."

Why are the teachers unable to teach? I asked.

"That love for the children, that need to impart knowledge is not there. The teachers do not care. Sometimes there is rotten food in the lunch boxes the children bring to school and the teachers do nothing! It makes me so sad. It is not because teachers are badly paid. They get seven hundred to eight hundred rupees a month and the pay scales have gone up. The teachers are part of the lower middle class. They have an SLC pass [School Leaving Certificate] plus a diploma in teaching that they get after two years of study. Education is well paid now and the teachers are organized—but they do not teach. If we don't respect them it is because we see them doing other business than teaching."

Why do the teachers lack motivation?

"I have visited many schools and spoken to many teachers. The teachers say that parents do not cooperate. They say that attendance is not regular and parents do not care. I ask them, 'Why don't you go to meet the parents?' But the teacher says to me, 'It is not my job.' So I say, 'Send a note to ask the parent to come.' And she says to me that the child will not take the note, or if the child does, then the parents do not know how to read. And she tells me that the parents do not see that their children do homework. I hear teachers say that the parents are from the lower castes and that the children 'have no mind.'

"The teachers do not do anything outside the classroom. The schools are like the medical system. Medicine here is clinically based. Doctors think people should come to the clinic. Teachers think parents should come to the classroom. They say they have no responsibility to go to see the parent. No doubt there are exceptions among the teachers—and among the doctors—but I am speaking of the general situation."

Are teachers from the lower castes better with the children?

"No, they are not sympathetic. When low-caste children are educated in the private schools, they want to become babus [clerks]. They don't want to look back. They don't want to work with people in their own community. There are a few educated lower-caste graduates who are voicing some protest, but most do not care."

I see many children working in households in Ahmedabad. Who are they and where do they come from? I asked.

"A lot of boys are brought in from Rajasthan to work in households. They sweep the floors, clean clothes, clean utensils. They come to each house twice a day, usually work for five or six families, and earn about three hundred rupees a month. They're a good lot. They never steal. They do not misbehave. They are mild boys. They speak Rajasthani, sort of, but it is difficult to communicate with them. They are sixteen or seventeen, but sometimes they bring their younger brothers, as young as ten, even as young as six. The younger boys work with one family and earn about one hundred rupees a month. If they become sick they rush home. They are very nervous and are scared of doctors, so the older boys send the younger ones home if they are ill.

"The boys who work in these houses are searching for a job in the textile mills or in one of the other factories. They do household work until they get into the factories so that they have some income and a place to sleep at night. But when they get a factory job they move to a slum. They cannot read or write, they have no education. We have this feeling here that if you can read and write you do not need to do this kind of work!

"Many children are also in the recycling trade, sorting out scrap and junk. The children work with their mothers. That is how they learn their trade. They are learning their future work."

Even if the schools are as bad as you say they are, I asked, wouldn't it be better if the children went to school rather than started to work at such early ages?

"These are precious years for learning their trade," she replied, "and these preparatory years would be gone if they went to school. The poor children who go to school will not complete their education and they will not get a degree. Most probably they will drop out of school and not go to college. So if they go to school then they are suited for nothing."

Ella Bhatt's criticism that the elementary schools have failed because they do not prepare children to work reflects the sentiments of Mahatma Gandhi in articles he wrote in the 1930s on what he called "Basic Education." Gandhi's views were subsequently endorsed by the nationalist movement in the Zakir Hussain Committee Report on Basic National Education. The report said that education

> should be imparted through some craft or productive work, which should provide the nucleus of all the other instruction provided in the school. This craft, if taught efficiently and thoroughly, should enable the school to pay the cost of its teaching staff. According to [Gandhi], this would also help the State to introduce immediately the scheme of free and compulsory education. . . . Modern educational thoughts are practically unanimous in commending the idea of educating children through some suitable form of productive work. . . . Psychologically, it is desirable, because it relieves the child from the tyranny of a purely academic and theoretical instruction against which its active nature is always making a healthy protest. It balances the intellectual and practical elements of experience and it can be made an instrument of educating the body and the mind in coordination. The child acquires not the superficial literacy which implies, often without warrant, a capacity of using hand and intelligence for some constructive purpose.
>
> Socially considered, the introduction of such practical productive work in education, to be participated in by all the children of the nation, will tend to break down the existing barriers of prejudices between manual and intellectual workers, harmful alike for both.[3]

Gandhi believed that schools could be made self-supporting by imparting education through a productive craft. "Literacy," wrote Gandhi, "in itself is no education. I would, therefore, begin the child's education by teaching it a useful handicraft, enabling it to produce from the moment it begins its training. Thus, every school can be made self-supporting, condition being that State takes over the manufacture of these schools."[4]

Gandhi and his followers regarded Basic Education as a system for all social classes, not simply as a form of vocational education for the poor. Gandhi was committed to ending the sharp differentiation that exists in Indian society between those who work with their hands and those who

[3] Quoted in C. B. Bhatia, *Indianisation of our Education* (Calcutta: All India Federation of Educational Associations, 1981), p. 14.

[4] Quoted in Shiv Kumar Saini, *Development of Education in India* (New Delhi: Cosmo, 1980), p. 72.

do desk work. In contrast, those Indians who now advocate integrating manual labor with formal education are not pressing for a common-school approach to education, as did Gandhi, but are seeking a means of ensuring that the children of the urban and rural poor are properly prepared for working with their hands. Ella Bhatt, as we have seen, regards child labor itself as a form of education. She does not regard work in cottage industries, in handicrafts, or on farms as "child labor," but as a form of apprenticeship, that is, as part of the educational process.

In Ahmedabad I tried to find out if anyone had done research on what kind of skills were acquired by working children and was told to see two scholars, Mr. B. B. Patel and Mr. Mukherjee, both on the research staff of the Gandhi Labour Institute. Mr. Mukherjee said that "we find that children do not acquire skills in these jobs. Many of the children work in restaurants and in hotels, where they acquire no skills. Others work at the brick kilns as carriers, and some are working at the stone quarries. Children also work in the cotton-ginning factories, where their job is to push the cotton into the machines, work that requires no skills and where they learn nothing. They get paid about five to six rupees a day. These jobs require no skills and, in fact, when the children get older, they generally leave these jobs to find something else. We did a survey of children working in the Ahmedabad area and in our sample we found that they were not developing any skills that prepare them for careers or for any others jobs."

Mr. Mukherjee's findings were promptly illustrated when a young boy entered the room with a tray of tea. Mr. Patel explained that the Gandhi Labour Institute employs a number of boys who come from the rural area of Rajasthan. This young boy was ten. His mother died the previous year. His father, an agricultural laborer, sent him to Ahmedabad with another villager just ten days earlier. The boy had never been to school and could not read or write. He sleeps in the canteen at the institute with several other boys. The boys are paid eighty rupees a month.

An Ahmedabad Educator

A sophisticated view of what might be done to integrate academic studies and manual work into the educational system was put forth by Miss Jayshree Mehta, a bright and articulate young woman working at the Science Center in Ahmedabad. Miss Mehta's job is to develop educational materials in the sciences for schools in Gujarat. The Science Center is part of the Children's Museum in Ahmedabad, founded by Vikram Sarabhai, one-time science advisor to the prime minister and director of India's space and nuclear programs.

Miss Mehta said that there are 25,000 primary schools in the state. About 40 percent are single-teacher schools, each with about sixty children. In the larger schools there is usually a teacher for every forty to forty-five children. "In my village," she said, "many children do not come to school because parents say that they do not have money to buy clothes or books or slates for the children. The teachers say the children must wear a shirt in school. There are programs to give clothing to school children and the government has established a midday meal program. The school feeds the children and the teachers spend a lot of their time arranging for the food.

"Children who are seven or eight years old take responsibility in the village. They collect firewood, take the animals for grazing, work in the kitchen and on the farm, care for younger brothers and sisters, and go to the well to get water. Many families do not see education as important. Teachers are told to go to the villagers to get the children into school. But when parents ask how will education be helpful, the teachers are unable to answer. There is some feeling in the village that children who go to school for some years are not useful in the village. They cannot do pottery, they have not learned a craft, and they are unable to get a job in the town either.

"Many children drop out of school at the end of the third grade when there are exams. Those who pass go on. I worked in one village where out of forty children in the third class who took the exam, eighteen failed. If a child fails more than one subject he cannot continue. We have compulsory primary education in Gujarat, but if a child fails the exam the parents take him out of school. Most of the fifteen- or sixteen-year-old boys you meet here have spent a few years in school but they cannot read or write. The dropouts are highest for girls. Parents here believe that if girls study more than boys they cannot get married. They say what use is it to have girls study when they can only work in the household? Also, boys do not want girls with much education because they think that the girls will become too independent!"

Miss Mehta explained that the state has a single curriculum for all government-run primary schools, which use the same textbooks. She has prepared manuals and videotapes for teaching math in primary school. "We need to impart skills to make the children independent. The school should teach carpentry, pottery, and carpet weaving. There should be a vocational program in every school, so the children would not just become laborers. We need to integrate work and study in the schools. But our educational system has not changed since the British were here. We talk about reforming the curriculum, but if I showed you the textbooks we used thirty years ago and what we use now you will see that all we have done is put eighth-grade materials into the third grade! We have

not reformed the curriculum. We have not changed the educational system. We should bring craft people into the school. Every village has a
potter, a tailor, a smithy, a man who makes shoes, but they are not associated with the school. And there are also women who know how to make
embroidery and do knitted work who could be attached to the school.
The people who run our educational system are not sensitive to the needs
of the children or to the skills that exist in the village. When we introduce new teaching materials that the teachers are not accustomed to they
don't want to use them, and their supervisors do not encourage them.
Our education people are not concerned with quality. I get upset when
I talk to them, but they say I am young and will get over it!"

A Secretary of Primary Schools

After talking with Mrs. Bhatt, Miss Mehta, and other critics of the school
system, I went to meet Mr. Gordhanbhai, secretary of primary education
in the state of Gujarat. Mr. Gordhanbhai, a member of the state administrative service, has spent many years in the state education department.
The state government finances and determines the curriculum in public
primary and secondary schools.

I asked Mr. Gordhanbhai if primary education was compulsory in Gujarat. In 1961, he explained, compulsory education was established
throughout the state for the first seven grades, covering children from
ages six to fourteen. In each district a district education officer was empowered to make parents send their children to school; the district education officer, in turn, delegated this power to local education inspectors.
Legally, the inspectors could prosecute parents who did not send their
children to school. "But," he went on to explain, "after the act was passed
the government decided that it was not in the interests of the backward
classes that defaulters be prosecuted because the socioeconomic conditions are such that poor people cannot send their children to school.
Fourteen percent of our population is tribal, seven percent are scheduled
castes, and another twenty-eight percent belong to other backward
castes; so forty-nine percent of the population is backward. If we made
education compulsory it would adversely affect these people. So the government gave instructions to all officers that there be no prosecutions.
The act is not operative. Now the government of India says that instead
of compulsory education we should go for universalization through persuasion."

How, I asked, do you use persuasion to achieve universal education?

"The state primary-education act of 1947 entrusts primary education to
the district panchayats. They run the schools but the costs are borne by

the state government. The local bodies have launched enrollment campaigns so we expect more and more childen to enroll in school. Already,
ninety-three percent of children in the six-to-eleven age group are in
school."

Are that many actually attending school?

"Well, there are a lot of dropouts. Only thirty-five percent of those
who enroll in the first grade make it to the fourth. Out of one hundred
admitted into grade one, only twenty will pass through grade seven." I
mentally noted that by this calculation the ninety-three percent enrollment figure made no sense.

"We have an enrollment drive. But in tribal areas children work in the
fields and look after younger brothers and sisters. Even if we compelled
these people to send their children to school they will take their children
out of school. They live hand-to-mouth and they need help from their
children. We will have to run evening classes for two hours for the children who work so they can get some education. We have selected topics
that are useful if they are to have a happy life, topics like health and
cleanliness. That is more important than the subjects taught in the regular schools, like language and arithmetic. To encourage the children to
come to school we are giving free textbooks and uniforms to needy children. We cannot do it for all children. The textbooks cost about ten rupees per set for each child. If we gave free books to all the children it
would cost six crore [60 million rupees] a year and the total expenditure
for primary education in Gujarat is only 191 crore."

Do you provide free food for children?

"We thought that especially in tribal areas free food would increase
enrollment. There are fifty lakhs [five million] children covered by the
midday lunch program. We also give cash to the scheduled castes to get
them to send their children to school. It is hard to say whether these
programs are increasing enrollments."

Why are there so many single-teacher schools in Gujarat, I asked? I
have heard it said that the single-teacher schools are poorly run and that
they have a higher dropout rate.

"It is the same all over the country. We have one hundred forty-five
thousand primary-school teachers for six point two million children, and
another forty thousand secondary-school teachers. In many schools we
have one teacher for fifty or sixty children. In schools from grades one to
four we say the children should not have to walk more than one and a
half kilometers, but that means many small schools with a single teacher.
Then, of sixty children, only twenty will reach the fourth standard, and
only fifteen will go to the fifth standard, especially in the tribal areas.
Grades five to seven have one teacher for fifteen pupils. The ratio im-

proves because of the dropouts, and we have to keep one teacher in the village for the higher grades, otherwise the school would close."

Where do you send your own children to school, I asked?

"They go to a private school. Academically it is not better. I don't think the standard of education is better in private than in public education. But in the private schools the approach of the staff to the parents is more personal. In the government schools the teachers and headmasters say that it is not their duty to deal with the parents, only with the children. The teachers in the government schools are indifferent. They have their unions and they do not think about academics. Once teachers enter the school system they cannot be terminated. No one is ever terminated. The crux of the problem in education is the lack of interest by the teachers in the children. They don't care about results and they don't worry about whether the teaching methods they use are effective. We cannot compel the teacher to teach!

"There is no personal relationship between the teachers and the children. We need to emphasize moral values in education, but how do we teach moral values to the students until we first train the teachers."

And how do you propose to do that?

"We need to teach the teachers about the life of Gandhiji and we have to emphasize the values of honesty."

Nana Chowk Municipal School

A few days later I visited Nana Chowk Municipal School in Bombay. It was difficult finding the school. It is located in a crowded section of Bombay near, I was told, the Grant Road railway station in Nana Chowk (bazaar). I stopped a number of people on the roadside to ask where the school is located, without success. Then I asked the driver of my car to inquire of a woman walking with a child wearing a school uniform. He looked at this clean, well-dressed, middle-class woman and her child, then turned to me and said, "No, they wouldn't know."

The municipal school, as my driver correctly surmised, is only for the city's poor since the middle classes send their children to private schools. The municipal school is located in a large brick building near a crowded street, not unlike school buildings in congested and poor American urban centers, though the one noticeable difference was the absence of any playground. I toured the building with the headmistress of the school, a heavy set, stern, and articulate middle-aged woman. As we walked around the building it was clear from the deference shown to her by teachers and pupils that she had a commanding presence.

I told her that I was particularly interested in the problem of retaining children in the school. She said that each year 15 to 20 percent of the children dropped out of her school in each class. "The children," she explained, "are not motivated. They want to join the family business. If the children don't come we send letters to the parents asking them to come to the school. But the parents are working and they are not in a position to come. Mostly, it is the girl students who drop out, since they do household work. We teachers are helpless to do anything."

Do teachers ever visit the parents?

"No, how can we? After school the teachers leave to return to their own home. Anyway, the parents do not have that urge for education. Many children fail in the first grade so they drop out. The government is thinking of examining only in the fourth grade. Most children who drop out have failed their exams, and maybe half drop out because of household need. Most of the children here live in the slums. Their parents are not literate. They need to have more income, so that is why the children are not coming to school."

The Nana Chowk school has both a primary and a secondary school. Classes have forty to fifty children each. The classrooms have blackboards, but no materials for either study or play. There are no play areas within the school. The teachers in the lower school were pleased to demonstrate how effective they were by asking the children to recite poems and provide rote answers to their questions.

I was shown the third-grade science reader for the English-medium stream (there are also streams in Marathi and Hindi). The section on anatomy had obviously been taken from a book for a higher standard for it was much too advanced for an average nine year old.

The lower school is free, but the secondary school has tuition fees, though these are waived for children whose parents earn less than five thousand rupees a year. Textbooks are provided for all children up to the seventh grade, but parents must provide notebooks and slates. Only one-third of the children in the school are girls.

The teachers in the lower grades have a high-school diploma and a teachers' training certificate. The high-school teachers have a college degree. Only the municipal education department can appoint, transfer, or remove teachers. Teachers are paid 1,000 to 1,700 rupees a month, which puts them into the lower middle class. The teachers can supplement their salaries by earning what are called "tuitions," or fees for tutoring students. One advantage of working in private schools, though salaries are sometimes lower, is that the teachers can earn more "tuitions." But even in the municipal schools, the headmistress noted, teachers can earn extra money teaching the children after school.

The National Council of Educational Research and Training

The inability of the school system to retain children who have enrolled in the first grade has been the single greatest impediment to the achievement of universal primary-school education. To find out why the dropout rate has been high, I visited the National Council of Educational Research and Training (NCERT) in New Delhi, India's paramount educational research institution. It conducts curriculum research, develops teaching materials, and has prepared programs for reducing dropout rates. NCERT has a large campus on the outskirts of New Delhi where, in addition to its research facilities, it houses training programs for teachers and educational administrators. I met with a senior staff person, a professor well-known for his studies of the problem of dropouts. NCERT, he said, advocated the use of incentives to increase enrollments and reduce dropouts: free uniforms and dresses, free textbooks, free education for girls, and midday meals. He also felt that the situation in the 200,000 single-teacher schools in India was unsatisfactory. "We have about six hundred thousand villages and, in all, about nine hundred thousand 'habitations,' including small hamlets, but there are only five hundred thousand schools, and in some communities children have to go some distance to get to school, so it is hard to get rid of single-teacher schools without making the problem of access more difficult." He went on to say that "the big program in Indian education now is to expand nonformal education, so children at work can get some education."

The professor, an elderly scholar and an observant Hindu—I could see the sacred thread under his dhoti, and his forehead was marked with ashes—has spent many years at NCERT doing research on Indian education. "Seventy percent of the children in the six to fourteen age group are not in school," he said. (A substantially higher figure, I mentally noted, than the 50 percent reported in the 1981 census.) "But we do not want to withdraw these children from the labor force because the parents need their income. We are not in a position to provide parents the income they would lose if their children were in school. So how can we take them out when they are helping their families? They are also helping the middle classes and upper-middle classes by working in their homes, in shops, and in factories. These children are the productive members of society.

"We don't speak of 'compulsory' education anymore. We have eliminated that word. We now speak of education for all, or universal education, not compulsion. We cannot compel education. The government has enacted laws to punish parents who do not send their children to school, but they do not work. The public does not want compulsion. We are trying to develop an interest in education, but we are against compulsion. We try to prepare materials in a form that would be interesting to children. And we want more children in the nonformal program. In the nonformal program we can focus on problems like health and cleanliness, on quality of life, not on the academic disciplines, and not on giving certificates. The children can go for certificates by transferring to the formal program. About ten percent or so of the children in the nonformal program go into the formal program. The nonformal education program was started in 1978 for children who dropped out of school. There are forty lakhs [four million] children in the program in one hundred sixty thousand centers, each with about twenty to twenty-five children. As far as money is concerned the emphasis will continue to be on the formal education system, but we are trying to expand nonformal education."

The professor was one of many educational officials I met who regarded the school dropout rate as a demonstration of the inadequacy of the schools and as evidence that the poor are in such need of the income and work of their children that they must withdraw them from the schools. Other Indian educators I met shared his view that the high dropout rate demonstrated that it is undesirable to impose compulsory education.

A Scientist-Turned-Educator

Not everyone agreed that poverty forces children to leave school. An alternative view was put forth by Dr. V. G. Kulkarni, a physicist-turned-educational researcher, who has been attempting to improve India's secondary-school science textbooks.

Dr. Kulkarni is the director of the Homi Bhabha Science Center, located in a wing of the Nana Chowk Municipal School. The center was organized by Bombay scientists concerned with improving the teaching of science in the municipal schools. Its staff is also interested in why the dropout rate is so high and what can be done to reduce it.

"We found that science is not really taught in our schools," Dr. Kulkarni began. "We Hindus have been chanting mantras for years and so now in the schools we teach our children to recite other mantras. We teach our children to repeat what we say, we don't teach them to experience science. The greatest difficulty with the children from the slums is that they don't know how to ask a question. They don't raise their hands. They haven't learned the 'formal' language that you need in school, and those who don't learn that language drop out. The municipal schools run by the Bombay Municipal Corporation mainly teach socially deprived children. All the other children go to private schools. We went to the Muncipal Corporation Education office to propose that we train teachers how to teach science. They said it was a good idea. There was to be a meeting of science teachers. Some of the headmasters attended but they said that they could not send their teachers so none of them came! We decided to work in the Nana Chowk Municipal School since the headmistress here is helpful. But the problem is with the teachers. They are not accountable to the students. If the students say they do not understand what the teachers are saying, then the teachers simply repeat the same lectures!

"Some of the teachers in the lower grades try to do well, but most of the secondary-school teachers would prefer to do something other than teach. Like work in a bank as a clerk.

"We have this idea that our schools should bridge the gap between ourselves and the West, so we want to teach science and technology to our children. The municipal school board says the schools should 'upgrade' the primary schools by introducing science and English subjects into the lower grades. All that means is taking materials from the upperclass texts and giving them to the younger children. The education department took materials from Russian and American texts and didn't pay any attention to what levels they were for and what labs we have, or how trained our teachers are.

"I say that the dropout rate is zero, but the pushout rate is high. It is the fault of the educational system that the children are pushed out of school. When they 'upgraded' the teaching of science and English, more children failed the exams, and the dropout rate went up. Our center developed a program for teaching science and tried it in some rural schools with success. The dropout rate went down. We offered the program to the Municipal School Board to use in the schools, but they declined."

Why?

"I don't know. That's a sociological question. We discovered that the teachers don't have a language of their own, but that they use the language of the textbooks. We decided that we could simplify the language of these books. That improved the language used by the teachers as well as made the materials easier for the children. We are trying to get the government to use these simplified texts, but without much success. You know, we do research on science education here, but we do not spend our time trying to persuade the government. I know that that is important, but we haven't done it yet. We are trying to bring in a concern for research in science education. We have brought in many people here but we haven't used our manpower for salesmanship."

I told Dr. Kulkarni that I was often struck by the fact that people in India often say the right things but so little seems to get implemented. The relationship between rhetoric and behavior in India seems so different from in the West. Speaking of mantras, in the West we have the impression that Indians see mantras as potent, that if they say the right words often enough they will change the world.

"Yes, that is true," replied Dr. Kulkarni. "The Indian mind expresses the thought beautifully. When we say something well we think, 'I have done my job.' If I can write an essay to explain why we are poor, then I have done my job. The rest is the responsibility of the government. We like elegant language. Take J. P. Naik's books [the government's chief educational advisor, and the author of many books on Indian education] or the Kothari Commission report [a government report on Indian education]. The expressions are so eloquent, so beautiful. They are typical of the Indian mind. No one can beat us in constructing epigrams. We repeat words with no idea of what they really mean because we don't understand that events occur because of describable and understandable causes. That outlook is lacking. We don't really look into causes, so we don't do anything. Maybe by doing nothing we contribute to the stability of society!"

Pushouts or Dropouts?

I heard a variety of opinions on the causes for the high dropout rate. The primary differences were between those who argued that poverty was paramount and those who attributed the dropout rate to the character of the schools; or, as Dr. Kulkarni put it, the issue is one of "pushouts," not "dropouts."

There are no reliable official national data on the magnitude of the dropout rate from Indian schools since school enrollment figures are notoriously unreliable. Enrollment figures are produced in each school, then sent to the *taluka* (subdistrict) office, and forwarded to the district educational officer, who transmits them to the state education departments. As one researcher put it, "each office pushes the figures up."

Moreover, government figures on the percentage of each age group attending school are often wrong because of inaccurate projections as to the number of children in each age group. For example, the Ministry of Education reported that 71 million out of 85 million children, or 83.6 percent of all children between the ages of six and eleven, were in primary school in 1979–1980. But the 1981 census reported that there were 108.8 million children in this age group, pushing the percentage of enrollment down to 65.3 percent. Thus, while the ministry estimated that 14 million children in this age group were not in school, actually there were 37.8 million six-to-ten year olds not in school. (To make the figures even more problematic, the 1981 census reports only 36 million children

in the five-to-nine age group in school, which makes the ministry's estimates of the number of six-to-eleven year olds attending school improb-
ably high.)

In the absence of reliable data on actual attendance, it becomes particularly difficult to estimate how many children entering primary school
fail to complete the fourth, fifth, or sixth grade. Consider the situation in
Karnataka, where the passage of a so-called compulsory education law in
1961 for the six-to-eleven age group resulted in an official enrollment rate
of 98 percent! A field study conducted in Karnataka at the Institute for
Social and Economic Change in Bangalore found that 35 percent of the
children dropped out of school in the first two years. The dropout rates
at the end of four years for boys and girls was 68.3 percent and 78.5
percent respectively. The actual numbers completing four years of primary education was less than 33 percent.[5] What is meant, then, by "98
percent" enrollment?

The authors of the Karnataka study explain that "a dropout is defined
as a child who after having enrolled in a primary school left before completing the full term of seven years of primary education. . . . At present
a child's name will not be struck off from the attendance register for a
period of seven years from the date of admissions to the first standard of
primary education whether he attends the school or absents himself
thereafter."[6] In other words, "enrollment" means that the child has at
one time been registered for school. It does not mean attendance. Attendance is enrollment minus dropouts.

The authors conducted a state-wide survey of 1,876 primary-school
dropouts. They reported that 60 percent of the dropouts were unable to
read, write, or count, while the remaining 40 percent "learned something."[7] As expected, the parents of dropouts were illiterate, especially
their mothers (93.5 percent of whom were illiterate). They were also
poor, with average family incomes below 300 rupees per month.

One of the most interesting findings is that the children who dropped
out of school did not enter the wage-labor force. Most helped their parents by looking after cattle, pigs, and poultry, collecting cow dung and
firewood, carrying water, and caring for younger children, activities characterized by the authors as "home management." Contrary to the view
that improved family income would increase school attendance, the authors report that projects to improve self-generated rural income such as
raising dairy cattle tended to increase child labor. They found that only
20 percent of the school dropouts were engaged in paid work, and three-

---

[5] A. S. Seetharamu and Usha Devi, *Education in Rural Areas: Constraints and Prospects*
(New Delhi: Ashish Publishing House, 1985), p. 3.

[6] Ibid., p. 5.

[7] Ibid., p. 25.

quarters of them were in agriculture. The working children's income averaged twenty-five rupees per month in agricultural work, fifty-three rupees for nonagricultural work.

These findings for Karnataka were confirmed by another study conducted at the Institute for Social and Economic Change by S. Nayana Tara. This study was conducted in Tamkur district in Karnataka. Dr. Tara reported that there was a two-day enrollment drive in the district among children in the six-to-ten age group. Of those who enrolled, attendance was irregular (45 percent of enrolled scheduled-caste children in first grade did not attend school). In the village primary schools the average dropout rate in first grade was 31 percent, and from grades 2 to 4, 16 percent.[8] A particularly interesting finding, confirming Dr. Kulkarni's observation, is that dropouts were largely children who had failed their exams at the end of the first and second grades (34 percent of the children failed exams at the end of the first grade, another quarter at the end of the second grade).

The findings in Karnataka were replicated in India's most populous state, Uttar Pradesh. Though the U.P. government reports that 11.5 million out of 16.7 million children (69 percent) between the ages of six and fourteen attend elementary school, a study conducted at the Giri Institute of Social Sciences in Lucknow found that for every 100 children admitted into the first grade, only thirty-five passed into the fifth grade, and only twenty completed eight years of schooling. Muslims and scheduled castes do badly, and girls have a particularly low enrollment and high dropout rate among all groups. The increase in rural income in western U.P. (which, along with Punjab and Haryana, has been a center for the green revolution in agriculture) has not resulted in rising school enrollments or a decline in dropouts.

The Giri Institute study also confirmed the Karnataka study's findings that most children who drop out of school do not enter the labor force. The largest number of dropouts, Dr. T. S. Papola, director of the study, reported, is in grades 1 and 2, the six-to-eight year olds. Few of these children engage in productive work. "As economists would say," Dr. Papola explained, "the direct opportunity costs in the form of foregone earnings is not a significant factor in the high dropout rate in the early grades."

Girls of ten to twelve who drop out usually do housework and look after younger brothers and sisters. There is, Dr. Papola found, a relationship between enrollments and the number of children in the family. When there were many young siblings the enrollment dropped, since the older

[8] S. Nayana Tara, *Education in a Rural Environment* (New Delhi: Ashish Publishing House, 1985), p. 58.

children stayed at home to take care of the younger ones. If there are grandparents in the family, it is more likely that the older children will remain in school. "There is a need," concluded Papola, "for arrangements for taking care of the younger preschool children, since that is an important factor affecting enrollments."

While there is no evidence that an increase in family income results in a rise in enrollments and a decline in dropouts, Dr. Papola found evidence that the educational level of the household does affect school enrollments. If there is an educated member in the family, then children are more likely to be kept in school. "That suggests," he said, "that adult-education programs may indirectly affect school enrollments for children as adults realize the value of education not just for themselves but for their children."

Dr. Papola said that as he visited the schools he was struck by how unattractive they were. "The schools do not have any play facilities. I did not find any open spaces around the schools. Just give children a place for them to fight among themselves—isn't that a favorite game among all children! I think the lack of play space reduces attendance. I have been trying to put together some data showing the relationship between play space and dropouts. The schools don't give enough attention to programs that would interest the children. I have heard of cases of children beaten by parents because they won't go to school, but I have never heard of a parent beating his child who wanted to go to school!"

The Karnataka and Uttar Pradesh studies agree that only a third of the children entering first grade complete four years of schooling. Both findings are reasonably consistent with the slightly higher all-India estimates made in 1975 by J. P. Naik, for many years special advisor to the government of India on educational policy. "Of every 100 children enrolled in Class I," he wrote, "only about 40 reach Class V, and only about 25 reach Class VIII."[9]

This low retention rate is the reason why India has been so unsuccessful in achieving universal primary-school education and why illiteracy remains so high in spite of the apparent impressive increase in school enrollments. The high dropout rate means that substantial portions of India's educational expenditures are for children who fail to have enough schooling to achieve functional literacy. With only 33 percent to 40 percent of those who enroll in the first standard completing four years of school, the costs of producing a literate child are substantially higher than if the school system was able to retain all of the children. As the former vice-chancellor of Allahabad University bluntly put it, "Would one be-

---

[9] J. P. Naik, *Elementary Education in India: A Promise to Keep* (Bombay: Allied Publishers, 1975), p. 10.

lieve that in free India after 33 years of independence we are turning out
of our primary schools every year two million not literate but illiterate
pupils!"[10]

An Educational Planner

In an interview with the director of the National Institute of Public Cooperation and Child Development, we discussed the issue of where it is
best to educate children, in school or in the work place. NIPCCD is run
and financed by the central government. It conducts research and training in child health, nutrition, and preschool education. The institute has
organized crèches in factories and mobile crèches for women working on
construction sites. It has also been active in developing an "integrated
child development scheme" to improve the health and mortality rate of
preschool children. The director is a tall, imposing man who speaks with
great conviction. The interview was conducted in his office in the presence of several members of his staff, who occasionally interjected support
for his views or gave examples.

The director described the variety of primary and secondary schools in
urban India. These include: (1) municipal corporation schools, funded by
an educational tax on urban property; (2) higher secondary schools, starting at grade 7, under the education department of the state government;
(3) private secondary schools receiving grants from government ("government-aided schools"), which are not permitted to charge fees; (4) central
schools run by the Ministry of Education for employees of the central
government; and (5) private fee-charging secondary schools that are recognized but not funded by the government. This last group includes what
he calls the "five-star" schools, like the Doon School attended by Rajiv
Gandhi.

In the last few years, he said, there has been a "craze" for "convent"
or "saint" schools—private, English-medium, unisex schools that charge
fees, are usually run by Hindus (their name notwithstanding), and attract
the upper-middle classes. The lower classes, he said, send their children
to the government schools and especially to the municipal schools.

NIPCCD, he explained, is concerned with the educational problems of
the lower classes. They have helped to organize some 110,000 preschool
centers, containing 4.5 million children, to improve the health and well-
being of preschool children, but also to increase primary-school enrollment. He said that they did not know yet whether these preschool centers had affected enrollments. He repeated the familiar view that "poor

---

[10] Bhatia, *Indianisation of Our Education*, p. 134.

people say it is better for their ten year old to learn to become a carpenter or carpet weaver, or graze the cattle, than go to school." He was skeptical of the benefits of the midday lunch program to get children into school, partly because it did not address the economic needs of the parents, and partly because teachers had become preoccupied with the logistics of running the program to the neglect of teaching. Like others with whom I spoke, he emphasized the need to develop programs for improving the welfare and education of the working child.

"Child labor is a reality we must accept because children learn crafts by working with the family. We do not frown on child labor in India. It is neither possible nor desirable to end child labor, because it is a way that children acquire skills. What is missing when children work is their education, so there needs to be some input for the education of the working child."

But is it necessary or desirable that children start to learn skills at work at the age of eight or ten, when they could start work at age fourteen?

"That's too late," he replied. "Look at the tribal children, for example. They have a tradition of learning crafts at home. But once we put them into school they won't go back to their own culture to learn their crafts. This new culture we teach in the schools has given them nothing. They can't even get a job as a peon! The problem is that the schools pull the children out of their own culture. The life-style of these people changes, but it is not for the better. We should let them learn crafts in the village, crafts that prepare them for life. The children learn skills by apprenticing in the family profession. When you learn skills this way you are graded not in marks but in what income you bring into the family. We should call it training, not work.

"If these low-income people had a chance, they would send their children to schools to get degrees, rather than learn the family craft. But that would be a mistake because then we would have more educated unemployed. Schools just add to the ranks of the unemployed. At home the children can learn skills that the schools do not teach. The ideal system would be to have schools that prepare children for work."

If you think that is the solution, why don't you and your colleagues try to change the school system? I asked.

"We should, but we can't, because low-income parents, want the schools to prepare their children for white-collar jobs."

5

Child Labor and Compulsory-Education Policies

In 1986 and 1987 the government of India adopted a new set of policies toward working children, which for the first time reflected the privately held views of officials in the ministries of Labour and Education. The government would no longer ban child labor (with some exceptions) but would instead seek to ameliorate the conditions of working children. The government would also endeavor to provide voluntary part-time nonformal education for working children rather than press for compulsory universal primary education. The new policies won legitimacy from several international agencies in the form of quasi-official statements and grants for specific programs. This chapter first reviews the government's new approach toward child-labor laws, then turns to the government's new education policy.

Child-Labor Policy

The official expression of the new child-labor policy is the Child Labour (Prohibition and Regulation) Act, approved by the Indian parliament in January 1987. The act prohibits the employment of children in certain occupations and processes, while regulating the conditions of work in other jobs. Children are prohibited from employment in bidi making; carpet weaving; cement manufacturing; cloth printing, dyeing, and weaving; match manufacturing; explosives and fireworks; mica cutting and splitting; shellac manufacturing; soap manufacturing; tanning; wool cleaning; and building and construction work. The central government can add to the list upon the advice of a newly constituted Child Labour Technical Advisory Committee. The prohibition applies only to children who are not yet fourteen. The act replaces the various age limitations set in earlier acts (e.g., fifteen in merchant shipping and transportation, twelve on plantations).

The act provides for the protection of working children not employed in specified hazardous occupations and processes. It sets limits on the number of hours children can work continuously ("an interval for rest for at least one hour" after three hours of work), limits the number of days of employment ("every child employed in an establishment shall be allowed in each week, a holiday of one whole day"), and restricts the times of work ("no child shall be permitted or required to work between 7 p.m. and 8 a.m."). Central and state governments are permitted to set rules for cleanliness in the place of work, the disposal of wastes and effluents, ventilation, temperature, dust, fumes, and so forth. Employers are required to maintain a register with the names and birth dates of all children they employ. Under the act any citizen may file a complaint with the local court if he or she believes that children under fourteen are being employed in prohibited occupations and processes—but it is necessary to produce a certificate from a government doctor that the employed children are under fourteen.

Critics of the legislation said that the government had legalized child labor. The bill did precisely that. The new act imposes no age limit on the employment of children. It simply specifies that children are prohibited from being employed only in certain occupations and processes. Even this restriction is carefully circumscribed. The act says that "nothing in this section shall apply to any workshop wherein any process is carried on by the occupier with the aid of his family." Thus, the act prohibits the employment of children in the making of matches in workshops, but not if the work is carried out in family-run workshops.

Even the regulations pertaining to conditions of work are circumscribed with the same qualification that none of these restrictions "shall apply to any establishment wherein any process is carried on by the occupier with the aid of his family or to any school established by, or receiving assistance or recognition from, the government." This latter phrase exempts government-run apprenticeship programs to teach children carpet weaving.

The act represents the culmination of a long debate within and outside the government between those who argued that government should take steps to enforce the many laws that prohibit the employment of children and those who argued that "existing socioeconomic conditions" make enforcement unrealistic and that government should instead seek to ameliorate the conditions of work. The debate became public in 1979 with the appointment by the government of India of a Committee on Child Labour to examine "the causes leading to the problems arising out of the employment of children" and to review existing legislation. To understand the debate we must first review the policies adopted by the British and the postindependence government that have been reconsidered.

Child-Labor Laws: A Legislative History

Restrictions against the employment of children were introduced by the British in the Indian Factories Act of 1881, which imposed a minimum age of seven years. Partly under the influence of the International Labor Organization in the 1920s and 1930s, India subsequently passed a series of acts for the protection of children. The Factories Act as amended in 1922 raised the age limit to fifteen years. The Indian Mines Act of 1923 raised the minimum age for employment in mines to thirteen years. A Royal Commission on Labour, appointed in 1933, examined the practice of parents pledging the labor of their children by taking advances in return for bonds—a practice called bonded labor. The practice was common in the carpet factories of Amritsar and the bidi factories of Madras. Though the government of India had eliminated the system of indenture, under which adults pledged their own labor on contract, the government had not banned the pledging of child labor by parents.

Subsequent acts regulated the employment of children in specific sectors of the economy, in each instance imposing a minimum age for employment. The Employment of Children Act (1938) was the first act devoted entirely to child labor. It listed occupations and processes in which children could not be employed, all of which were later incorporated into the 1987 legislation. The act similarly exempted family-run workshops. The Factories Act of 1948 set fourteen as the minimum age of employment in factories, defined as a premise employing at least ten persons where manufacturing is being carried on with the aid of power, and above twenty where no power is employed. A "fitness" certificate was required from a doctor for children over fourteen and under eighteen. No birth certificate or certificate of school attendance was required. The law also restricted the number of continuous hours of work, night work, and the use of machinery by young persons.

India's Constituent Assembly wrote into the constitution specific protections for children. Article 24 provides that "no child below 14 shall be employed in any factory or mine or engaged in any hazardous employment." Article 39 promises that the state shall direct its policy toward ensuring that "children are not abused and that citizens are not forced by economic necessity to enter avocations unsuited to their age or strength," that "children are given opportunities and facilities to develop in a healthy manner and in conditions of freedom and dignity, and that childhood and youth are protected against exploitation and against moral and material abandonment." Article 45 says that the state shall endeavor to provide by 1960 free and compulsory education for all children until they reach fourteen years of age.

A series of acts further extended protection to children: The Plantations Labour Act of 1951 prohibited the employment of children under twelve; the Mines Act of 1952 prohibited employment under fifteen; the Factories Act of 1954 prohibited the employment of adolescents under seventeen at night; and the Beedi and Cigar Workers Act of 1966 prohibited the employment of children under fourteen in any factory manufacturing bidis or cigars. These central government acts were applicable throughout the country. State governments also passed acts regulating the conditions of work for young people in restaurants, hotels, and shops, setting age limits ranging from twelve to fifteen.

In response to a United Nations General Assembly resolution proclaiming 1979 as the International Year of the Child, the government of India appointed the Committee on Child Labour to review existing legislation. The sixteen-member committee included members of parliament, representatives from institutions dealing with children, and officials of state and central labor departments. In his inaugural speech to the first meeting of the committee the central government labor minister called for a new set of policies toward working children. He noted that the government had not enforced legislation banning child labor.

> It is not that this is not a desirable objective . . . but we have to think of two sets of problems related with a proposal for an immediate legal ban on the employment of child labour. One set of problems can be described as economic problems, flowing from the problems of poverty. The fact remains whether an immediate prohibition of the employment of child labour will not lead to the closing of some channels of supplementing incomes for extremely poor families who live below the poverty line. . . . Another set of problems can be described as administrative problems, because you may pass a law in your wisdom, but the law has to be implemented. What is a law's worth if it is to remain imprisoned in the Statute Book? Social reform has to be practical. . . . In spite of all these laws you find in some areas, especially where you have to deal with far flung areas, where the representatives of the administration can reach only with great difficulty, where there can be connivance and complicity, then it becomes very difficult to enforce a law unless conditions are such that there is a tendency to accept the sanctions of the law. Therefore, if we say tomorrow that all child labour should be abolished in this country, make it punishable, it will be very difficult to see that it is enforced.[1]

The Committee on Child Labour listened to this argument sympathetically. In an exceptionally frank statement, the committee in its report agreed that most of the legislation was not enforced:

> In the course of its spot inspections and discussions, the Committee got a clear impression of several inadequacies in the existing administrative setup for the implementation of various laws. The jurisdiction of individual inspectors was too extensive for them to keep a regular watch on activities within their purview. In several States one inspector was required to cover a group of sev-

[1] Ministry of Labour, *Report of the Committee on Child Labour* (New Delhi: Government of India, 1979), p. 54. For a review of British policies, see Rajani Kanta Das, "Labour Legislation in Indian States," *International Labour Review* 38, no. 6 (December 1938).

eral districts. He was also burdened with very wide ranging other responsibilities pertaining to labour legislation. The results of this situation were apparent. There were practically no prosecutions in most parts of the country of any violation of existing laws pertaining to child labour. In one of the States it was pointed out with pride that the first prosecution ever launched by them was only in the International Year of the Child! The Committee itself during spot inspections noticed children of very tender age working in certain factory premises in total disregard of the statutory provisions. In the course of the discussions with different interests, including officials of labour departments, it was pointed out that the entire situation was being overlooked because of certain inherent factors. There was, in fact, a vicious circle. The Labour Inspector, whenever he got a chance to book any violation, had difficulties in collecting evidence for proper prosecution. The fact of employment of a child against law was denied both by the employer and the parents of the children. Social acquiescence in the existing conditions also made it difficult to enlist support of other independent witnesses. A general sympathy was prevalent amongst people towards any one employed. It was also argued that if the child was not so employed he would really be in the streets and thus become a more dangerous hazard for the community at large. By keeping the child occupied, he was kept away from becoming a vagabond. Some also argued that since the parents also were involved in occupations, it was not possible for the child to be left all by himself in the house and the parents, therefore, preferred to make the child work in some establishment. Some even took the view that the environment in which the child was working was distinctly better than the environment in which he lives and, therefore, discouraging him from such a situation was not being helpful to him.[2]

The committee nonetheless urged the government to strengthen its enforcement machinery and to make use of voluntary organizations and trade unions. The committee proposed that the government increase the number of prosecutions and increase the penalties, including one-year jail sentences and fines of up to 2,000 rupees. It also suggested that attention be given to creating an institutional framework for collective bargaining for working children, though the committee offered no such framework. The committee noted that the elimination of child labor would benefit employment of those in the age group of fifteen to fifty-nine, but regarded such an approach as "radical and perhaps not feasible at first sight." Instead, the committee pressed for the enforcement of minimum-wage laws for adults ("If parents' earnings increase, they would be less inclined to allow their children into service"). The committee supported primary education for children but repeated the familiar argument that "serious doubts are raised about the usefulness of the present

[2] Ibid., p. 39.

system of education," which "does not prepare them for future occupations. In fact it raises amongst children aspirations and hopes only for 'white collared' jobs. . . . The educational curriculum must be geared to bring the maximum of skill and competence in the child keeping in view the environment in which he is living."[3]

The committee called for a strengthening of nonformal education facilities for working children. "Employers should be urged to include education as one of the necessary ingredients of labour welfare measures in their establishment. It would also be worthwhile in the view of the Committee, to impose a cess on industry to raise funds for this purpose; or alternatively to allow concessions in taxes, etc. to employers who undertake to implement educational schemes."[4]

There was a debate within the committee over whether there should be a uniform minimum age for employment and, if so, whether it should be fixed at fifteen years or less. One member of the committee, the development commissioner in charge of small-scale industries, pointed out that there was no minimum age for employment except for occupations specified by existing laws. Thus children of any age could be employed as domestic helpers, while in some sectors of the economy (plantations, shops, and establishments) the age limit was twelve. Given the economic circumstances and the fact that so many children were not in school because "the type of education that is now being imparted in schools makes it completely unattractive to the parents of children particularly in the rural areas where children are considered an economic asset," he recommended that the minimum age for employment in all occupations be lowered to twelve.[5] Other members of the committee questioned whether any age limit should be imposed, except in selected hazardous occupations. The committee concluded, however, that the minimum age for entry into *any* employment should be fifteen years, that existing laws be consolidated, and that the ministry should enforce legislation relating to the employment of children.

The government rejected the recommendation that the minimum age of entry into employment be fifteen years, but agreed with those recommendations aimed at improving conditions for working children: health schemes in areas with concentrations of child labor, supplementary nutrition provided by employers to working children with tax concessions from the government, and the establishment of nonformal education for working children.[6]

[3] Ibid., p. 42.
[4] Ibid., p. 44.
[5] Ibid., p. 49.
[6] For the response of the government of India to the committee's recommendations, see

In 1983 the planning minister, S. B. Chavan, stated the government's position that banning child labor was "not feasible due to the prevailing socio-economic constraints and exigencies."[7] The seventh five-year plan (1985–1990), approved by the National Development Council, said that since it is not feasible to eradicate child labor, the government should try to make the conditions of working children more acceptable. The plan proposed a greater role for voluntary agencies in providing child workers with health care, nutrition, and education. The abolition of child labor, it said, could only be achieved when there is sufficient improvement in the conditions of the families whose children are compelled to work.

In its annual report (1983–1984) the Ministry of Labour said that the government had accepted child labor as a "harsh reality" and that it was neither "feasible nor opportune" to prevent children from working in the present stage of economic development.[8]

In November 1985 a Bangalore-based organization created by trade-union activists, the Concerned for Working Children (CWC), held a national seminar in Bangalore under the auspices of the central government's Department of Education in the Ministry of Human Resource Development. The seminar's final report made a distinction between "child work," which should be regulated, and "exploitation of child work," which should be prohibited. Government policy, the report said, should aim to protect the working child and make provision for the working child's education.[9] The CWC prepared a draft bill on child labor, which became the model for the act the government subsequently brought to parliament. The widely circulated committee proposal started with the familiar premise, "It is now a well recognised fact that high incidence of child labour is essentially a problem of development. . . . In developing countries like India, the families with no or meagre income are forced to send their children to the labour market as soon as they are old enough to get out of their houses, often at the age of 4 or 5."[10] The CWC draft bill recommended that no age limit be imposed on child labor except in hazardous occupations where there would be a fifteen-year-old age limit. They recommended that wages for children be set by a government board, that the terms of employment for child workers be put in writing and sent to parents and to government inspectors, that a child-

P. M. Shah, ed., *Child Labour: A Threat to Health and Development* (Geneva: Defence for Children International, 1985), pp. 99–100.

[7] *Deccan Herald* (17 July 1983).

[8] Ministry of Labour, *Annual Report 1983–84* (New Delhi: Government of India, 1985).

[9] The Concerned for Working Children, *The Report of the National Seminar on Education for Working Children* (Bangalore: CWC, November 1985).

[10] *The Concerned for Working Children Present the Child Labour (Employment, Regulation, Training, and Development) Bill, 1985* (Bangalore: CWC, 1985).

labor development fund be created with funding from employers, that evening and weekend schools for child workers be created, and that child labor unions be established.

The Bangalore seminar report concluded that child labor and education had to be seen

> in relation to the power structure and the social system in which it is embedded. It is a product and a part of under-development and its vicious circle of parental poverty and of low productivity. The abiding solution can lie only in long term economic regeneration so that employers will not have to seek such minimally paid labour nor parents be compelled to drive their children to the indignities of forced labour to supplement their low incomes.[11]

The seminar participants faulted the education system as totally irrelevant, the yearly school timings inappropriate ("a full day schedule of school obviously keeps away working children"), and supported proposals for nonformal education ("it is obvious that the educational needs of working children can be best served by nonformal education"). Education for all, said the report, depended on dealing with such issues as agrarian relations, rural indebtedness, bonded labor, and the payment of minimum wages. The general thrust of the seminar was that the elimination of poverty was a precondition to the ending of child labor.

The bill drafted by the Concerned for Working Children and the revised version subsequently proposed by the government generated opposition from some activists and journalists. Dr. Neera Burra, a sociologist who had extensively researched child labor, wrote a series of sharp attacks against the proposed new policy.[12] She faulted the proposed Child Labour Bill on the following grounds:

> 1. The list of hazardous occupations is drawn almost entirely from the Employment of Children Act of 1938 and fails to include new hazardous occupations. Nor is it clear what criteria will be used for defining what is hazardous. Garbage picking (commonly described in India as "Ragpicking"), for example, is not classified as hazardous though thousands of children collecting scraps of iron, glass, paper, and rags often pick up bits of food to eat and are prone to tetanus and skin diseases.

[11] The Concerned for Working Children, *The Report of the National Seminar* (Bangalore: CWC, November 1985), p. 7. The CWC put the figure of child laborers higher than had other groups. It regarded as too low the 1983 government figure of 17.3 million and the Operations Research Group estimate of 44 million, arguing that since 90 million children in the five-to-fifteen age group do not attend school, virtually all of them should be regarded as working children.

[12] Neera Burra, "Old Flaws in New Child Labour Bill," *Times of India* (7 November 1986). See also Walter Fernandes and Neera Burra, "A Law That Will Not Protect," *Indian Express* (18 August 1986).

2. Hazardous work is exempt if it is part of family labor, though in many industries, such as bidi making and match making, owners operate through a putting-out system, with households and small shops doing hazardous work under unsatisfactory working conditions. Under the pretext of family labor, employers can get around restrictions on the employment of children. For children working in these small shops, no safeguards are provided at all.

3. In spite of constitutional provisions banning child labor in hazardous occupations, existing legislation has not been enforced. Is there any reason to believe that the government will enforce the new legislation?

4. The legalization of child labor in so-called nonhazardous occupations without regard for age is a violation of articles 24, 39, and 45 of the Constitution, which ban child labor and call for compulsory schooling.

Dr. Burra went on to criticize the government's proposed National Child Labour Program (NCLP). The proposed NCLP would provide free lunches for working children, a scheme she noted that would undermine the government's existing program of providing free lunches to school children as an inducement to school attendance. Similarly, the provision of medical and other welfare services in the match and fireworks, industries meant that the government was inducing children to continue to work in hazardous industries (this provision was subsequently dropped).

In a hard-hitting address at a seminar on child labor in New Delhi organized by the Indian Social Institute to protest the proposed bill, Dr. Walter Fernandes, the institute's director, argued that the proposed legislation would legitimate the government's decision not to enforce existing child-labor laws in such hazardous industries as match making, carpet weaving, and bidi making. The government, he said, should first demonstrate its commitment to abolishing child labor by dealing with these industries, then move on to implement the Rural Indebtedness Abolition Act to end bonded labor. He accused the government of lacking the political will to enforce existing child-labor legislation since politicians are receiving financial support from employers of child laborers.

The concluding report for the conference urged the government to enforce existing child-labor legislation and to implement the constitutional directive for free and compulsory education until the age of fourteen. "If the constitutional directive on universal and free primary education were to be implemented, then children would automatically be away from full-time work."[13] The decline in expenditures on elementary education demonstrates, the report said, the lack of the government's concern with ending child labor.

[13] Walter Fernandes, Neera Burra, and Tara Anand, *Child Labour in India: A Summary of a Report Prepared by the Indian Social Institute* (New Delhi: Indian Social Institute, November 1985).

The role of "vested interests" in not implementing the Employment of Children Act of 1938 or the constitutional protection provided to children was another theme of Dr. Burra's.

> From the urban middle class housewife to the landlord in the village, from the parents to the employers in the unorganised sector—everyone wants child labour. After all if you can pay less and get more work done, why not! The only person who suffers is the child who doesn't count. Socially minded people salve their conscience by employing children ostensibly to save them from starvation and look upon it as a social service! Whatever the CWC may have to say about regulating hours of work, better conditions of work, health facilities, etc. it is an impossible task. We are dealing with millions of children all over the country and not just a few in an urban slum. . . . It is totally unrealistic to think that children will benefit by this bill. It will just give a carte blanche to employers and parents to exploit the poor child with the benign indulgence of the State.

The argument that child labor should be made legal in order to regulate, concluded Dr. Burra, was a false promise.[14]

Within the government, however, the overwhelming sentiment in the relevant ministries was support for the new initiative. The general manager of the Handloom and Handicrafts Export Corporation said that a ban on child labor in the carpet industry would be suicidal for exports. The HHEC is a government organization that runs 200 training centers for children, many well below age fourteen. The union minister for labor, Mr. P. A. Sangma, said that a move to ban child labor would cause hardships to those who depended on their income and would be impossible to implement. Instead, the government proposed to make the conditions of work less arduous. The minister called upon employers in Sivakasi to support the government's 14 crore ($10 million) national child-labor welfare project, saying that "I dictate to the conscience of the industrialists to look at the problem from a humane angle." He expressed his appreciation to managers in the match industry in Sivakasi who were supporting the scheme, saying that "we realise that child labour exists because of economic necessity and because a family has to earn somewhere from somebody."[15]

---

[14] Neera Burra, "Pay Less, Get More Work," *Hindustan Times Sunday Magazine* (19 January 1986). See also Neera Burra, "Child Labour in India: Poverty, Exploitation, and Vested Interest," *Social Action* 36 (July–September 1986), pp. 241–263; and Sheela Barse, "Legitimising Child Labour," *Indian Express* (28 July 1985).

[15] *Hindu* (17 August, 25 January, and 21 April 1986).

India and the International Labor Organization

The new legislation, by legalizing child labor in nonhazardous employment, appeared to violate the ILO convention on child labor. But officials of the ILO, along with officials of other international organizations, expressed their support for India's new strategy of regulation rather than abolition. In November 1985 the United Nations held a seminar in Geneva "on ways and means of achieving the elimination of the exploitation of child labour in all parts of the world."[16] The seminar, organized by the Secretary General of the United Nations in cooperation with the ILO, was called at the initiative of the United Nations Commission on Human Rights. Twenty-nine countries participated, and there were representatives from the major international organizations concerned with children, including the ILO, UNESCO, UNICEF, and WHO.

The seminar subscribed to the Indian distinction between child labor and the exploitation of child labor. Speakers said that "in many developing countries, child labour was unavoidable, in particular child labour performed within the family, mostly in rural areas, in order to supplement the family's income. This type of work could not be considered as exploitative. . . . It was further observed that there were certain positive aspects of some forms of child labour. In certain particular contexts, work formed a part of the training process of the child and prepared him for adult life and did not involve exploitation."[17]

Much of the discussion at the seminar centered around the problem of how to distinguish between child labor and the exploitation of child labor, considering such issues as the age of the child, the nature of the work, whether work was essential for the survival of the child or the child's family, the conditions of safety and health in which the child worked, the working hours, and whether wages were discriminatory.

Kurt Herndl, assistant secretary general for human rights, raised four issues: (1) whether exploitation is merely the existence of child labor or whether it refers to specific exploitative elements in the employment of children. Should one, he asked, consider the employment of all children under the age of twelve by definition exploitative? (2) What is meant by a "child"? In practice, he noted, three categories are used: children under twelve, children between twelve and fifteen, and children between fifteen and eighteen. (3) How should we distinguish between labor that

---

[16] *Seminar on Ways and Means of Achieving the Elimination of the Exploitation of Child Labour in All Parts of the World* (Geneva: United Nations, ST/HR/Ser.A/18, 22 January 1986).

[17] Ibid., p. 6.

is dangerous, hazardous, and morally outrageous (e.g., child prostitution) and acceptable forms of child labor? (4) What would constitute the "elimination" of exploitative practices? Banning the employment of children under twelve, he reported, and the banning of child labor in all hazardous and unsafe activities is the minimum standard advocated by the ILO.

The seminar recommended that "States . . . should review their legislation in the field of child labour with a view to absolute prohibition of employment of children in the following cases: employment before the normal age of completion of primary schooling in the country concerned; sexual exploitation of children; night work; work in dangerous or unhealthy conditions; work concerned with trafficking in and production of illicit drugs; work involving degrading or cruel treatment." Other recommendations dealt with improving the conditions for working children. These included "undertaking development programs aimed at achieving equitable distribution of income, generating opportunities for employment, creation of small businesses, and agrarian reforms; and abolish, wherever possible primary school fees; introduce flexible school timetables to enable children who work to receive education; . . . establish or improve medical services for school children and children at work."[18] No mention was made of introducing compulsory education.

The ILO, since its inception, has been an advocate of legislation prohibiting the employment of children. In 1919 the ILO adopted its first Minimum Age Convention, which fixed a minimum age of fourteen for employment in industry. Subsequently, the ILO approved conventions regulating the age and conditions of work of children in particular sectors and occupations. A declaration issued in 1979, the International Year of the Child, reiterated the ILO's commitment to the elimination of child labor but also declared that pending its attainment the ILO would work for the improvement of the conditions of working children. In 1983, the annual report of the director general of the ILO, Francis Blanchard, was devoted to the issue of child labor. He reiterated the ILO's stance on child labor and noted the "close correspondence between school attendance rates and the incidence of child labor," which underscored the ILO's 1973 minimum-age recommendation that "full-time attendance at school or participation in approved vocational orientation or training programmes should be required and effectively ensured up to an age at least equal to that specified for admission to employment." He agreed with those who said that "child labour is embedded in poverty and it is through sustained increases in standards of living that it will be abolished," but, he went on to say, "recognition of this reality must not serve as a pretext for inaction. The problem of child labour is so grave and is often manifested in forms

---

[18] Ibid., p. 26.

so unacceptable that it cannot be left aside until economic conditions and social structures are fundamentally improved."[19] He urged states strictly to enforce their child labor laws and called upon member states to ratify the ILO Minimum Age Convention of 1973 which established fifteen as the minimum age of employment in most sectors, while permitting light work from age thirteen.

But other officials of the ILO and other international organizations took a position more sympathetic to the new Indian policy. In a number of widely circulated papers, Assefa Bequele, a senior research economist at the ILO from Ethiopia, argued that governments should carry out a two-pronged approach of protecting children from extreme forms of exploitation while improving the conditions of employment for others. "The close link between poverty and the incidence of child labour suggests the strong complementarity of anti-child labour policies and those aiming at employment creation and poverty alleviation."[20] Rural development programs and income generating and income maintenance programs were thus necessary, he wrote, for eliminating child labor. More broadly, he concluded, "changes in the structure of the present international system, including a more equitable distribution of economic opportunities among

[19] *Report of the Director-General to the International Labour Conference*, 69th sess., 1983 (Geneva: International Labour Office, 1985). For a global survey of child labor, see *Conditions of Work Digest: The Emerging Response to Child Labour*, vol. 7, no. 1, 1988 (Geneva: International Labour Office, 1988). ILO conventions are conveniently summarized in *Child Labour: A Briefing Manual* (Geneva: International Labour Office, 1986). For a bibliography, see *Annotated Bibliography on Child Labour* (Geneva: International Labour Office, 1986).

[20] Assefa Bequele, *Towards a Global Programme of Action on Child Labour* (Geneva: Conditions of Work and Welfare Facilities Branch, Working Conditions and Environment Department, International Labour Office, September 1985). See also Assefa Bequele and Jo Boyden, eds., *Combating Child Labour* (Geneva: International Labour Office, 1988), esp. Ramesh Kanbargi, "Child Labour in India: The Carpet Industry of Varanasi," pp. 93–108. For an ILO analysis of the Indian situation, see *Towards an Action Programme on Child Labour. Report to the Government of India of an ILO Technical Mission* (Conditions of Work and Welfare Facilities Branch, Working Conditions and Environment Department, International Labour Office, Geneva, April 1984). This report supports the Indian view that "the abolition of child labour . . . is not attainable in the short run in many developing countries; millions of children will continue to be working for many years to come. Measures to regulate and humanise child labour are therefore essential during the transitional period until its elimination" (p. 1). Other international organizations have supported the Indian position. See, for example, Sumanta Banerjee, *Child Labour in India* (London: Anti-Slavery Society, 1979), who writes that "however outrageous the presence of child workers might be to liberal sentiments, Indians will have to live with the phenomenon as long as the level of the country's economic development remains what it is now." Similar views can be found in Garry Rodgers and Guy Standing, eds., *Child Work, Poverty, and Underdevelopment* (Geneva: International Labour Office, 1981); and *Exploitation of Working Children and Street Children* (New York: United Nations Childrens Fund, 1986).

nations . . . and other changes advocated by the International Development Strategy can, by enhancing national efforts aimed at poverty alleviation and rapid growth, provide significant impetus to the struggle against child labour."[21]

To what extent the international organizations should throw their political weight behind efforts to end "exploitation" and to ameliorate child labor rather than pressing for its abolition has been an issue within the ILO, UNICEF, WHO, and the UN Commission on Human Rights. A handful of officials in each of these agencies has given considerable attention to these questions, notably Assefa Bequele in the ILO, William Cousins in UNICEF, Dr. P. M. Shah at WHO, and Abdelwahab Bouhdiba of the UN Commission on Human Rights. Among these officials there are subtle differences, but in the main they have tended to emphasize the need by governments to end the worst forms of exploitation and to ameliorate the conditions of working children rather than press for abolition. Dr. P. M. Shah, an Indian pediatrician, has pressed for programs of health care for working children, believing that such programs can be developed through cooperation between government agencies and employers. Officials at UNICEF have suggested that the agency give special attention to providing services to children in especially difficult circumstances, such as street children and children of refugees and immigrants. At the ILO the emphasis is on protection rather than abolition, at least for the short run. Work in hazardous and unsafe activities, wrote Bequele, should be prohibited. For other children, protective measures are advocated, including the provision of fair remuneration, strict limitation of hours of work, and the maintenance of satisfactory standards of safety and health. Steps should be taken to expand educational opportunities, including "increased access to it by the relatively deprived sectors and socio-economic groups, improvements in the quality of education so as to make it more relevant and attractive to the poor, and reducing the real cost of education to the poor."[22] Once again, the theme is incentives, not compulsion.

Thus, the Indian government's position on child labor, while not in accordance with the 1973 ILO convention (India, along with most developing countries, has not ratified the convention), has won considerable support at international conferences and among officials in the ILO.

Rajiv Gandhi's New National Policy on Education

Rajiv Gandhi's announcement in January 1985, only a few weeks after his election as prime minister, that he had asked the Ministry of Education

---

[21] Bequele, *Towards a Global Programme of Action on Child Labour*, p. 51.
[22] Ibid., pp. 48, 49.

to review the country's educational system and to propose a new national policy on education to take India into the twenty-first century was greeted with both enthusiasm and cynicism: enthusiasm that the young prime minister had made educational reform a high priority early in his administration; cynicism in that once again another committee would be appointed, whose recommendations were likely to go unheeded. Since this new education policy has relevance for our understanding of the government's policy toward child labor, we shall examine the policy and the debate surrounding it.

In August 1985 the ministry's review, called *Challenge of Education—A Policy Perspective*, was released.[23] The 119-page document provided a host of recommendations for what it called "educational restructuring": universalizing elementary education, reducing the school dropout rate, creating a network of "model schools" in every district in the country for the most meritorious children from rural areas, using new communications technologies in schools, vocationalizing secondary education, expanding nonformal education for those who had not attended or completed school, delinking degrees from jobs, making education more "socially relevant," and depoliticizing the universities. There followed months of public discussion on these proposals, innumerable conferences of educators, and the appointment of twenty-three task forces by the government to make detailed recommendations for specific subjects covered by the proposed National Policy on Education.[24]

While there was much criticism of the government's proposals for education, there was agreement that the *Challenge of Education* provided an extraordinary—and disarming—critique of the government's own failure to carry out the reforms and targets set by earlier government commissions. The report noted that from 1950 to 1983 there had been a massive increase in the number of primary schools, from 210,000 to 504,000, and a vast increase in the student population of the country, from 28 million in 1950–1951 to 114 million in 1982–1983, a growth rate of 4.5 percent per annum. Most states reported more than 100 percent enrollment of boys and 75 percent for girls.

In a spirit of self-criticism, the report documented the following failures in educational development:

1. A quarter of the pupils enrolled in primary school are underage or overage, and if these are excluded from the rate of growth of enrollments for 1971–

[23] Ministry of Education, *Challenge of Education—A Policy Perspective* (New Delhi: Government of India, 1985).

[24] The detailed recommendations appear in Department of Education, Ministry of Human Resource Development, *National Policy on Education 1986—Programme of Action* (New Delhi: Government of India, 1986).

1981 (2.5 percent per annum) the growth rate is below the age-specific population growth rate. "This implies that the backlog of illiterate population in absolute terms keeps on increasing with time."[25]

2. Though there has been an increase in the enrollment of girls in primary schools, the situation in many states remains unsatisfactory. In Uttar Pradesh, India's largest state, the gross enrollment ratio (which includes underage and overage children) for girls is 49 percent. In Jalore district in Rajasthan enrollment of girls is as low as 17 percent.

3. While most children have a primary school within one kilometer of their home, nearly one-fifth of all habitations in India do not have schools. The schools themselves are often unsatisfactory: 40 percent of the schools have no *pacca* (brick or cement) buildings; 9 percent have no buildings at all; 40 percent have no blackboards; 60 percent have no drinking water; 70 percent have no library facilities; 53 percent are without playgrounds; 89 percent lack toilet facilities; 35 percent of the schools have only a single teacher to teach three or four different classes; "many schools remain without any teacher for varying periods of time and some teachers are not above sub-contracting teaching work to others who are not qualified."[26]

4. Nearly 60 percent of the children drop out between classes 1 and 5. Of 100 children enrolled in class 1, only 23 reach class 8. "The magnitude of wastage is emaciating the educational development of the country."[27] While there has been a marginal decline in the dropout rate in some states, in Uttar Pradesh the dropout rate is increasing.

5. While the literacy rate has increased from 16.7 percent in 1951 to 36.2 percent and the number of literates has increased fourfold from 60 million to 248 million, the absolute number of illiterates has grown from 294 million at the time of independence to 424 million in 1981. There is also a glaring disparity between male and female literacy, the former being 46.9 percent, the latter 24.8 percent. In rural areas the literacy rate for males is 40.8 percent and for females 18 percent; in urban areas it is 65.9 percent and 47.8 percent respectively.

6. The regional variations are large, from Kerala, which has a literacy rate of 70.4 percent, to Rajasthan, with a literacy rate of 24.4 percent (only 11.4 percent of the females in Rajasthan were literate in 1981). Eight states have literacy rates five or more percentage points above the national average: Gujarat, Himachal Pradesh, Kerala, Maharashtra, Manipur, Nagaland, Tamil Nadu, and Tripura. Five states have literacy rates that are five or more percentage points below the national average: Andhra, Bihar, Madhya Pradesh, Rajasthan, and

[25] Ministry of Education, *Challenge of Education*, p. 18.
[26] Ibid., p. 36.
[27] Ibid., p. 22.

Uttar Pradesh (for state literacy rates, see table 5.1; for school attendance rates by state, see table 5.2).

7. India spends 3 percent of its gross national product on education, similar to that of other countries in South Asia, but well below the percentage spent in many developing countries and well below the 6 percent recommended by the Educational Commission in 1966. While in 1950–1951, 43 percent of the educational budget was for primary education, by 1976 the expenditure on primary education had declined to 27 percent. More than 90 percent of the ex-

TABLE 5.1
School Enrollments and Literacy Rates by State (percent)

	Enrollment (1978)		Literacy Rate (1981)	Male	Female
	Ages 6–10	Ages 11–13			
Andhra Pradesh	60.2	30.1	29.9	39.3	20.4
Assam	63.7	37.9	28.1[a]		
Bihar	54.4	25.9	26.2	38.1	13.7
Gujarat	69.8	56.9	43.7	54.4	32.3
Haryana	60.7	45.0	36.1	48.2	22.3
Himachal Pradesh	79.0	62.3	42.5	53.2	31.5
Jammu and Kashmir	58.3	41.4	26.7	36.3	15.9
Karnataka	75.1	47.4	38.5	48.8	27.7
Kerala	86.0	76.8	70.4	75.3	65.7
Madhya Pradesh	47.7	33.7	27.9	39.5	15.5
Maharashtra	79.4	56.2	47.2	58.8	34.8
Manipur	76.4	54.5	41.4	53.0	29.1
Meghalaya	60.3	53.5	34.1	37.9	30.1
Nagaland	70.4	62.8	42.6	50.1	33.9
Orissa	56.5	40.7	34.2	47.1	21.1
Punjab	93.2	64.1	40.9	47.2	33.7
Rajasthan	45.2	29.1	24.4	38.3	11.4
Sikkim	68.9	59.9	34.1	43.7	22.2
Tamil Nadu	87.6	50.7	46.8	58.3	35.0
Tripura	73.9	37.7	42.1	51.7	32.0
Uttar Pradesh	53.4	33.4	27.2	38.8	14.0
West Bengal	67.6	39.7	40.9	50.7	30.3
All India	64.1	41.7	36.2	46.9	24.8

Source: Enrollment figures from *Fourth All-India Educational Survey* (New Delhi National Council of Educational Research and Training, 1980), pp. 944–947. Data from survey conducted in 1978. Literacy figures from O. P. Sharma and Robert D. Retherford, *Recent Literacy Trends in India, Occasional Paper No. 1 of 1987* (New Delhi: Registrar General and Census Commissioner, 1987), p. 17; the authors estimate that it will take seventy years for the goal of complete literacy to be achieved if current trends continue—Kerala will take fifteen years, Rajasthan a century.

[a] 1971 figure.

TABLE 5.2
School Attendance by State, 1981

	Age Group	Total Attendance	Male	Female
			(Percent of population)	
Andhra	5–9	42	47	34
	10–14	41	52	30
	15–19	19	27	10
	20–24	5	8	2
Bihar	5–9	26	33	18
	10–14	41	55	25
	15–19	24	38	9
	20–24	8	15	2
Gujarat	5–9	45	50	39
	10–14	61	70	50
	15–19	29	37	19
	20–24	7	10	3
Haryana	5–9	39	47	31
	10–14	55	71	36
	15–19	27	37	14
	20–24	5	7	3
Karnataka	5–9	43	49	38
	10–14	48	58	38
	15–19	23	32	14
	20–24	7	12	3
Kerala	5–9	75	75	75
	10–14	86	88	84
	15–19	44	49	40
	20–24	10	12	8
Madhya Pradesh	5–9	30	38	22
	10–14	41	55	25
	15–19	21	32	9
	20–24	5	9	2
Maharashtra	5–9	52	58	47
	10–14	63	73	51
	15–19	30	40	19
	20–24	7	12	3
Punjab	5–9	52	54	49
	10–14	63	69	56
	15–19	29	34	23
	20–24	6	8	5

TABLE 5.2 (*cont.*)

Age Group	Total Attendance	Male	Female
		(Percent of population)	
Rajasthan 5–9	27	37	16
10–14	40	59	19
15–19	23	36	8
20–24	6	11	2
Uttar Pradesh 5–9	25	32	17
10–14	44	58	25
15–19	26	39	10
20–24	8	14	2
West Bengal 5–9	37	41	33
10–14	53	60	45
15–19	30	37	21
20–24	10	14	5

Source: Data compiled from *Census of India. Part II-Special. Report and Tables Based on 5 Per Cent Sample Data*, Series numbers 2, 4, 5, 6, 9, 10, 11, 12, 17, 18, 22, 23 (New Delhi, 1983).

penditure is for teachers' salaries and administration. Total expenditure per student per year by the center and the states has declined in real terms. Very little money is available for science equipment, kits, posters and charts, or books, even blackboards. (For data on expenditures on elementary education from 1951 to 1985, see table 5.3.)

8. Educational expenditure is disproportionately lower in rural areas. In 1970–1971, when 4.9 billion rupees were spent on education in rural areas, 6.2 billion rupees were spent in urban areas, so that "the quality and maintenance of school and college buildings in urban areas are very much better than in rural areas."[28] Urban–rural disparities are further magnified by the presence of privately managed quality institutions in the urban areas.

9. From a share of 56 percent in the first five-year plan, the expenditure on elementary education over most of the successive five-year plans has declined. By the sixth five-year plan (1980–1985), it was down to 36 percent. On the other hand, between the first and sixth five-year plans the share for university education rose from 9 percent to 16 percent. With 70 percent of the total plan expenditure for education coming from the states there is great variation among the states in how much they spend on education, from as low as 40 rupees in Uttar Pradesh to 120 rupees in Kerala (with the all-India average at 68 rupees).

10. The goal of universalizing elementary-school education remains elusive

[28] Ibid., p. 57.

96

CHAPTER 5

TABLE 5.3

Expenditures on Elementary Education

Plan	Expenditures (Rupees in Millimi) Total Education	Elementary Education	Percent on Elementary Education
first (1951–1956)	1,530	850	55.6
second (1956–1961)	2,730	950	34.8
third (1961–1966)	5,890	1,780	30.2
annual (1966–1969)	3,220	650	20.2
fourth (1969–1974)	8,230	2,350	28.6
fifth (1974–1979)	12,850	4,100	31.9
sixth (1980–1985)	25,230	9,050	35.9

Source: Dr. T. N. Dhar, "Elementary Education in India," unpublished paper (New Delhi: Planning Commission, Government of India, n.d.). Sixth-plan data represents proposed outlays, not actual expenditures, which are usually lower. In the sixth plan, 30 percent of the total plan outlays in education but only 7 percent of the plan outlays for elementary-school education were from the central government.

as the population grows. The number of children in the six-to-fourteen age group will be 174 million by 1990. Were elementary education universal in 1990, 110 million pupils would be in lower primary school, 64 million in middle primary; this would be 1.5 times and 3.2 times the present size, respectively. To achieve this increase, the number of school teachers in elementary education will have to increase from 2.9 million in 1990 at the existing level of educational growth (there were 2.2 million elementary-school teachers in 1980) to 4.4 million. The budgetary requirements for 1990, assuming no change in per capita expenditure, will have to double, from 15.4 billion rupees in 1980 to 32 billion rupees in 1990. With an 8 percent per annum rate of inflation, the 1990 education budget at current prices will have to be more than four times the 1980 allocations.

In some respects what was more depressing than these hard numbers was the reference to the Education Commission of 1964–1966. Over a two-year period this commission (often called the Kothari Commission after its chairman, Professor D. S. Kothari of the University Grants Commission), made up of India's leading educationists and a number of distinguished foreign participants, with twelve task forces, scrutinized India's educational system. The central thrust of their 615-page report was its call for "a higher priority than that given so far to education in our national plans for development" and its plea for "vigorous and sustained implementation."[29]

[29] National Council of Educational Research and Training, *Education and National De-*

Among the commission's strongest recommendations was that all areas of the country provide five years of education to all children by 1975–1976 and seven years by 1985–1986. Enrollments for grades 1 to 4 should rise from 37 million in 1965 to 72 million in 1975 to 76 million in 1985, while higher primary classes 5 to 8 should increase from 13 million in 1965 to 32 million in 1975 to 49 million in 1985. The goal of universal education by 1960 that had been proclaimed in article 45 of the Constitution was now to be achieved by 1985. The commission was particularly distressed at the high dropout rate in the midsixties, and it set as a target an 80 percent completion rate for class 7. On the basis of the commission's recommendations the government of India announced a National Policy on Education in 1968. The government reconfirmed its commitment to provide free and compulsory education for all children up to the age of fourteen and to reduce the dropout rate.

As is well known, none of these targets was achieved. The Fourth All-India Educational Survey conducted by the National Council of Educational Research and Training reported the following data for September 1978: 61 million children in grades 1 to 4, and 25.6 million in grades 5 to 8.[30] In other words, in 1978 there were 86.6 million children in elementary school as against the targeted 104 million for 1975.

It is not surprising, therefore, that the government's announcement in 1986 that the National Policy on Education had as its "new thrust" the achievement of universal enrollment and universal retention of children up to fourteen years of age by 1995 was greeted with skepticism. The skepticism was not unfounded, especially in the light of two programs announced by the government. The first was the proposal for creating model district schools for high-achieving rural youth. Each district was to have a single residential high school, a Navodaya Vidyalaya, which would provide free boarding and lodging to gifted students chosen on the basis of competitive examinations. In these schools 75 percent of the seats would be reserved for rural children and an effort would be made to ensure that one-third of the students would be girls. The schools would be well-equipped, with large playgrounds, lawns, hostels, audiovisual aids, and computers. Classes would be in English, but the children would learn the regional language and Hindi. Some children would be moved from their home district to a school elsewhere in the country as a way of promoting national integration through regional interaction.

Rajiv Gandhi was an enthusiastic supporter of the Navodaya Vidyalayas. Speaking at a conference on education in New Delhi on 26 June

velopment: Report of the Education Commission 1964–66, vol. 2: School Education (New Delhi: NCERT, 1970).
    [30] National Council of Educational Research and Training, Fourth All-India Educational Survey. Some Statistics on School Education (New Delhi, 1980).

1986, he defended himself against the charge that the proposed new schools were elitist.

> The education system that we have today is more elitist than anything that we could imagine. . . . It only makes good education available to those people who have not just adequate resources but plenty of resources. If you are lacking that, if you cannot afford seven thousand or ten thousand rupees a year to educate your child from the primary to secondary level, then what is available to you is really a very bad, unorganised, pathetic perhaps is the only word, system. . . . We are attempting in this new education system to break this double standard and to try and bring good education to the weakest, the poorest sections of our society. The only measure of elitism that will be kept is that of the brilliance of the individual child and not of its economic background or its social background. And this elitism, I think, must be built into our society if the best in our society is to come out.

For the prime minister egalitarianism meant providing gifted rural youth without financial means the same quality education that he and others of his social class had obtained at such privately run institutions as the Doon School.

Critics of the Navodaya Vidyalayas said that the schools would divert substantial sums away from efforts to increase elementary-school education, and that the children in the schools would be recruited largely from among the more prosperous rural, landed classes. The cost of the school buildings for the Navodaya Vidyalayas is estimated at 10 billion rupees, while the annual central education budget is only 8.3 billion rupees. The annual cost of running 433 Navodaya Vidyalayas, each with 500 students, is estimated at 2 billion rupees after 1995. The director of the program, J. N. Sharma, expressed his concern that "the scheme will die under its own financial weight." Critics noted that the national per capita expenditure on school children by the government is 150 rupees per year, while the proposed cost for each Navodaya Vidyalaya student is 9,500 to 10,000 rupees. In defense of the scheme, Mr. Sharma said: "Two per cent of children in every society are mentally superior to others. To cater to their greater appetite for learning, a free environment has to be given."[31]

The government did have a program for the universalization of education: Operation Blackboard and Non-Formal Education. Under Operation Blackboard 1 billion rupees was allocated in 1987 for basic amenities for village schools, or 2,200 rupees for each government-run primary school. But the major effort to bring dropouts and other nonenrolled children into the education system is to be made through the Non-Formal Education system (NFE), especially in the nine states that are regarded as

[31] "Navodaya Schools—Chalking a New Path," *India Today* (15 June 1988).

educationally backward: Andhra, Assam, Bihar, Jammu and Kashmir, Madhya Pradesh, Orissa, Rajasthan, Uttar Pradesh, and West Bengal, states with 75 percent of the country's nonenrolled children. NFE was put in place in 1979. A key objective is to provide education for working children. Anil Bordia, secretary of the Department of Education and previously an official in the Labour Ministry, argued that expenditures on improving the facilities of primary schools would do little to help the poor who drop out, whereas the system of nonformal education was targeted to meet the needs of working children.[32]

The intended clientele of nonformal part-time education was laid out in some detail earlier in the report of the Working Group on Universalisation of Elementary Education appointed by the Ministry of Education (1977):

(a) Children of the weaker sections like the scheduled castes, scheduled tribes, those in hilly areas, tribal areas, urban slums and other economically backward rural areas. There are a large number of children among these sections in the age-group 6–14 who have either never entered the formal school or have dropped out. They are helping the family in a number of ways and the school time does not suit them. Given the facility of schooling at a suitable time and place and with relevant curriculum, they might like to avail themselves of the educational facility and might like to rejoin the formal school system at some appropriate stage.

(b) Girls in the age group 6–14 who are not attracted by the existing programme of education being offered by the formal elementary school. These girls may generally not be interested in joining the formal school at any stage. Thus they would need an additional programme tailored to suit their requirements as housewives, mothers and citizens.

(c) Boys and girls (generally boys) in the age-group 6–14 who are employed in professions like carpet-weaving, pottery, etc. These children need only a part-time programme of general education which may be focussed around literacy, numeracy and citizenship training.[33]

NFE is to have a more flexible curriculum, one directed at the needs of working children and youth. According to the proposed program children will move at their own pace. Classes will be held at hours that take into

[32] Anil Bordia, *Working Paper on Child Labour in India—Implications for Educational Planning,* ILO Asian Regional Tripartite Workshop on Practical Measures to Combat Child Labor, Bangkok, September 1986 (New Delhi: Ministry of Human Resource Development, Government of India, 1986), p. 17. This paper provides a systematic analysis of the linkage between the Child Labour (Prohibition and Regulation) Bill and the proposed National Policy on Education. As an official in both departments, Mr. Bordia played an important role in formulating the new policy.

[33] Ministry of Education and Social Welfare, *Working Group on Universalisation of Elementary Education* (New Delhi: Government of India, 1977), pp. 11–12.

account the children's work schedule; and nongovernmental organizations will be encouraged to help plan the curriculum. The costs of NFE are split evenly by the central and state governments. From 1979 to 1984 the central government's expenditure on NFE totaled 777 million rupees. In 1985–1986, according to the government, 3.67 million children were enrolled in 128,000 centers around the country.

Observers of the program noted that states had failed to match the funds that the center had budgeted, that teachers in the program were not properly trained, that many of the centers had closed down, that a large proportion of the children in the program were below the age of nine and thus were supposed to be attending regular schools, and that there was no effective monitoring and evaluation of the centers.[34]

Critics were skeptical that the goal of enrolling and retaining all school-age children was achievable through the government's new policy on education. There was no evidence that the government was planning the kind of massive increase in elementary-school education expenditure that was needed to achieve universalization. One critic said that the government was making token investments in nonformal education without any real commitment to developing the existing primary schools. Other critics regarded the district model schools, with English as the medium of instruction and classroom computers, as no substitute for mass education. One critic doubted that the government was really concerned with ending illiteracy. Professor Upendra Baxi, a well-known professor of law, wrote that "after acknowledging that in A.D. 2000 there would be 500 million illiterates in India, and that such magnitude of illiteracy is a drag on development towards the 21st century, the NEP document says that we should decide 'once and for all' after 'careful consideration' whether the perception that 'removal of illiteracy is . . . an essential precondition for the meaningful participation of the masses in the process of political decision making and national reconstruction' would be 'valid for India'! In other words, the authors of the Report aren't sure! Some 'policy perspective', this!"[35]

These doubts about the very objectives of the government were reinforced by a statement made by the prime minister while in the United States that was widely quoted in the Indian press. In a prepared public address at Harvard University in October 1987, Rajiv Gandhi extolled Indian democracy for its success in a society that remained poor and whose population was largely illiterate. In the question period that followed an Indian student asked if it was not a blot on Indian democracy that so many people were illiterate years after independence. Gandhi

---

[34] "Education for All at Snail's Pace," *Overseas Hindustan Times* (30 May 1987).

[35] Upendra Baxi, "Draft Graduates for Adult Literacy," *Yojana* (January 1986), p. 66.

replied: "I don't think literacy is the key to democracy. . . . Wisdom is much more important. We have seen—and I'm not now limiting myself to India, I'm going beyond to other countries—literacy sometimes narrows the vision, does not broaden it."[36]

In the January 1986 issue of *Yojana*, a government-run journal of education, eighteen of India's leading educationists critically reviewed the government's proposed national policy on education and suggested measures to universalize education and eliminate illiteracy: using the government surplus foodgrain to provide each child a kilo of rice or wheat each day of school as an insurance against dropping out, a massive increase in budgetary allocations for elementary schools, a shift in education expenditures from higher education to mass education and greater attention to nonformal education, greater attention to vocationalization in the schools and more involvement of all development agencies in adult literacy programs, greater educational decentralization, a national model act on primary education, the expansion of part-time literacy centers, the creation of preprimary classes, the use of college students for literacy classes and adult education, and a greater effort to recruit and motivate dedicated teachers. None of the critics, it should be noted, proposed making elementary-school education compulsory.

Compulsory Education: A Legislative Review

As noted earlier, compulsory-education laws in India do not make education compulsory: they merely establish the conditions under which state governments may make education compulsory in specified areas. Thus, the Assam Elementary Education Act of 1974 contains a provision that "the State Government may, by notification, declare that elementary education shall be compulsory up to certain age to be prescribed in any area or areas of the State as specified in the notification. In such an area of compulsion the guardian of every child resident in such area shall . . . be bound to cause the child to attend a recognised Elementary School in such area." When this provision is in effect, "the State government may appoint the attendance authorities for the purpose of enforcing attendance in the schools." Fines are then prescribed for those who contravene the provisions of the law.[37]

Similarly, the Tamil Nadu Elementary Education Act (1920, amended in 1973) provides that "any local authority may . . . resolve that elemen-

---

[36] "Gandhi, at Harvard, Extolls Virtues of India's Democracy," *Boston Globe* (19 October 1987).

[37] The Assam Elementary Education Act, 1974 (Gauhati: Government of Assam, Education Dept., 1974).

tary education shall be compulsory within the whole or a specified part of the local area under its jurisdiction," but only with the approval of the state government.[38] The Mysore Compulsory Primary Education Act of 1961 actually permits the state government to notify areas that primary education is to be made compulsory. A related set of rules (the Mysore Compulsory Primary Education Rules) specifies in detail how compulsory education is then to be enforced, including the appointment of an attendance authority, procedures for the enumeration of all children within the prescribed area, the compulsory registration of the names and birth dates of children, the publication of an enumeration register, procedures for revising and updating the enumeration register, procedures for issuing notices to parents and guardians whose children are not attending school, conditions under which children are exempt (e.g., illness or the lack of a school within a mile of their home), and, finally, penalties for failing to send children to school. However, most other state laws merely provide that initiative for the establishment of compulsory education rests with the local authorities.

A few local governments made education compulsory. As early as 1893 compulsory education was legally imposed in a division of the state of Baroda, then a princely state led by Maharaja Sayajirao Gaekwar of Baroda. The Maharaja of Baroda was an enthusiastic supporter of universal education. He regarded his experiment with compulsory education in one division as a success, and in 1906 he made education compulsory throughout the state. Earlier, the British had debated the question of introducing compulsory education into India but concluded that it was contrary to British jurisprudence, a position that was weakened by the introduction of the principle of compulsory education in England in 1870. Some Indian and British officials argued for introducing compulsory education before the Indian Education Commission in 1882, but the proposal was never seriously considered. A proposal to introduce compulsory education was taken up in Bombay in 1906, but rejected. Shortly before World War I, Gopal Krishna Gokhale, a leading Indian liberal and Congress Party president, took up the issue in the central legislature in New Delhi. He introduced a private bill proposing that local bodies, subject to prescribed conditions, be authorized to introduce compulsory education in their areas. The bill was widely circulated and while it received some support from leaders of the Indian National Congress and the Muslim League, a majority of the central legislature, most officials, and representatives of the princely states were opposed. The government regarded the proposal as utopian on financial and administrative grounds.

[38] The Tamil Nadu Elementary Education Act (Madras: Government of Tamil Nadu, 1973).

In 1918 a leading nationalist, Vithalbhai Patel, introduced a bill in the Bombay legislative council permitting municipal areas of the state to make education compulsory, with grants-in-aid to be provided by the state government. The Patel Act was passed and thereafter every state under British rule passed a similar compulsory-education law, as did many of the Indian states. By the early 1930s the principle of compulsory education was written into state law; the 1950 Constitution, in article 45, made it officially a matter of national policy.

All these laws permit, but do not require, local authorities to introduce compulsory education. To ensure that local authorities did not zealously introduce compulsion in an area that was not ready, these laws require that two-thirds of those present or one-half of the total number of members of the local authority have to approve, and that the state government also has to give its approval. The acts also specify the procedures for making education compulsory: the preparation of a census of nonattending children, the issue of notices to parents, hearings to consider exemptions, a report from the school headmaster, persuasion of parents by teachers and attendance officers, another hearing with the parents, and, only as a last resort, prosecution. Describing these acts, J. P. Naik (and his two coauthors) wrote that "the early legislators were more anxious to prevent harassment to parents than to increase attendance and, except in Baroda where simplified procedures were prescribed in the light of actual experience, these early views on the subject have continued unchanged to this day."[39]

No one need have been concerned with overzealous local bodies, for as it turned out few of them made education compulsory. In 1921–1922, when the British transferred education to Indian control, education was made compulsory in eight towns and not a single village. By 1936–1937 education had been made compulsory in 167 out of a total of 2,700 urban areas and only in a handful of rural areas. Opposition to compulsion was strongest among the officers of the Indian Educational Services, and on financial grounds state governments rejected a number of proposals from local authorities.[40]

[39] K. G. Saiyidain, J. P. Naik, and S. Abid Hussain, *Compulsory Education in India* (Paris: United Nations Educational, Scientific, and Cultural Organization, 1952), p. 33. Naik reviews the data on enforcement and prosecutions in the various states for 1948–1949 on pages 68–72.

[40] For an account of the preindependence history of efforts to introduce compulsory education into India, see *Compulsory Education in South Asia and the Pacific. Report of the Bombay Conference* (December 1952), Studies in Compulsory Education (Paris: United Nations Educational, Scientific, and Cultural Organization, 1954). For a postindependence analysis of the unsuccessful efforts to universalize elementary education, see John Kurrien, *Elementary Education in India: Myth, Reality, Alternative* (New Delhi: Vikas Publishing, 1983).

Moreover, even when local authorities did succeed in making education compulsory, there was little enforcement. In Baroda, for example, many of the villages in which education was supposed to be compulsory had no schools, so the question of enforcement was moot. Bombay province made education compulsory for the city in 1939 but, wrote J. P. Naik,

> the municipality has consistently refused to prosecute defaulting parents on the ground of trying persuasion before prosecution. . . . Ever since 1926–1927, when a quinquennial review first discussed the results of compulsory education, the official reports have been continuously complaining that no attempts are made to enforce compulsion in practice and that it has remained, more or less, on paper. It has been said, for instance, that the census of children of school-going age is not regularly taken and that procedures adopted for it leave several loopholes for truants to escape; that attendance officers are untrained and too few to cope with the situation; that local committees are always unwilling to launch prosecutions; that exemptions are granted too freely, and that the arrangements for trying cases under the compulsory law are generally defective, so that inordinate delays which defeat the very object of the Acts are common. The conclusion is, therefore, justified that in no area under compulsion is a vigorous attempt made to enforce it rigidly, that in several cases compulsory education exists only on paper, and that in most areas, the dividing line between voluntary and compulsory education is very thin.[41]

J. P. Naik noted that there was some enforcement in Baroda (though many villages continued to lack schools) with the result that by 1921 the literacy rate in Baroda exceeded that of Bombay and in the country as a whole was only behind Travancore and Cochin.[42] The Travancore government was perhaps the most aggressive in India in its efforts to spread elementary education. In 1935–1936 the Travancore government began a scheme of grants to pupils belonging to the backward communities. In the early 1940s a midday meal program was introduced. And in 1945, when enrollment in primary schools (classes 1 to 5) reached 80 percent, the government made education compulsory.[43] The dropout rate was the lowest and literacy the highest of any of the states.

[41] Saiyidain, Naik, and Hussain, *Compulsory Education in India*, p. 33.

[42] Baroda (now called Vadodara) had a literacy rate of 68 percent in 1981, substantially higher than the 57 percent rate for urban India. Other cities with populations above 500,000 with literacy rates above 65 percent included Calcutta (66 percent), Bombay (68 percent), Madras (66 percent), Pune (67 percent), Nagpur (66 percent), Coimbatore (66 percent), Madurai (67 percent), Cochin (78 percent), Ulhasnagar (66 percent), Tiruchirapalli (69 percent), Calicut (73 percent), and Trivandrum (76 percent).

[43] P. R. Gopinathan Nair, *Primary Education, Population Growth, and Socio-Economic Change (A Comparative Study with Particular Reference to Kerala)* (New Delhi: Allied Publishers, 1981).

The low investment in primary education before independence, the absence of primary schools in much of the country, the high dropout rate and the absence of any system of compulsory education combined to keep illiteracy at a near constant rate. Between 1881 and 1931 literacy increased from 3.5 percent to 8.0 percent, or 1 percent per decade. In spite of the growth in primary schools and an increase in school enrollment between 1921 and 1931 the literacy rate during the entire decade continued to rise by only 1 percent. A committee appointed by the government to review the growth of education in British India (the Hartog Committee) concluded that "in the primary system, which from our point of view should be designed to produce literacy and the capacity to exercise an intelligent vote, the waste is appalling. So far as we can judge, the vast increase in numbers in primary schools produces no commensurate increase in literacy, for only a small proportion of those who are at the primary stage reach Class IV, in which attainment of literacy may be expected. The waste in the case of girls is even more serious than in the case of boys."[44]

The assumption of office in seven provinces by the Indian National Congress in 1937 led to a discussion of how to expand primary education. Provincial finances were a problem, especially since Congress was committed to introducing prohibition, a policy that substantially cut a major source of government revenue. It was at this time that Mahatma Gandhi proposed his famous scheme of Basic Education. In a series of articles in his journal *Harijan* he laid out his views on how to establish mass education at low cost:

> As a nation we are so backward in education that we cannot hope to fulfill our obligations in this respect in a given time during this generation if this programme is to depend on money. I have, therefore, made bold, even at the risk of losing reputation for constructive policy, to suggest that education should be self-supporting. By education, I mean an allround drawing out of the best in the child—in body, mind and spirit. Literacy is not the end of education nor even the beginning. It is only one of the means whereby men and women can be educated. Literacy in itself is not education. I would, therefore, begin the child's education by teaching it a useful handicraft, enabling it to produce from the moment it begins its training. Thus, every school can be made self-supporting, condition being that State takes over the manufacture of these schools.[45]

[44] Quoted in Shiv Kumar Saini, *Development of Education in India: Socio-Economic and Political Perspectives* (New Delhi: Cosmo Publications, 1980), p. 64.

[45] Ibid., p. 73. The notion of vocational training for the masses in the early years of school has been a central theme of most recommendations for educational reform in India. For a critical assessment of vocational education in the early grades, see George Psacharopoulos,

Gandhi's proposals were endorsed by a conference of education ministers from the seven provinces with Congress governments. A committee chaired by Dr. Zakir Hussain (later, president of India) subsequently prepared a detailed description of the curriculum for the scheme of Basic Education (or *Nai Talim*). "It is significant," commented J. P. Naik, "that during the whole discussion, there was no mention of making education compulsory as the idea of compulsion in any form was repugnant to Gandhian philosophy."[46]

A major new proposal was made in a plan called Post-War Educational Development in India (1944), prepared by Sir John Sargent, educational advisor in the Central Advisory Board of Education. The Sargent plan proposed the adoption of Gandhi's Basic Education scheme, but rejected the view that elementary-school education could pay for itself through the sale of articles produced by pupils. It called for a substantial increase in expenditures in elementary education to enable India to bring all children from six to fourteen into the school system over a forty-year period, and proposed that education during this period be made compulsory. The report noted that in areas where there was legal compulsion, there was no organized system of trained attendance officers to see that children attended school, and the courts were disinclined to enforce the law. Sargent proposed that compulsory education could be made to work if the government carried on an extensive educational propaganda campaign among parents and that it was also important to have "attendance officers who know their duty and courts which are ready to do theirs."[47]

The postindependence government regarded the Sargent plan as too conservative. The government's position was that compulsory universal elementary-school education should be achieved not in forty years (1945–1984), but by 1960. The provision of compulsory education in the Constitution notwithstanding, successive Indian governments have sought to universalize elementary-school education but without making it compul-

---

To Vocationalize or Not to Vocationalize? That is the Curriculum Question (Washington, D.C.: World Bank, Education and Training Department, report no. EDT31, 1986). Psacharopoulos questions the value of incorporating vocational training into general education and argues instead for separate vocational institutions or employment-based training for the higher grades. He notes that attempts to "ruralize" the curriculum as a means of enhancing farm productivity do little more than the use of a general curriculum, with its emphasis on rudimentary arithmetic and literacy, at the primary level. Moreover, an examination of a number of country studies leads Psacharopoulos to conclude that graduates from both vocational and general education streams are absorbed equally well by the labor market and that the returns from traditional academic education are greater on average than the returns to investment from vocational training.

[46] Saiyidain, Naik, and Hussain, *Compulsory Education In India*, p. 132.

[47] Report by the Central Advisory Board of Education, *Post-War Educational Development in India* (New Delhi: January 1944).

sory. None of the states has sought to compel local authorities to make education compulsory. By the early 1950s officials within the government of India concluded that the financial resources for the establishment of universal compulsory education by 1960 were not available as a consequence of the government's decision to undertake large development projects. The first five-year plan noted that a program to provide education for all children in the six-to-fourteen age group would require an annual expenditure of 4 billion rupees, an additional 2 billion rupees for teacher training, and another 2.72 billion rupees for the construction of buildings.[48] But the plan only provided 1.56 billion rupees for education over the five-year period.[49] Neither the Planning Commission nor the Ministry of Education proposed that the recommendation of compulsory education by the Sargent Committee be adopted. Many educators—J. P. Naik being one of them—continued to be persuaded that much of the resources for the expansion of education could still come from the Basic Education scheme proposed by Gandhi, under which schools would raise enough money from the sale of crafts produced by children to pay for the cost of teachers. Basic Education was seen by some educators not simply as an educational program but as a financial program to make schools partially self-supporting.

The authority to set policies, priorities, and programs in education moved from the states to the central government as the Planning Commission and the Ministry of Education set targets and proposed financial allocations. There was little or no educational innovation by the state governments, which looked toward the center for resources and policy. Education, initially listed in the Constitution as a state subject, was subsequently transferred to the list of concurrent subjects. Though there were variations among the states in their expenditures on education, the major constraint on the expansion of elementary-school education was the limited budgetary allocations made by the central government. The allocations for elementary education declined in successive five-year plans, even as the budget for higher education grew. Whatever the rhetoric, clearly the government regarded higher education a greater priority than the establishment of mass elementary education. Education, said each of the five-year plans, is an "investment in human resources," essential to economic growth. Though the plan documents alluded to other benefits from education, the planners evidently saw education primarily in the

[48] Government of India Planning Commission, *First Five Year Plan* (Delhi: Government of India, 1952).

[49] Indian Committee for Cultural Freedom, *Studies on the Plan Frame* (Bombay: ICCF, 1956). The authors of the report, notable economists, officials, and other intellectuals, were regarded at the time as conservatives when they criticized the plan for its attention to large-scale projects and its neglect of education and other social services.

context of a development strategy that emphasized large development projects and the training of skilled workers rather than mass education. Governing elites in many other countries have had a more positive and broader view of the purpose and importance of mass education than India's governing elites.

6

Historical Comparisons:
Advanced Industrial Countries

THE notion that the children of the poor should be removed from the labor force and placed into schools is a very modern one. Until only a few centuries ago, children everywhere worked alongside their parents, learning to gather food, hunt, cultivate crops, to fetch water, collect firewood, tend the cattle, and help in the household. Only the children of the privileged classes could escape manual work, and in this they emulated their parents—priests, landlords, and rulers—whose control over wealth, knowledge, and power enabled them to educate their children to assume the same roles as their parents. There was a process of social reproduction in which educational, social, economic, and political institutions reproduced social classes.

A distinctive feature of modern societies is that they break with the principle of social reproduction. It is no longer assumed that children necessarily ought to do what their parents have done. Indeed, given the ways in which the occupational structure of modern societies constantly changes, it is essential for the continued expansion of the economy that children be educated to take jobs that are different from those of their parents. One key to such generational mobility is education. Education does not ensure occupational mobility, of course, but without education occupational mobility in modern industrial societies is exceedingly difficult.

Child labor was not created by industrialization, nor is it the result of capitalism. It represents the persistence of traditional preindustrial conceptions of the child in relation to work and to parents. The traditional conception in most societies is that children should be socialized to contribute to the maintenance of the family. Early in life children begin the process of entering adulthood through a period of work apprenticeship. The family, not the individual, is the unit of social action as the family develops a strategy that is conducive to its collective well-being.

Child labor in nineteenth-century Europe was qualitatively different from what had preceded it. Children were employed in factories, for employers, for wages. Some worked in cottages and in tenements with their parents, who in turn were paid for the output of the household. Industrialization increased job opportunities for working-class families. Urban working-class families dependent on daily wages sought to reduce risk through the employment of their children. Children's work became more dangerous: machines and chemicals endangered their well-being, ventilation was poor, hours long, and wages low (though higher than what children could earn in money or in kind by working on the farm with their parents).

Even before these conditions became widespread there existed some sentiment for restrictions on the conditions under which children should be employed. As early as 1284 a statute of Venetian glass makers forbade the employment of children in certain dangerous branches of the glass-making trade, and in 1396 a Venetian ducal edict prohibited work for children under thirteen in certain trades. As Philippe Aries has documented, childhood was discovered ("invented?") in Europe in the thirteenth century, but it became more significant by the end of the sixteenth and early seventeenth centuries.[1] In the eighteenth century the concept of adolescence, as distinct from that of childhood, emerged. In time, the central concern of the family became its own children. Children became, as Viviana Zelizer has written, "priceless."[2] Children were transformed from valuable wage-earners to economically useless but emotionally priceless objects. The transformation did not occur without considerable public debate, and while the upper and middle classes held this view of their own children they did not readily apply it to the children of the poor.

It was not until the nineteenth century that governments began to regulate the conditions of employment for children and to restrict the ages at which children could work. However, much of the early legislation proved to be ineffective, although the passage of the legislation itself was indicative of changing attitudes toward children and work, and toward the responsibility of the state as protector of children against employers and parents.

Attitudes toward the employment of children were closely linked to sentiments regarding their education. With the Protestant Reformation came the view that everyone ought to be able to read the Bible. Protestant churches and parishioners took on the responsibility of teaching chil-

[1] Philippe Aries, *Centuries of Childhood: A Social History of Family Life* (New York: Random House, 1962). Aries provides a history of changing adult attitudes toward children, based largely upon an examination of portraits, medical treatises, and literature. A similar study in India would be useful, though it is not clear that such a study would reveal comparable changes in adult attitudes.

[2] Viviana Zelizer, *Pricing the Priceless Child: The Changing Social Value of Children* (New York, Basic Books, 1985). Zelizer argues that in the late nineteenth century, as a consequence of a variety of cultural forces rather than changes in the structure of the labor market, American children began to undergo a process of "sacralization," that is, the separation of children from the cash nexus.

dren to read and write. Long before the state entered the field of education, civil society created its own schools. When the state created
schools it was to supplement, not to replace, private education. But at
some historical moment every industrializing country introduced the
principle of compulsory education. Parents, no matter how poor, were
not permitted to use the labor of their children in lieu of sending them
to school. Children could continue to help at home, work in the fields,
even be employed in factories or in putting-out shops, but for part of the
day they had to attend school. How many hours of school they had to
attend, and for how many years, varied from country to country, and
there were differences too in what they were taught and where religion
fit into the state-run schools. But once the principle of compulsion was
established as a matter of state policy, these questions became matters of
public debate. Compulsory education was introduced initially for children from ages six to eight or ten. In time it was extended from primary
to secondary school. As the minimum years of schooling was extended,
restrictions were imposed on the employment of children: the number of
hours they were permitted to work, the kind of work they were allow to
do, and the minimum age for employment. The public sphere was rede-
fining the very definition of childhood.

Every contemporary developed country underwent this process, but
the manner and timing varied greatly from country to country. The pace
of industrial development and urbanization were important, but what is
more striking is that mass education—and sometimes compulsory education—often preceded industrialization and urbanization. One might say
that the conception of modernization, at least with respect to education,
sometimes preceded the reality of a modern society and economy. Mass
education diffused in Japan, for example, in the eighteenth and early
nineteenth centuries, and the Meiji regime imposed universal and compulsory education before the initiation of large-scale industrialization.
The state promoted education in Scotland in the eighteenth century, and
both the Swedish and Prussian states moved toward establishing compulsory education and the regulation of child labor early in the nineteenth century.

Since the nineteenth century—and in some countries earlier—the major driving force for popular education was the intervention by the state
to provide free tax-supported schools and to *enforce* legislation *compelling* parents to send their children to them. In Scotland, colonial Massachusetts, and in Germany, Protestant leaders, believing that education
was essential to salvation, successfully persuaded governments to make
education compulsory. In 1524 Martin Luther sent a letter to German
municipalities insisting it was their duty to provide schools, and the duty
of parents to educate their children. In Scotland a similar religious influ-

ence was exercised by John Knox. In 1647 Massachusetts passed the Old Deluder Satan Law, so-called because the preamble said that the old deluder Satan kept men from knowledge of the Scriptures, compelling local authorities to set up compulsory elementary schools. In Sweden a royal decree in 1723 instructed parents and guardians to "diligently see to it that their children applied themselves to book reading and the study of lessons in the Catechism." Failure to do so could lead to fines used for the "instruction of poor children in the parish."[3] In Europe, one country after another—Scotland, Prussia, Austria, and Sweden early; France, England, and Italy later—made education compulsory. At the end of the nineteenth century Japan became the first non-Western country to make elementary-school education compulsory, with a declaration by the Meiji government in 1872 and the promulgation of the Imperial Rescript on Education in 1890. Subsequently, other non-Western countries made education compulsory, most notably and successfully South Korea and Taiwan.

---

[3] Egil Johansson, "The History of Literacy in Sweden," in Harvey J. Graff, ed., *Literacy and Social Development in the West: A Reader* (Cambridge: Cambridge University Press, 1981), p. 163. By the early part of the eighteenth century more than 50 percent of the Swedish population was literate. Similar high rates of literacy were reported in Protestant England, Scotland, and the Netherlands, all prior to the Industrial Revolution, but not in the Catholic and Orthodox regions of southern and eastern Europe. For a review of the data on the spread of literacy in Europe, see Carlo M. Cipolla, *Literacy and Development in the West* (Penguin Books, 1969).

There is an academic cottage industry on the diffusion of literacy in Europe. The pioneering article that set the terms of much of the subsequent debate is Lawrence Stone, "Literacy and Education in England, 1640–1900," *Past and Present*, no. 42 (1969), pp. 69–119. See also Harvey J. Graff, *The Literacy Myth: Literacy and Social Structure in the Nineteenth-Century City* (New York: Academic Press, 1979); John Markoff, "Some Effects of Literacy in Eighteenth-Century France," *Journal of Interdisciplinary History* 17, no. 2 (1986), pp. 311–333; Michael Sanderson, "Literacy and Social Mobility in the Industrial Revolution in England," *Past and Present*, no. 56 (1972), pp. 75–104; Lawrence Stone, "The Educational Revolution in England, 1560–1640," *Past and Present*, no. 28 (1964); Brian V. Street, *Literacy in Theory and Practice* (Cambridge: Cambridge University Press, 1984); Lawrence Stone, ed., *Schooling and Society: Studies in the History of Education* (Baltimore: The Johns Hopkins University Press, 1976); Harvey J. Graff, *The Legacies of Literacy: Continuities and Contradictions in Western Culture and Society* (Bloomington: Indiana University Press, 1987); Egil Johansson, "The History of Literacy in Sweden," in Harvey J. Graff, ed., *Literacy and Social Development in the West: A Reader* (Cambridge, Cambridge University Press, 1981); Harvey J. Graff, *Literacy in History: An Interdisciplinary Research Bibliography* (New York: Garland Publishing Co., 1981); Michael Sanderson, *Education, Economic Change, and Society in England, 1780–1870* (London: The Economic History Society, 1983), p. 53; Phillip McCann, ed., *Popular Education and Socialization in the Nineteenth Century* (London: Methuen, 1977); E. G. West, *Education and the Industrial Revolution* (New York: Harper and Row, 1975); Kenneth Charlton, *Education in Renaissance England* (London: Routledge and Kegan Paul, 1965); G.A.N. Lowndes, *The Silent Social Revolution: An Account of the Expansion of Public Education in England and Wales, 1895–1935* (London: Oxford University Press, 1937).

The historical cases raise three issues. The first is the question of what constituted the driving force toward literacy and universal education. Could state intervention have succeeded had not certain fundamental economic and technological changes taken place? Technological changes, so it has been argued, reduced the need for unskilled labor, and therefore of child labor. As the income of the working class increased, the parental need for the income of children was reduced. Parents were then in a position to invest in the future income of their children by entering them into the school system. While these changes do not explain state intervention, it is argued, state intervention without them would not have been possible.

While this argument appears to fit several cases it does not stand up in a comparative analysis, for there are far too many instances where states compelled education prior to a reduction in the need for unskilled labor or a rise in family income. Indeed, in many instances the reverse can be argued: a reduction in the availability of child labor increased the need for technological change, and a reduction in the employment of children increased adult employment and income. Seen from a comparative perspective, the timing of state intervention was unrelated to a country's level of development. Moreover, the diffusion of mass education sometimes preceded state intervention as well as economic development. Scotland and Sweden, for example, achieved near-universal education in the eighteenth century before either became industrialized and without state intervention. Similarly, in Japan a high level of literacy was attained prior to that country's development, though it took state intervention to achieve universal mass education. In Taiwan and South Korea the state created a system of national elementary education when per capita incomes were comparable to what they are in India today and when literacy rates were low. In contrast, industrial Britain did not make education compulsory until 1881, stymied by opposition from the Anglican church and a strong ideological tradition of voluntarism. If any generalization is to be made of timing it is that mass literacy more often than not has preceded industrialization. Countries of western Europe were largely literate early in the nineteenth century and Japan had a high level of literacy on the eve of the Meiji restoration. It was the high level of literacy rather than a declining need for unskilled labor that facilitated the introduction of compulsory education by the state.

Second, what was the relationship between the spread of mass education and the reevaluation of the child in relation to the family's social and economic aspirations? Did increased opportunities for mobility lead families to conclude that they should invest in their children's education rather than place them into the labor force at an early age, or alternatively, did the widespread availability of education, pressures for education from religious leaders and institutions, and sanctions by the state lead families to rethink the relationship between education and work for their children? How did it happen that children came to be regarded as "priceless," their education and well-being given precedence over that of their parents? Did cultural change—the impact of religion, liberalism, secularism—create these new attitudes toward children and thereby ease the passage into state intervention, or did changes in the economy and in the behavior of the state precede and shape family attitudes toward children?

The answer, one suspects, is surely not uniform for all societies. In some cultures parents of low income are keen on the education of their children, while in other cultures, with similar economic conditions, parents choose instead to place their children into the labor force. Moreover, in some cultures education is regarded as an intrinsic good, in others it is valued for its instrumental benefits. What is clear is that in many societies a shift does take place in which income within the family is no longer transferred from the young to the old but from the old to the young. This generational shift in income transfers is central to an understanding of the demographic transition from large to small families. Once children are viewed as a cost rather than a benefit and, to use the language of economists, as a consumerable good rather than an investment, then fertility rates decline. While not all societies with universal education have low fertility rates (other factors may intervene), all societies with low fertility rates have universal education.

Third, what was the relationship between the diffusion of mass education, the introduction of compulsory education, and the abolition of child labor? Can child labor be eliminated in a society in which education is not universal? The historical examples described here point to the links between compulsory education and child-labor laws. With the diffusion of mass education, state compulsion was introduced to deal with those children whose parents, invariably of the lower classes, chose to place their children into the labor force rather than into school. Child-labor laws proved to be unenforceable unless all children were required to attend school. Then, as the minimum age of schooling was extended, so was the minimum age for entrance into the labor force. Country after country established a system of rules as to when and under what conditions children could enter the labor force, usually with work permits granted by the state. Only upon proof of age or the completion of a specified number of years in school could young people be given work permits that entitled them to seek employment.

State intervention to remove children from the labor force and require that they attend schools was often politically contentious. Many regarded it as improper or unrealistic to compel the parents of the poor to send their children to school. The notion that children ought not to work, that they ought to be in school, and that the state should assure both, was in some societies rejected by both conservatives and leftists, each from quite different perspectives. On the Left were those who argued that child labor was inherent in the system of capitalist exploitation and that parents needed the income of their children. On the Right were those who argued that industry needed low-wage child labor, that the state ought not to disrupt the social order by educating poor children beyond their station, that the education provided by schools was ill-suited to the needs of the poor, and that child labor relieved the state of caring for the poor. Still others pointed to the unenforceability of child-labor legislation and on a more philosophical level to the inappropriateness of state interference in the rights of parents.

Opposition to state intervention was thus tied to conceptions of children and work, to the question of the rights and obligations of the state versus the rights and obligations of parents, and to the character of the capitalist order itself. A review of the nineteenth-century debate is instructive for it demonstrates how powerful were the arguments—and the political forces behind them—against state intervention, and how in time they were overcome. It is striking how similar these debates were to contemporary debates in India, especially with regard to the question of whether the state should force the parents of the poor to send their children to school; and yet how different are the sociopolitical forces between India and those countries that did intervene on behalf of children.

The Debate

Education versus Work

One argument against compulsory education was that education would make the poor unsuited for the boring manual work that society requires. Voltaire wrote that "it is absolutely necessary that a great proportion of mankind is destined to drudgery in the meanest occupations, that nothing but early habit can render it tolerable, and that to give the meanest of people an education beyond the station in which Providence has assigned them is doing a real injury." English conservatives argued that schooling was inappropriate for the working class, whose children could better acquire skills as apprentices. To many of London's poor, elementary education seemed irrelevant since for generations the working class had been urged not to look beyond their station, with the result that parents—and conservatives who subscribed to this view—saw no practical value to education.

The British Parliament sought to reconcile education with work for the lower classes by creating a system of part-time education. The 1833 Factory Act provided that children employed in the textile industry (other industries were subsequently added) were to receive two hours of schooling, six days a week. This system of part-time education remained in place for another half century. An alternative solution was followed by the Prussian government, which emphasized vocational training for working-class children. The children of the poor were compelled to attend the *Volksschule*, where they were taught skills that would enable them to remain in the working class. It was a policy that probably contributed to the technical quality of German products. Similarly, both the Japanese and Korean governments opted for educational systems that emphasized basic vocational training at the elementary-school level.

Child Labor and Poverty

A second objection to compulsory education was that child labor is necessary for the well-being of the poor when the state is unable to provide relief. Thus, in a country with large numbers of poor people and inadequate poor laws, the state ought to promote the employment of the children of the poor rather than remove them from the labor force. From this point of view the more that could be done to place children into the work force the greater the likelihood that poverty could be ameliorated. The 1601 English Poor Law, designed to banish idleness, authorized the involuntary "binding out" of needy children as apprentices to masters. Poor-law officials paid keepers several pounds for each child taken off their hands. One of the arguments for part-time education was that the children of the poor could continue to work even as they attended school. As one of the poor-law commissioners put it, "children who have to live by their labour should be trained to labour early . . . boys should be accustomed to work at the earliest practicable age."[4]

A similar position was argued by the governor of New York, who in 1767 proudly stated that "every house swarms with children set to work as soon as they could spin."[5] New York imposed a tax on carriages to support a linen-making shop to provide employment for the poor, "es-

[4] Harold Silver, "Ideology and the Factory Child: Attitudes to Half-Time Education," in McCann, ed., *Popular Education and Socialization in the Nineteenth Century*, p. 146.

[5] Walter I. Trattner, *Crusade for the Children: A History of the National Child Labor Committee and Child Labor Reform in America* (Chicago: University of Chicago Press, 1970), p. 26. In 1789 a petition on behalf of a cottage factory in Beverly, Massachusetts, stated that it would "afford employment to a great number of children, many of whom will be otherwise useless, if not burdensome to society" (ibid., p. 26).

pecially women and children and thus lessen the burden of caring for them." And Alexander Hamilton argued for protecting infant industries, noting that "children are rendered more useful by manufacturing establishments than they otherwise would be."[6] One of the arguments for industrialization was that it would uplift the poor by providing employment opportunities to women and children.

Opposition to child-labor legislation came not only from employers but from those who believed they were protecting the interests of the poor. As late as the 1920s the New York state legislature killed a proposal that cigar making in tenements should be prohibited, persuaded by manfacturers that the proposed bill would throw needy families out of work. Officials in mill towns were reluctant to enforce compulsory-education laws on the grounds that poor parents needed the earnings of their children. The same argument was used in the London School Board after education was made compulsory in 1871. Many labor and socialist members of the board who advocated the abolition of school fees and provision of free school meals were hesitant to enforce compulsory attendance. Annie Besant, a member of the board, wrote that many families needed the income of their children. "One has to choose," she wrote, "between leaving the child ignorant or having it starve, so that one must do harm anyway. . . . It makes one heartsick."[7] One analyst of the workings of the London School Board in the 1890s noted that "it is not surprising that in prevailing social conditions those who believed more ardently in the value of educating working class children should on occasion attempt to prevent its effective execution. But this meant that the Board's teachers and officials, already under severe pressure from the right, faced opposition too on their left, thus rendering their work even more difficult."[8]

Both in the United Kingdom and in the United States, trade unions fought against the argument that the poor gained from the employment of their children. Union leaders recognized that child labor forced wages down and displaced adult workers. The Knights of Labor and the American Federation of Labor actively supported legislation for compulsory education and for banning the employment of children under fourteen. In the 1920s Herbert Lehman, lieutenant governor of New York and a leading member of the National Child Labor Committee, which led the campaign, noted that 125,000 children under seventeen were holding jobs in the state. If many of these "employed boys and girls remained in

---

[6] David Rubinstein, "Socialization and the London School Board, 1870–1904: Aims, Methods, and Public Opinion," in McCann, ed., *Popular Education and Socialization in the Nineteenth Century*, p. 244.

[7] Ibid., p. 245.

[8] Ibid.

school," he said, "that would leave jobs for their elders to fill."[9] The following decade, in the midst of the depression, state after state extended compulsory education to age sixteen or seventeen in an effort to reduce adult unemployment by deferring children from entering the labor force.

Child Labor and Marginal Industries

A third argument was that without low-wage child labor certain industries would be forced to close, outcompeted by more efficient industries at home or abroad, and that exports would then fall and unemployment increase. This argument was particularly troublesome in the United States, where child-labor laws were passed by state governments and were not nationally uniform. It was frequently argued in state legislatures that the passage of a particularly stringent child-labor law would lead a mill to move elsewhere, usually to the south, where legislation was more lenient. Trade unions sought to counter this tendency by pressing for a constitutional amendment that would enable the federal government to pass national legislation, and when that failed they successfully pressed for such legislation under the interstate commerce clause of the Constitution.

The threat of international competition was also used against legislative reforms. In Prussia, where legislation restricted the employment of children under twelve (and in some industries for those under fourteen), the government hesitated to extend child-labor laws into industries with export markets. Much of the pressure for extending the legislation, curiously enough, came from military officers concerned that the health and physical well-being of their recruits (military service was compulsory in late-nineteenth-century Prussia) was damaged by the premature employment of children in the industrial regions of the country. In an extraordinary development, Emperor William II called for an international workers-protection conference on the grounds that the difficulties in passing child-labor legislation because of fear of international competition could be resolved only through an international agreement. In March 1890 representatives from fifteen European countries met in Berlin, where they passed numerous resolutions on the protection of children. While these resolutions were nonbinding, the conference proved to be a precursor of later efforts by the International Labor Organization to create common international rules concerning the employment of children.

[9] Trattner, *Crusade for the Children*, p. 26.

Child Labor and Capitalism

A fourth argument against state intervention to end child labor came from those who believed that child labor was the result of capitalism and the technologies it created. Karl Marx, the leading exponent of this view, argued that child labor is a source of profit to employers and is thus inherent in a capitalist system of wage labor. At some length Marx described the cruelties of child labor: in steel, where children were employed at night; in glass manufacturing and in coke heaps, where young girls are "begrimed with dirt and smoke"[10] in brass foundries; in book binding; in candle factories; in the sorting of rags; and in the household production of lace. Time and again, Marx returned to two central arguments: that the new technologies increased the demand for cheap, unskilled labor; and that the decrease in the rate of profit led capitalists to increase their exploitation of labor.

As profits declined, he wrote, the capitalist buys "with the same capital a greater mass of labour power, as he progressively replaces skilled workers by less skilled, mature labour-power by immature, male by female, that of adults by that of young persons or children." Children, along with the unemployed, were part of the "industrial reserve army." "Pauperism," he wrote in an eloquent passage, "forms a condition of capitalist production and of the capitalist development of wealth. Within the capitalist system all methods for raising the social productivity of labour are put into effect at the cost of the individual workers . . . so that they become means of domination and exploitation. They transform his life-time into working-time and drag his wife and child beneath the wheels of the juggernaut of capital."[11]

Marx's documentation of the cruelty of child labor and his analysis of its causes was not for the purpose of amelioration. Marx was not interested in reform, but in drawing up a charge sheet against capitalism. He therefore dismissed as irrelevant Parliament's decision to require that children be in school up to age fourteen before they could be employed in factories. "The spirit of capitalist production," he wrote, "emerges clearly from the ludicrous way the so-called educational clauses of the Factory Acts have been drawn up, from the absence of any administrative machinery, whereby this compulsory education is once again made for

[10] Karl Marx, *The Marx-Engels Reader*, Robert C. Tucker, ed. (New York: W. W. Norton, 1978), p. 353. Marx drew much of his description from the 1864 Children's Employment Commission Report. He took issue with the report's conclusions that children need to be protected by the state against exploitation by parents, attributing instead the exploitation of children to the capitalist mode of production (see p. 415).

[11] Ibid., p. 799.

the most part illusory, from the opposition of the manufacturers themselves to these education clauses and from the tricks and dodges they use
to evade them."[12]

In a letter to the leaders of the German Social Democratic movement,
Marx took issue with their proposal to press the German government to
prohibit child labor. "A general prohibition of child labor," he wrote, "is
incompatible with the existence of large-scale industry and hence an
empty, pious wish."[13] Marx also took issue with the view that parents
exploited children. In 1866 the Commission on the Employment of Children issued a report saying that "it is unhappily, to a painful degree,
apparent through the whole of the evidence, that against no person do
the children of both sexes so much require protection as against their
parents." Child labor in general and home labor in particular are "maintained only because the parents are able, without check or control, to
exercise this arbitrary and mischievous power over their young and
tender offspring. . . . Parents must not possess the absolute power of
making their children mere machines to earn so much weekly wage. The
children and young persons, therefore, in all such cases may justifiably
claim from the legislature, as a natural right, that an exemption should
be secured to them, from what destroys prematurely their physical
strength, and lowers them in the scale of intellectual and moral beings."

No, replied Marx, "It was not the misuse of parental authority that
created the capitalistic exploitation . . . of children's labour, but on the
contrary, it was the capitalist mode of exploitation which, by sweeping
away the economic basis of parental authority, made its exercise degenerate into a mischievous misuse of power."[14] For Marx, then, state intervention to abolish child labor and implement compulsory education were
meaningless within a capitalist system. Only the removal of capitalism
could end the evils associated with child labor.

Time proved Marx to be wrong. In one industrial capitalist country
after another the participation rate of young people in the labor force
declined, partly the result of a growing demand for an educated and
skilled labor force, and partly the result of increased school enrollments
and attendance. The growth in manufacturing technology, the associated
demand for skilled workers, and the expansion of opportunities for middle-class employment all made education more attractive. At the same
time, and sometimes earlier, the state itself made education compulsory.

[12] Ibid., p. 523.
[13] Ibid., p. 541.
[14] Ibid., p. 415.

Law Enforcement and Child-Labor Laws

A fifth argument against state intervention was that child-labor laws could not be enforced since the number of manufacturing establishments and small shops was so large. Government bureaucrats despaired of administering child-labor legislation. In New York state, for example, the Factory Act of 1886 prohibited the employment of children under thirteen in manufacturing establishments. New York then had over 42,000 manufacturing establishments with 630,000 workers, but the state legislature provided funds only for the appointment of a chief factory inspector with one assistant, no office, and no transportation! It took twenty years before the state legislature increased the number of inspectors to fifty.

To a considerable extent these objections were overcome by government-enforced compulsory-education laws. Reformers argued that compulsory education was necessary if child-labor laws were to be enforced. Reformers also noted that enforcing school laws, though by no means simple, was easier than enforcing child-labor laws and factory acts. Teachers, social workers, truant officers, school census takers—the school bureaucrats responsible for the enforcement of compulsory-education legislation—knew their community. Once a child was enrolled in the local school, truant officers could go to the child's home if the child failed to appear. Parents were also less willing or able to bribe truant officers than employers were to bribe factory inspectors. Moreover, parents of young children in the six-to-ten or six-to twelve age group were less likely to resist the pressures for compulsory education than the parents of older children.

The enforcement of compulsory-education laws was facilitated by the system of compulsory birth registration. In England compulsory birth registration was established in the 1830s, in New York state in 1853. As birth registration records became available, the task of enforcing truancy laws and issuing working papers was made easier.

On the Rights versus Duties of Parents

Of all the arguments against state intervention to ban child-labor and impose compulsory education, the most powerful came from those who argued that the state ought not to interfere with the rights of parents to choose what is best for their children and their families. The Scots intellectuals Adam Smith, James Mill, Thomas Macaulay, Thomas Malthus,

W. T. Thornton, and John Stuart Mill were responsible for developing the case for state intervention.

Adam Smith, the theoretician of the market, was the first to present systematically the case for state intervention in education. In *The Wealth of Nations*, he wrote: "Ought the public . . . to give no attention, it may be asked, to the education of the people? Or if it ought to give any, what are the different parts of education which it ought to attend to in the different orders of the people? And what manner ought it to attend to them?"

Smith's answer: "In some cases the state of the society necessarily places the greater part of individuals in such situations as naturally form in them, without any attention of government, almost all the abilities and virtues which that state requires, or perhaps can admit of. In other cases the state of the society does not place the greater part of individuals in such situations, and some attention of government is necessary in order to prevent the almost entire corruption and degeneracy of the great body of the people."

Had society created such a situation? Smith argued that the division of labor had created such a situation and he explained why and with what consequences:

> In the progress of the division of labour the employment of the far greater part of those who lived by labour, that is, of the great body of the people, comes to be confined to a few very simple operations, frequently to one or two. But the understandings of the greater part of men are necessarily formed by their ordinary employments. The man whose whole life is spent in performing a few simple operations, of which the effects too are, perhaps, always the same, or very nearly the same, has no occasion to exert his understanding, or to exercise his invention in finding out expedients for removing difficulties which never occur. He naturally loses, therefore, the habit of such exertion, and generally becomes as stupid and ignorant as it is possible for a human creature to become. The torpor of his mind renders him, not only incapable of relishing or bearing a part in any rational conversation, but of conceiving any generous, noble, or tender sentiment, and consequently of forming any just judgment concerning many even of the ordinary duties of private life. Of the great and extensive interests of his country he is altogether incapable of judging; and unless very particular pains have been taken to render him otherwise, he is equally incapable of defending his country in war. The uniformity of his stationary life naturally corrupts the courage of his mind, and makes him regard with abhorrence the irregular, uncertain, and adventurous life of a soldier. It corrupts even the activity of his body, and renders him incapable of exerting his strength with vigour and perseverance, in any other employment than that to which he has been bred. His dexterity at his own particular trade seems, in

this manner, to be acquired at the expense of his intellectual, social, and martial virtues. But in every improved and civilized society this is the state into which the labouring poor, that is, the great body of the people, must necessarily fall, unless government takes some pains to prevent it.[15]

What can government do to remove the torpor into which the laboring classes descend as a consequence of the division of labor? Adam Smith continued:

The education of the common people requires, perhaps, in a civilized and commercial society, the attention of the public more than that of people of some rank and fortune. . . . [The common people] have little time to spare for education. Their parents can scarce afford to maintain them even in infancy. As soon as they are able to work, they must apply to some trade by which they can earn their subsistence. That trade too is generally so simple and uniform as to give little exercise to the understanding; while, at the same time, their labour is both so constant and so severe, that it leaves them little leisure and less inclination to apply to, or even to think of anything else.

But though the common people cannot, in any civilized society, be so well instructed as people of some rank and fortune, the most essential parts of education, however, to read, write, and account, can be acquired at so early a period of life, that the greater part even of those who are to be bred to the lowest occupations, have time to acquire them before they can be employed in those occupations.

For a very small expense the public can facilitate, can encourage, and can even *impose* [emphasis added] upon almost the whole body of the people, the necessity of acquiring those most essential parts of education.[16]

The "public" can facilitate the acquisition of these "essential parts of education" by establishing in every parish or district a little school. These can be supported in part by the public and by charitable institutions.

Does the state itself benefit from mass education? Adam Smith had no doubt:

The state . . . derives no inconsiderable advantage from their instruction. The more they are instructed, the less liable they are to the delusions of enthusiasm and superstition, which, among ignorant nations, frequently occasion the most dreadful disorders. An instructed and intelligent people besides, are always more decent and orderly than an ignorant and stupid one. They feel themselves, each individually more respectable, and more likely to obtain the respect of their lawful superiors, and they are therefore more disposed to respect those superiors. They are more disposed to examine, and more capable

[15] Adam Smith, *The Wealth of Nations* (New York: Modern Library, 1937), p. 735.
[16] Ibid., p. 737.

of seeing through, the interested complaints of faction and sedition, and they are, upon that account, less apt to be misled into any wanton or unnecessary opposition to the measures of government. In free countries, where the safety of government depends very much upon the favourable judgment which the people may form of its conduct, it must surely be the highest importance that they should not be disposed to judge rashly or capriciously concerning it. [17]

There are thus two parts to Adam Smith's advocacy of state intervention in education. The first is that the division of labor by confining workers "to a few very simple operations" destroys the intellectual abilities of workers, and that the common people, left to themselves, are unlikely to remedy these defects by tending to their own education, for they lack the time and would not choose to defer entering the labor force in order to acquire an education. But the case for government attention rests on the second part of his argument, namely that there are a variety of public goods, not simply private benefits, that come from mass education. These public goods include an increase in public order by making the masses less liable to the "delusions of enthusiasm and superstition," teaching them to respect their superiors and disposing them to be critical of those who are in opposition.

A related argument, put forward by other Scots intellectuals, was that law and order were maintained as a result of popular education. Scotland, it was noted, with more education than either England or Ireland, had a lower crime rate. "The quiet and peaceful habits of the instructed Scots peasant," wrote Malthus, "compared with the turbulent disposition of the ignorant Irishman, ought not be without effect upon every impartial reasoner."[18] In the same vein W. T. Thornton suggested that state education was less expensive than maintaining prisons.

The link between education and the protection of property rights was addressed by Thomas S. Macaulay, speaking to Parliament in 1848. "It is the sacred duty of every government," he said, "to take effectual measures for securing the persons and property of the community; and that the government which neglects that duty is unfit for its situation. This being admitted, I ask, can it be denied that the education of the common people is the most effectual means of protecting person and property?"[19]

[17] Ibid., p. 740.

[18] Ibid., p. 113.

[19] Quoted in E. G. West, *Education and the State: A Study in Political Economy* (London: Institute of Economic Affairs, 1965), p. 32. For Bentham, the rationale for compulsory education was that it would ensure that the poor would become educated and that ordinary people would become acquainted with the law. In his *Principles of Penal Law*, Bentham wrote, "Education is only government acting by means of the domestic magistrate" (quoted ibid., p. 124). Utilitarian educationists did not regard literacy as an end in itself, but as a means of reducing crime, curbing strikes and riots, encouraging church attendance, and nurturing the values of self-help, thrift, sobriety, and cleanliness. On the relationship be-

The classic liberal case for state responsibility for education—and for compulsory education—was made forcefully by John Stuart Mill in his *Principles of Political Economy* (1848) and *On Liberty* (1859). Mill argued for both state provision and compulsion in education, resting his argument on two principles: (1) that since education was necessary for a child to fit him "to perform his part well in life," parents were as obliged to provide their child with "instruction and training for its mind" as they were to provide "food for its body"; and (2) that education was necessary for "the members of the community general, who are liable to suffer seriously from the consequences of ignorance and want of education in their fellow citizen." For Mill, education for the poor was essential for self-improvement, social mobility, and citizenship, reflecting his own egalitarian socialist and democratic political philosophy.

In *On Liberty* Mill addressed the question of compulsion, since as an advocate of liberty ("A person should be free to do as he likes in his own concerns") he needed to justify state interference with individual rights. Mill argued that a person

> ought not to be free to do as he likes in acting for another, under the pretext that the affairs of the other are his own affairs. The State, while it respects the liberty of each in what specially regards himself, is bound to maintain a vigilant control over his exercise of any power which it allows him to possess over others. This obligation is almost entirely disregarded in the case of the family relations, a case, in its direct influence on human happiness, more important than all others taken together. . . . It is in the case of children that misapplied notions of liberty are a real obstacle to the fulfillment by the State of its duties. One would almost think that a man's children were supposed to be literally, and not metaphorically, a part of himself, so jealous is opinion of the small interference of law with his absolute and exclusive control over them.

Mill went on to argue that the state should compel the education of "every human being who is born its citizen," and that the state "ought not leave the choice to accept or not to accept education in the hands of parents." Mill wrote of the double duty of parents, toward the children themselves and toward the members of the community who suffer from the consequences of ignorance and want of education in their fellow citizens: "It is therefore an allowable exercise of the power of government to impose on parents the legal obligation of giving elementary education to children."[20]

---

tween education and the working class in England, see J. M. Goldstom, "The Content of Education and the Socialization of the Working Class Child, 1830–1860," in McCann, ed., *Popular Education and Socialization in the Nineteenth Century.*

[20] John Stuart Mill, *On Liberty* (1859), in *The English Philosophers from Bacon to Mill* (New York: Modern Library, 1967), p. 128.

That those who advocated state intervention ultimately won does not mean that the policies were the result of their arguments. Mill may have had logic on his side, but the Anglican church—which feared a secular state-run compulsory-education system—had the power to impede the adoption of compulsory-school legislation for another quarter of a century. The British experience reminds us that *who* makes the arguments matters. The differences in when various Western countries made education compulsory and legislated and enforced child-labor laws depended on the attitudes of those within the state apparatus and upon those outside who could successfully influence state policies. The opinions of politically influential forces, the kinds of coalitions that were constructed on behalf of or in opposition to state intervention, and the institutional structure of the state appear to be more important in explaining the timing of state intervention than the level of industrial development, per capita incomes, or the prevalence of poverty.

The Policies and Politics of State Intervention

While the debate over child labor was often similar from one country to another, the political forces arrayed for and against intervention varied considerably. Religious institutions supported compulsory education in some countries, opposed it in others. Trade unions; teachers' associations; social activists; the military; political parties; and education, labor, and health ministries played varying roles. Social democrats generally fought against child labor and advocated compulsory education, but in some countries they had conservative support while in others they were stymied by conservative opposition.

The patterns of policy intervention in education also varied considerably. England, for example, with its emphasis on voluntarism in organization, localism in administration, private financing, hierarchy in the educational system, character formation as an educational goal, social criteria in educational admissions, and unstandardized curricula, was at one pole; France, with an emphasis on state organization of education, centralized administration, major financing by the state, career orientation as an educational goal, meritocratic admissions, and standardized curricula was at the other.[21]

Ultimately, all the advanced industrial countries (and others) adopted a system of compulsory, universal, largely (though not exclusively) state-

[21] This useful typology is from Michalina Vaughan and Margaret Scotford Archer, *Social Conflict and Educational Change in England and France, 1789–1848* (Cambridge: Cambridge University Press, 1971), p. 203.

run education, and a ban on the employment of children under fourteen, with restrictions on employment of adolescents over fourteen. Each country produced its own policies, the products of divergent interests and social values. In the pages that follow we shall outline the major policies, political forces, and social values at work in Germany, Austria, England, the United States, and Japan. In the subsequent chapter we shall consider some of the more recent, successful examples of state intervention among contemporary developing countries.

Germany

Germany and Scotland were the first European countries to establish the principle of compulsory school attendance—and they did so for the same reason. Though neither country adopted compulsory education for some time, the religious pronouncements of Luther and Knox linked the national religion to the educational duties of both the state and its citizens.

As early as 1528 the government of Saxony provided for the establishment of Latin schools in every village and town. But systematic, large-scale state intervention in education was to await the rise of the Prussian state. In 1817 King Frederick William III issued a decree ordering all children from ages five to twelve to attend school if a school existed nearby, and in 1836 the Prussian state initiated a program of building elementary schools, leaving the local community responsible for the salary of the teachers and the maintenance of the schoolhouse. Local, secular boards answering to the state administration were formed, with the local clergy serving as superintendents and school inspectors. The clergy, keen on educating the poor to work, created industry or work schools that emphasized vocational training in workshops in which children produced goods for sale. These schools became the dominant form of education for poor and working-class children. As noted earlier, these developed into *Volksschulen* (elementary schools). Cleanliness, industriousness, and order were the values inculcated by the industry schools. By 1837 over 80 percent of Prussia's school-age children were enrolled in some form of *Volksschule*.[22] By 1849 adult literacy in Prussia was 80 percent, compared with 70 percent for England and 55 to 60 percent for

[22] Thomas Alexander, *The Prussian Elementary Schools* (New York: Macmillan, 1918). See also Eugene N. Anderson, "The Prussian Volksschule in the Nineteenth Century," in Gerhard A. Ritter, ed., *Enstehung und Wandel der moderne Gesellschaft* (Berlin: 1970); and Gerald Strauss, "Techniques of Indoctrination: The German Reformation," in Graff, ed., *Literacy and Social Development in the West*.

France. It was equalled by Scotland and exceeded only by Sweden's 90 percent rate.[23]

The growth of the central Prussian state was reflected in the establishment in 1817 of a new Ministry for Religious, Educational, and Medical Affairs. Beneath, and responsible to, the ministry were the district administrations, which were given extensive authority for implementing and promoting mass education. Where there was no school, the district administration was empowered to create a local school board and given the responsibility for creating an elementary school to be funded by the community. Where state or private schools existed, the district administration was responsible for the appointment of teachers and the local school inspector (usually the local clergy), approval of texts and curriculum, and the school budgets.

After the 1848 revolution the school system was placed under the direct supervision of the state, teachers became civil servants, and new regulations were issued requiring that schools emphasize religious instruction. By 1871, following the unification of the German states, school attendance was universal. Adult illiteracy for the country as a whole was only 3.4 percent. The state paid only 5 percent of public elementary-school costs, 75 percent came from local communities, and 20 percent came from school fees. Under Kaiser William II the *Volksschule* was given a central role in the fight against the growing socialist movement in Germany. Religious instruction was stressed and the ethical immorality of socialism and communism was emphasized. History instruction portrayed the positive development of the German nation and the concern by the monarchy for the well-being of the working class. Under the Prussian School Supervision Law of 1872, which governed the *Volksschulen* until the World War I, a weekly plan was decreed, requiring seven to eleven hours of religion, four to five hours of German, one to two hours of mathematics and recitation, two hours of drawing, and six hours of sports. At the middle level there was an additional six hours of history, geography, biology, and physics.

A three-track system was developed corresponding to the three broad social classes. The lower classes sent their children to the *Volksschule*, which had eight grades. The children in the lower classes attended school approximately twenty hours per week while the middle and upper classes received about thirty hours of instruction each week. Instruction was primarily in German language, religion, mathematics, and singing for the lower classes; and in the upper classes, drawing, natural sciences, sports, and vocational training. In rural schools with more than eighty children, the school could be divided into two half-day classes, with each class at-

---

[23] Cipolla, *Literacy and Development in the West*, p. 115.

tending school about sixteen hours per week. Working-class children who attended the *Volksschule* could go on to the continuation school. These schools appeared in the last third of the nineteenth century to fill the need for skilled workers. In 1874 the Prussian state offered to build these schools if the community in which they were located made them obligatory. The Trade Workers Protection Law of 1897 obligated all masters to send their apprentices to the continuation schools.

Parallel to the *Volksschule* was the *Mittelschule*, intended for the middle classes. By charging tuition, the working class was effectively excluded. In some communities the *Mittelschule* began only in grade 4, while for the lower grades all the children attended the *Volksschule*. In 1911 there were 1,551 *Mittelschulen* in Prussia, with 255,000 students out of a school population of 6.5 million. Graduates of the *Mittelschulen* were qualified to attend high school; graduates of the *Volksschulen* were not.

A third track was created for the wealthy: elite preparatory schools known as the *Vorschulen*. A system of high fees and high admission standards ensured social segregation. Graduates of the *Vorschule* went on to high school and to higher education before taking on elite positions in Prussian society.

The earliest official concern over child labor occurred in 1817, when the Prussian state chancellor, von Hardenberg, sent a survey to all "high presidents" of Prussia. Von Hardenberg expressed his fear that children employed in factories would become "chained" to a particular factory for life. The result, he said, is that few workers would be available for agriculture, domestic services, construction, and other industries. He also expressed his concern that the hard labor done by working children might make them unfit to defend their country in an hour of danger. He therefore asked his "colleagues" for advice on possible countermeasures to the "enchainment of the worker in childhood."[24] In their official replies, many of the high presidents shared the state chancellor's concern that child labor would reduce Germany's military capabilities, a theme that was to recur frequently in the debate.

In the 1820s the Prussian culture minister undertook a campaign to eliminate the inhumane treatment of children in factories. Reports were prepared on the condition of child labor in a number of provinces, but his superior, the interior minister, refused to take action in the belief that it was improper for the state to intervene in private economic matters. The culture minister persevered by sending a circular to provincial gov-

[24] Juergen Kuczynski, *Die Geschichte der Loge der Arbeiter unter dem Kapitalismus* (Berlin: Akademie-Verlag, 1969). For translation of German sources I am grateful to Jennifer Nupp and Richard Deeg.

ernments reminding them of their duty to enforce compulsory-education laws.

At approximately the same time, General Lieutenant von Horn sent a military report to King Frederick William III complaining that the industrial regions were failing to provide their share of conscripts. This "degenerate physical state" was attributed to excessive working hours, the noxious substances swallowed by the children, the employment of children at night, the absence of open air, and other conditions that damaged the physical growth of children. Following a discussion in the Diet of both the economic and military aspects of child labor, the Diet sent an address to the Prussian king urging that action be taken. In 1839 the king signed into law the "Regulations for the Employment of Young Operatives in Manufactories." While it did not prevent child labor, the law required that five hours of daily schooling be provided to factory children. Similar measures were adopted by other German states. In 1853 legislation was passed raising the minimum working age from nine to twelve, forbidding night work, and limiting the work day to six hours for children between twelve and fourteen, with three hours of compulsory schooling.

As in England and the United States, child-labor laws were not effectively implemented, for there were few factory inspectors, industrialists regularly circumvented the law, and even the local clergy apparently made little effort to enforce the regulations. But with the unification of the German states into a single country following the war of 1870–1871, a commission was appointed to investigate the problem of child labor. The imperial Parliament subsequently banned the employment of children under twelve in any factory and restricted the employment of twelve-to-fourteen year olds. In subsequent legislation that further restricted the employment of children, increasing attention was paid to enforcement. More factory inspectors were appointed, employers were obligated to keep a register of all children employed in the factory, and fines were imposed on employers for violations. The enforcement of compulsory education laws also reinforced the child labor laws. While part-time child labor persisted for some time in agriculture and in the informal sector, school attendance was obligatory through the *Volksschule* and for those not going on to high school two or three years in the *Berufsschule* (trade school.)

Under pressure from the teachers' association, an occupational census was conducted in 1898, which reported that compulsory education notwithstanding 6.5 percent of all school-age children were employed, in textiles, cigar making, weaving, shoe making, assembling artifical flowers, and making costume jewelry and toys. The 1904 census found that of 9.2 million children under age fourteen, 1.8 million were employed, mainly in agriculture. However, the survey also reported that virtually all working children under fourteen attended school and were employed only a few hours a day. Fourteen-to-sixteen year olds could work no more than ten hours per day. Employers were required to register all young workers with the local police and to record the working hours of all their young employees.

Germany was among the more successful states in ending child labor and in establishing compulsory education because of an unusual coalition. The military and conservatives, eager to improve the health and educational skills of the conscript army, were concerned that child labor would reduce Germany's military capabilities. Teachers had professional concerns for expanding education. The Protestant clergy looked upon schooling as a place for religious education. The Social Democrats were guided by ideological and humanitarian considerations. The conservatives in turn pressed for reforms in order to undermine the socialist movement. Motives and interests were mixed: concern for military prowess and national power, religious considerations, professional concerns, humanitarianism, political rivalries. In short, there were powerful political forces at work, each for its own reasons, pressing for reform against the interests and opposition of some parents and sections of the business community.

Austria

In 1897 Mr. J. Russell Endean, a member of the London School Board, visited Austria to study its education system. He visited the major educational institutions—*Volksschule, Fortbildung* (evening schools), high schools, universities, teacher-training institutes, and trade and technical schools—that made up what the emperor of Austria once termed "the admirable system of [Austrian] public education." In the preface to his published report, Mr. Endean wrote: "My object . . . in the following pages is to give my fellow subjects a careful and complete resume of the Austrian system of education, so that they may see how greatly in advance of ours that system is, in all its general arrangements, and specially so in the arrangements for ensuring the best education for the masses."[25]

Whether the Austrian educational system was in fact "in advance" of the English system is beside the point—Mr. Endean used the comparison with a competing country in the well-established manner of trying to persuade his own government to put more resources into education—but

[25] J. Russell Endean, *The Public Education of Austria: Primary, Secondary, Technical, Commercial* (London: Simpkin, Marshall, and Co., 1888), preface.

Mr. Endean's report does provide us with a useful description of the state of Austrian mass education at the turn of the century.

Mr. Endean was particularly impressed by the ability of the Austrian government to enforce compulsory attendance in the elementary schools. He reported that education was compulsory in the *Volksschule* for both sexes from ages seven to fourteen. Because of the system of military conscription, he wrote,

> the numerical history of every family in the Empire is recorded in the books of the police of the district in which the subject resides; should he remove from one commune to another, or from one province to another, one of the first duties compulsorily discharged by the head of the family, on arriving at his new residence, is to report himself to the police bureau, giving particulars of himself and family, stating number, age, sex, etc., and he must also state to which school he proposes to send his child or children, should he have any of school age. On this being done, should it be necesseary to enquire if the child or children be at school, a note is sent from the school-attendance department to the Head Master or the Director of the school named; if not attending, further enquiries are made by the School-Managers, and so the question is pursued until the parent is compelled, if need be, to send his child or children to school, and thus costs to enforce attendance are avoided. In Austria no parent is permitted continuously to set the law at defiance, as do many in this country. The police on duty are instructed to report all school-due children found playing in the streets during school hours, should there by any.[26]

The Austrian school system was financed by the provinces and local communes. Teachers' salaries were covered by the province while the cost of school buildings, furniture, and local expenses were paid by the communes. Austria had seventeen provinces, each with its own educational board made up of members of the provincial Diet, clergy of different religious denominations, and distinguished professors and teachers. The names of members of the boards were submitted to the educational minister for his approval. Members of the communal educational boards were nominated by town councils or by communal representative councils for rural districts and were under the control of the provincial educational boards.

Students who completed elementary school could continue in the *Fortbildung*, which provided technical education "with reference to the trades of the locality in which the school is placed," or in the *Gymnasium* (high school). There were also *Gewerbeschulen* (public technical schools), where "every hour spent in the school is distinctly devoted to the acquisition of skilled knowledge under the eyes of a duly-recognized master of

[26] Ibid., pp. 8–9.

his art," such as drawing, engineering, architecture, building, and join-ery.[27] At the age of twenty, every physically qualified Austrian male en-tered the army for a three-year term.

Of special interest to Mr. Endean was the Imperial and Royal Inspec-torate of Schools. Inspectors—all schoolmasters or professors—were ap-pointed by the minister of education to engage in a once or twice yearly inspection of all *Volksschule*. No date was fixed for inspection and no advance notice was given to the school authorities. The inspector entered the school in the midst of its ordinary routine. "Entering unexpectedly he tells the teacher to proceed with his lesson, of which he takes special note, and of the progress of the class. . . . He sends a special report to the Education Department of the Province. His inspection or report has no effect upon the school funds, as 'payment by results' is entirely un-known."[28] A yearly conference was held of the teachers in the district, at which the inspector discussed his overall findings.

This "admirable system" was relatively new. In the latter part of the eighteenth century few Austrian children attended school. A census taken in Vienna in 1770 showed that only 25 percent of the city's children attended school. In the surrounding rural areas, 15 to 20 percent of school-age children were in school. The first school law was promulgated in 1774. It provided that every parish had to establish a lower primary school (*Trivialschule*) and larger towns had to establish a three-year up-per primary school (*Hauptschule*). Parish priests continued to take some responsibility for supervising local schools, but the law provided for country and provincial school commissions appointed by the government to supervise all schools.

Throughout the eighteenth and nineteenth centuries the Catholic church and state authorities fought over who should control local schools. Church officials expressed their concern that "demogogues" in state-run schools might "imbue the young, imprudent hearts, under the pretext of humanitarianism, with pernicious ideas, to disseminate these ideas even among the lowest classes and let them strike deeper and deeper roots," as Cardinal Migazii wrote to the emperor in 1793. The French Revolu-tion made state officials fearful of the consequences of a system of mass education devoid of a religious content. The Political School Law of 1805, confirming church control over education, warned that "it is one of the chief failures of popular education not to take into account the require-ments of the class of children whom it is educating and instructing, but to believe that knowledge is suitable for every class."[29]

[27] Ibid., p. 27.
[28] Ibid., pp. 48–49.
[29] Ibid. On the development of the Austrian school system, see Robert Dottrens, *The*

Not until 1867, when a new constitution was written, did the state become the sole educational authority in Austria. A Ministry of Education was formed and a National Public School Law was passed in 1869 providing for a state-run system of compulsory primary education for all children between the ages of six and fourteen. The law was opposed by the church and there was considerable opposition from rural areas to its implementation. Farmers wanted only six years of compulsory education so that their children could be employed on the farms. There was also local opposition to the school taxes used to hire teachers. Strong support for compulsory education and against Catholic clericalism in the Austrian schools came from the Social Democratic Labor party. Austrian school teachers were also among the most active supporters of compulsory public education. The Social Democrats, teachers, and various liberal reformers joined together in 1905 to form the Free School organization to promote educational reform and to press for the enforcement of the compulsory-education legislation.

As elsewhere, the issue of child labor was closely tied to the question of educational reform. While measures for the protection of working children were first introduced in the eighteenth century under Joseph II, it was not until the end of the nineteenth century that any serious legislative steps were taken to remove children from hazardous occupations. Legislation passed in 1884 and 1885 prohibiting the employment of children under the age of thirteen (under fourteen in mining), restricting night-time employment, and permitting the employment of thirteen and fourteen year olds only if they had fulfilled the legal school requirements. Subsequent studies revealed, however, that despite this legislation the employment of children was, for a time, actually increasing.

While there were expressions of concern within the state bureaucracy and among some politicians over child labor and the failure to enforce compulsory education, it was the associations of teachers, working with the bureaucracy, who took the lead in dealing with the problem. The initial focus was on ascertaining the magnitude of child labor. Studies of child labor were conducted by the Central Association of Viennese Teachers in 1897. An official investigation of child labor was undertaken by the Central Statistical Commission of Austria in 1900. The commission made use of statistics on student admissions to schools and, with the aid of teachers, collected data on the employment of children during the school year. The Viennese Teachers Association and the Lower Austrian Regional Teachers Association subsequently did another survey of child labor. In the next decade several child-labor laws were passed, aimed at

New Education in Austria (New York: John Day, 1930); and Ernst Papanek, The Austrian School Reform (New York: Frederick Fell, 1962).

tightening enforcement procedures, restricting (but not prohibiting) employment of children under fifteen, and imposing a limit of three hours per day for the employment of children in the compulsory-school-age group.

Under a 1918 law a system of work cards was created, similar to the system of work permits established in the United States. All children of working age were required to have a work card and to undergo a physical examination by a doctor at the expense of the employer. The cards had to list the name, occupation, and dwelling of the employer and the legal guardian of the child. The law required that employers keep the work cards up-to-date and make them available to regional officials, school directors, and a variety of government officials. Regional governments were required to establish an office under the Office of Business Inspection to enforce child-labor laws. School officials were required to send yearly reports on school attendance to this office while other agencies, including voluntary organizations, were charged with reporting to the regional offices of the Office of Business Inspection illegal employment practices involving children.

In Austria it was a coalition of a centralized and conservative bureaucracy, the monarchy, the school administration, the local police, associations of teachers, and the Social Democratic Labor party that overcame the objections of Catholic clerics, parents, and the business community to create a state-run system of compulsory primary education and enforceable child-labor laws.

England

Compared to Germany and Austria, the British government moved late and slowly into education and the regulation of child labor. A combination of forces impeded state action: the Anglican church, which feared that state intervention would reduce its hold over education; dissenting churches concerned that state education might be controlled by the Anglicans; factory owners reluctant to lose the economic benefits of low-wage child labor; a political system under which local authorities had considerable autonomy, especially with regard to education; and an ideology of voluntarism that made legislators and magistrates reluctant to force parents to send their children to school. Many critics of child labor mistakenly concluded that it was capitalism, rather than British politics, institutions, and ideology, that impeded reform. Had they looked across the channel to Germany, Austria, Sweden, and France, they might have drawn different conclusions.

As in other Protestant countries, mass education developed early in

England. Prior to 1833 education in England was wholly voluntary, financed by parents, charitable organizations, and religious institutions. The Church of England formed the National Society for Promoting the Education of the Poor, an organization committed to the diffusion of Anglican-dominated schools and opposed to state intervention. From the point of view of the Anglican church and the British upper classes, education for the poor was a religious and moral matter—to encourage church attendance; reduce crime; implant the virtues of self-help, thrift, sobriety, and cleanliness; and to condition the lower classes to passively accept their station in life. No professional training was required for becoming a teacher. The essential qualification for teaching at the beginning of the nineteenth century was certification by an Anglican bishop. There was less concern for pedagogical standards than for doctrinal orthodoxy. The contrast with developments in France could not have been greater. After the French Revolution, the French government sought to break the hold of the Catholic church upon education by creating state-run primary schools, placing religious schools under state control by compelling them to follow an official curriculum, and by creating a teaching profession differentiated from other parts of the civil service and free from clerical influence. Teacher training was obligatory and all teachers were employed by the state as civil servants.[30] Education in France became state organized, state administered, and state financed.

The English reliance upon voluntarism in education, which meant largely church-run rather than state-run schools, led to the successful diffusion of literacy and education. Even without state support an increasing number of children attended school throughout the nineteenth century. It is estimated that as late as 1869 two-thirds of all school expenditures in England came from voluntary sources, parents, charitable institutions, and churches. Primary education was largely under the control of Anglican parish schools, Sunday schools supported by Evangelicals and Dissenters as well as by Anglicans, and sundry church-supported charity schools.

The spread of mass literacy was the major achievement of the system, though the number of years of schooling for the lower classes remained limited. The 1851 census report on education estimated that the average length of a working-class child's school life was about four years.[31] Twice as many boys as girls were withdrawn from school to enter employment. Still, as early as the 1830s one-half to two-thirds of working-class adults

[30] Vaughan and Archer, *Social Conflict and Educational Change*, pp. 206, 211.

[31] Beryl Madoc-Jones, "Patterns of Attendance and Their Social Significance: Mitcham National School, 1830–1839," in McCann, ed., *Popular Education and Socialization in the Nineteenth Century*, p. 42. See also J. M. Goldstom, "The Content of Education and the Socialization of the Working Class Child, 1830–1860," ibid.

could read, and by 1870 illiteracy ceased to be a major problem in England.

The system provided appropriate forms of education for the different classes—church-run schools for the lower classes and a system of elite education that provided the upper class with a sense of their own role as an elite. There were few advocates (as there were in the United States) of a common educational system for all classes. James Mill expressed the prevailing view when he wrote that "there are certain qualities, the possession of which is desirable in all classes. There are certain qualities, the possession of which is desirable in some, not in others. As far as those qualities which ought to be common to all, there ought to be a correspondent training for all. It is only in respect to those qualities which are not desirable in all that a difference in the mode of training is required."[32]

To English moralists education and religion, the two closely related, were instruments for social order and political stability. Education was not regarded as a means of social mobility. Nor was investment in education regarded as a means of increasing the country's wealth. The major objection to child labor was that it prevented children from attending school, where they imbibed the proper values of their social class. The earliest legislation, therefore, provided for the establishment of part-time education for factory children (the Factories Act of 1833). Nine-to-eleven year old children employed in the textile industry were to receive two hours schooling, six days a week. Later legislation provided for part-time education for children in printworks, mining, lace, foundries, metal, tobacco, and other industries. The system of part-time education was intended to enable children to remain in the labor force.[33]

The British parliament appropriated funds for education for the first time in 1833. The sum was small (20,000 pounds) but it established the principle of state educational expenditures. Thereafter, liberals, utilitarians, radicals, and trade unions pressed for an expanding role of the state in education. The Education Act of 1870 was another landmark. It did not impose compulsory education, but it enabled school boards to do so. In 1871 the London School Board made education for all children up to the age of ten compulsory. There was considerable resistance to the enforcement of compulsory education from the poor themselves, from members of the Anglican clergy on the school board, and from the magistrates whose responsibility it was to levy fines upon parents who failed to send their children to school.

A detailed study of the London School Board describes how difficult it was to force parents to place their children in school. One official wrote

---

[32] Quoted in Vaughan and Archer, *Social Conflict and Educational Change*, p. 73.
[33] Silver, "Ideology and the Factory Child: Attitudes to Half-Time Education," p. 157.

at the time that parents had been accustomed to "make capital out of their children as soon as the little hands could make a match box, or paint a toy, and naturally resented any interference with their supposed rights." One member of the school board, a socialist teacher, wrote in 1902 about a conversation with a mother in Leicester who had kept her daughter at home to assist with the washing. He reflected on the "painful complexity of interests involved—the mother's need of help; the child's need of education; society's claim that the child, as its ward, shall be trained to intelligent citizenship. The mother must yield; and the mother must suffer; but, alas! no commonwealth can truly gain by the sufferings of mothers."[34]

"One London magistrate," reports Rubinstein, "commented in 1899 that if as many summonses had been granted in the 1870s as the Board had wished, 'we should have had an insurrection.' " "But most important and most significant," he continues, "magistrates refused to cooperate with the School Board because they did not believe in the value of compulsory elementary education. Conservative in their politics, upper middle class in their attitudes, they saw no reason to encourage the poor to rise above their station." Rubinstein describes a case involving a twelve year old, the daughter of parents described to the court as "sober, hardworking, respectable people." She was working as a nursery maid for three shillings a week. The magistrate decided that under section 74 of the Education Act of 1870 the girl's employment was a reasonable excuse for not attending school. The judge said that "she has been discharging the honourable duty of helping her parents, and, for my own part, before I held that these facts did not afford a reasonable excuse for her non attendance at school I should require to see the very plainest words to the contrary in the Act. I may add that there is nothing I should read with greater reluctance in any Act of Parliament than that a child was bound to postpone the direst necessity of her family to the advantage of getting a little more elementary instruction for herself."[35]

In 1880 Parliament enacted legislation that made education compulsory throughout the country.[36] School boards now were required to en-

---

[34] Rubinstein, "Socialization and the London School Board 1870–1904: Aims, Methods, and Public Opinion," p. 247.

[35] Ibid., pp. 236, 248, 250.

[36] The case for the expansion of education through compulsion was put forth by the Liberal vice-chairman of the London School Board in 1899: "We want our lower classes to be educated. . . . We want them in the schools and in the homes to learn the self-respect of citizens, to feel their responsibility as voters, to have the self-restraint, the thoughtfulness, the power of judging and weighing evidence, which should discipline them in the exercise of the great power they now wield by their industrial combinations and through their political action," ibid., p. 242. A particularly eloquent case for the compulsory education of the poor was presented in 1892 by a teacher in the Metropolitan Board Teachers' Association:

force compulsory education and it became a punishable offense for parents to keep their children out of school. Opposition to compulsion continued to come from parents who depended on the earnings of their children and from employers, especially farmers, who employed low-wage child labor. But reformers increasingly persuaded members of Parliament that the right of parents to dispose of the child's labor was of less importance than the needs of the child and the community for a minimum of education.[37] Many Tories who had previously been partisans of voluntary schools were now in favor of giving local authorities and school boards the power to compel attendance.

The procedure for enforcement of compulsory education in London was as follows: Defaulting parents who failed to send their children to school received an *A* notice. If this was unsuccessful, a *B* notice followed, in which the parents were required to attend a meeting with members of the school board to explain the reasons for the absence. In 1889, 96,000 *A* notices and 95,000 *B* notices were issued. In the same year there were 12,800 summonses. Between 1870 and 1903 the number of children attending elementary schools in London increased from 319,000 to 549,000, a 72 percent increase at a time when the school-age population had increased by only a third. In 1893 the minimum age of schooling was raised to eleven, then to twelve in 1899.

The enforcement of compulsory education in London was linked to efforts by the school board to make the schools more attractive. Slates were replaced by pencils, pens, and paper. Visual aids like maps and pictures were widely used. School libraries were established. There was an improvement in physical education and in sports. Manual training centers for the teaching of woodworking were created. The content of courses was upgraded. As the school board enforced compulsory education, truancy declined. Assaults on London attendance officers were less common by the turn of the century. Attendance steadily improved, from 80 percent in 1877 to 82 percent in 1900 and 88 percent in 1904. Much of the increase came from children employed in small workshops and homes, the "sweating dens" of East London. For the country as a whole literacy rose for males, from 67 percent in 1841 to 80 percent in 1871 to 97 percent in 1900.

Why was it possible to pass and enforce compulsory-education legisla-

---

"Poverty, however abject it may be, cannot be accepted as an excuse for keeping children from school. But a moment's thought will show that to accept poverty as an excuse would perpetuate the very conditions that are a disgrace to our boasted civilisation. . . . To leave them without education would be to leave them hungry and half-naked all their lives," ibid., p. 262.

[37] Gillian Sutherland, *Policy-Making in Elementary Education 1870–1895* (Oxford: Oxford University Press, 1973), p. 340.

tion after 1880 and not earlier? One explanation lies in the growing pressure from the labor movement, teachers, local government officials, and social reformers. These advocates of compulsory education both shaped and reflected popular sentiment that parents should not have the right to deny their children access to education in preference for immediate earnings. The new attitude was part of a broader public concern for the health and well-being of the children of the poor. And this new attitude was in turn a reflection of changes in the English class system, which had impeded efforts to legislate on behalf of children. The changing structure of the British economy also made the argument for compulsory education more appealing. The increasing demand for clerks and other white-collar workers provided opportunities for children of the working class to enter occupations different from those of their parents. Though many poor parents continued to prefer employment for their children to education, educators could now plausibly argue that parents should not be allowed to make wrong choices for their children. This is not to say that changes in the economy pushed children out of the labor force. There is no evidence that children were unable to find employment or that parents were on their own opting for education. The large number of truancy notices issued by the London School Board provide evidence to the contrary. But changes in the economy did make the reforms more palatable. Finally, the reforms were more enforceable by the 1880s because the number of children not attending school had declined substantially. The smaller the number of truants, the easier it became to enforce truancy laws.

The compulsory-education law of 1880 notwithstanding, England continued to move more slowly into child-labor reform than other European countries and the United States. Not until after World War I did England pass legislation making education compulsory for all children up to fourteen and restricting the employment of children under fourteen in factories and workshops. Other reforms affecting the children of the poor (e.g., widows' pensions) came later. The English experience thus suggests that beliefs and ideologies with regard to children and the poor played a more important role in shaping policies than any compulsions imposed by the labor market.

The United States

As in England, religious beliefs in the American colonies played a central role in the attitudes of parents toward the education of their children and in the attitudes of government officials toward the role of the state in education. As early as 1642 Massachusetts passed a law requiring all parents and guardians to see that their charges were taught to read. Five years later another law was passed requiring all towns of fifty or more families to appoint a teacher of reading and writing to be paid for by tax funds. The law also provided that towns of 100 or more families should provide a teacher of Latin grammar to prepare boys to enter college. These laws, in effect, established three principles that were to guide subsequent educational policies: that the state had the authority to compel parents to educate their children, that public moneys collected by local authorities could and should be used to establish and support schools, and that the state could require towns to establish schools using local taxes.

These laws did not restrict religious institutions or other private bodies from establishing their own schools. The close ties between the established churches and civil governments in the colonies throughout the seventeenth century legitimized the growth of sectarian and other private schools. Nor did these laws require compulsory schooling: They required that parents educate their children, not that children attend school. The distinction is an important one, for the earliest education laws permitted parents to educate their children at home. They contained no provision for compulsory schooling and its enforcement. Such legislation was not to come until late in the nineteenth century. Finally, it should be noted that the legislation in Massachusetts distinguished between elementary schools intended for the lower classes and secondary schools intended to enable the children of the upper classes to move on to the universities.[38]

While both compulsion and public education were from the very beginning part of American educational policy, it was the private sector— particularly religious institutions— that dominated the educational scene until well into the middle of the nineteenth century. Throughout the latter part of the eighteenth and early part of the nineteenth century school enrollments increased. One measure of how pervasive education had become—both through the teaching of children by their parents and through schooling—was the level of literacy reached by the middle of the

[38] There is a substantial literature on the development of education in Massachusetts. The major works include Carl F. Kaestle, *Pillars of the Republic: Common Schools and American Society* (New York: Hill and Wang, 1983); Carl F. Kaestle, *The Evolution of an Urban School System: New York, 1750–1850* (Cambridge: Harvard University Press, 1973); Stanley K. Schultz, *The Culture Factory: Boston Public Schools, 1789–1860* (New York: Oxford University Press, 1973); Carl F. Kaestle, "Ideology and American Educational History," *History of Education Quarterly* 22 (Summer 1982); Carl F. Kaestle and Maris A. Vinovskis, "From Fireside to Factory: School Entry and School Leaving in Nineteenth Century Massachusetts," in Tamara K. Hareven, ed., *Transitions: The Family and the Life Course in Historical Perspective* (New York: 1978); and Carl F. Kaestle and Maris A. Vinovskis, *Education and Social Change in Nineteenth Century Massachusetts* (New York: Cambridge University Press, 1980).

nineteenth century. Ninety percent of the white population over twenty years of age was, according to the United States census of 1850, literate. Only Sweden compared favorably with the United States. Adult literacy for England and Wales at the time was 70 percent, for France 55 to 60 percent, for Prussia 80 percent, and for Italy only 20 to 25 percent. (Among nonwhites in the United States, however, only 20 percent were literate as late as 1870).[39]

The commitment to education by the Puritans was based on their belief that salvation was the primary purpose of schooling. According to Puritan doctrine children were innately depraved. Education was seen as essential to remove the evil propensity of children, and discipline was the essential mechanism for placing children on the road to salvation. Religion was the first R, reading the second, 'riting the third, and, in colonial times, 'rithmetic was a poor fourth. First and foremost, prospective teachers had to be certified in the faith. Since the colonists were committed to education for discipline and salvation they welcomed the creation of denominational schools. The separation of church and state and the separation of religion from education were to come later.[40]

Legislation notwithstanding, in the early part of the nineteenth century not all American children were in school. It has been estimated that in 1832 two-fifths of the factory workers in New England were children. The 1870 census reported that 750,000 children between ten and fifteen years of age were working and subsequent census reports indicated that their numbers actually increased from 1870 to 1910.

The call for compulsory school-attendance legislation began in the 1820s. In the 1830s and 1840s Massachusetts, Connecticut, and Pennsylvania passed laws limiting the hours of employment of minors in textile factories. Legislation passed in Massachusetts in 1836 required that children under fifteen years of age working in manufacturing establishments were to have attended school for at least three months during the pre-

[39] Cipolla, *Literacy and Development in the West*, p. 94.

[40] On the spread of mass education in the United States in the nineteenth century, see Ernest E. Bayles and Bruce L. Hood, *Growth of American Educational Thought and Practice* (New York: Harper and Row, 1966); Michael B. Katz, *Class, Bureaucracy, and Schools: The Illusion of Educational Change in America* (New York: Praeger, 1975); Albert Fishlow, "The American Common School Revival: Factor or Fancy," in Henry Rosovsky, ed., *Industrialization in Two Systems* (New York: Wiley, 1966); Robert L. Church and Michael W. Sedlak, *Education in the United States* (New York: Free Press, 1976); Michael B. Katz, *The Irony of Early School Reform: Educational Innovation in Mid-Nineteenth Century Massachusetts* (Cambridge: Harvard University Press, 1968); John Perrin, *The History of Compulsory Education in New England* (Meadville, Penn., 1876). For an analysis of the spread of education that emphasizes the needs of the capitalist system, see Samuel Bowles and Herbert Gintis, *Schooling in Capitalist America: Educational Reform and the Contradictions of Economic Life* (New York: Basic Books, 1976).

ceding year and to have obtained a certificate of attendance. In 1842 school committees were instructed by the commonwealth to enforce the law. But there is no evidence that these laws, and others that were subsequently passed by other state legislatures in the middle of the nineteenth century, were widely or strictly enforced.

There was a further spate of legislation beginning in the 1870s, in part the result of a campaign by the Knights of Labor, then the major trade-union federation in America, to press states to prohibit the employment of children. And in Massachusetts, studies conducted by the newly created Massachusetts Bureau of Statistics and Labor stimulated legislative action. In 1873 the state passed legislation requiring that all towns provide for truant officers to enforce compulsory school education laws. An 1874 law made education compulsory up to the age of fourteen, for a minimum of twenty weeks a year. In 1876 Massachusetts passed a law prohibiting the employment of any child under ten in a manufacturing or mercantile establishment and stipulating that children between ten and fourteen thus employed must have attended school for twenty weeks in the preceding year. A deputy constable was assigned to enforce the child-labor laws and in 1878 a law was passed requiring employers to keep proof of their employees' birth and school attendance on file for inspection by truant officers. Still, according to data collected by the Massachusetts Bureau of Statistics and Labor, children under ten continued to work in factories, many children ten to fifteen had not been to school for years, and factory officials often falsified records.[41]

Perhaps the most concerted effort to extend public education was in Massachusetts. The leader of the movement for school reform was Horace Mann, a lawyer, member of the Massachusetts state legislature, and, in 1837, the first secretary of the newly created state board of education. Mann became the leader of what was known nationally as the common-school movement: a movement for free, universal education to be paid for by government; schools that would provide moral instruction but would be free of sectarian religious education, that would be open to children from all religious, social, and ethnic backgrounds, and that would have trained professional teachers who had mastered their subjects. The thrust of this movement was to expand public schooling at the cost of private schooling and to provide for greater central (i.e., state government as opposed to local government) control over schools in order to ensure common and minimum standards. Central to the notion of a common school was that an elementary school would serve all the children in an area. While in England school aid was seen as a means of

[41] Kaestle and Vinovskis, *Education and Social Change in Nineteenth Century Massachusetts*, p. 77.

providing education for the poor, Horace Mann argued that there should be a common provision for the education of all children, irrespective of social class. The common-school movement in America saw education as an instrument for the social integration of classes and of ethnic communities.

There were political differences over these proposals. The Democrats believed that private academies were adequate, while the Whigs wanted government intervention to improve the number and quality of private schools. Unitarians (of whom Mann was one) were for nonsectarian schools, while the clergymen of other religious groups were often opposed to the expansion of public education and deplored the creation of nonsectarian schools. Some politicians opposed state control as trespassing on the authority of local communities. Rural leaders were particularly opposed to Mann's concern for centralizing education for they believed that teachers should be accountable to the school trustees who hired them, the parents, and other taxpayers, and that the curriculum of the rural schools should be determined by the local community. The advocates of school reform wanted professionalization: teacher training schools, the creation of a bureaucratic educational structure that would remove authority over the schools from the hands of laymen and thereby "free education from politics," and state laws that would force rural communities to consolidate one-room schools into larger entities.

By the latter half of the nineteenth century the school reformers were winning. Free schooling became widely available throughout the country. Public education rose from 47 percent of total expenditures for schooling in 1850 to 79 percent in 1900. Most of this money came from local tax assessments. Studies by educational historians of school attendance reveal that an overwhelming proportion of children were in school. A study in St. Louis in 1880 reported nine out of ten children in the eight-to-eleven age group were in school. Other studies show that five years of schooling were commonplace for most children. But two problems remained of concern to educators: there was a minority of children who did not attend school and a large proportion of children in their midteens were in the labor force. Many of the truants were poor, of immigrant stock, and non-Protestants.

Political pressure grew for enforcing compulsory education. In 1873 Massachusetts passed legislation requiring that all towns provide for truant officers to enforce compulsory school education laws. In 1876 Massachusetts passsed a law prohibiting the employment of children under ten and stipulating that children between ten and fourteen must have attended school for at least twenty weeks in the preceding year. A deputy constable was assigned to enforce the child labor laws, and in 1878 a law was passed requiring employers to keep proof of their employees' birth and school attendance on file for inspection by truant officers. By 1885 sixteen out of thirty-eight states had compulsory schooling laws, and by 1900 thirty-one states required attendance from ages eight to fourteen. With the passage of compulsory education by the state of Mississippi in 1918, the process was complete for all the states.

There had been a shortage of classrooms, but by the first decade of the twentieth century accommodations had caught up with demand, the size of classes had diminished, and there was a widespread commitment to universal education. School aid to local communities was tied to average daily attendance and this reportedly stimulated local school boards to pursue truants. Journalists and reformers actively campaigned for the enforcement of compulsory schooling and child-labor laws. Attendance, however, was not universal and it took the effort of the school bureaucracies—school census takers, truant officers, and school social workers—to ensure full attendance. Their task was eased by the mechanization of operations that previously had employed children, although it is difficult to differentiate cause and effect. As children were withdrawn from the labor market many of their tasks were mechanized. The expansion of white-collar jobs after 1890 and the increasing demand for high-school graduates who could work in offices also made school more attractive. In short, the opportunity costs of staying out of the labor market declined, while the benefits of a high-school education were increasing. The number of children in the labor force, which had increased from 1870 to 1910, declined substantially thereafter.

The 1880 United States census reported 60,000 children in the ten-to-fifteen age group employed in New York state, but large numbers of unreported children living in tenements were also employed. Nor did the census provide data on newsboys, bootblacks, peddlers, messengers, or farmer laborers. One scholar of child labor estimated that a more realistic figure would be 200,000 child laborers in the state, and he concluded that between 1886 and 1900 the percentage of children under sixteen employed in New York's factories remained unchanged at 4 percent of the total number of factory workers.[42] The 1880 census reported that nationally a million children between the ages of ten and fifteen were employed, about one out of every six in that age group. The 1890 census reported an increase to 1.5 million children, or 18 percent of the age group. And the 1900 census reported 1.75 million children between ten and fifteen in the labor force. Child labor had increased particularly in the South, where there had been an expansion in textile mills. Several southern states with textiles mills—North and South Carolina, Georgia,

[42] Jeremy P. Feit, *Hostages of Fortune: Child Labor Reform in New York State* (Syracuse: Syracuse University Press, 1965), pp. 17, 35.

and Alabama—had neither child-labor nor compulsory-education laws until after 1900. As the economy grew in the latter part of the nineteenth century, child labor increased.

A variety of social-reform organizations set out to end child labor and enforce compulsory education: the National Child Labor Committee (NCLC), founded in 1904; the New York Child Labor Committee, the National Consumers' League (1890), and the General Federation of Women's Clubs (1890). The Knights of Labor actively pressed state governments to pass laws and enforce rules prohibiting the employment of children. The American Federation of Labor, at its first annual convention in 1881, called upon states to ban the employment of all children under fourteen. Both trade-union federations advocated a constitutional amendment to permit federal regulation of child labor. At its 1892 convention, the Democratic party called for state legislation prohibiting the employment in factories of children under fifteen years of age.

The National Child Labor Committee was among the most effective of the lobbying groups, in large part because it systematically engaged in studies of particular industries and the conditions of work of children. The NCLC launched a campaign to end the employment of children in the glass industry after they completed a study that refuted many of the claims made by glasshouse operators. Employers argued that their industry was dependent upon child labor, that children under sixteen were better equipped than adults to work, that training of good glass workers had to begin at an early age, that should child labor and night work be prohibited they would be forced to close down their plants, and, finally, the familiar argument that child labor relieved the poverty of the poor. The NCLC study revealed that productivity had increased more rapidly in states that had forbade the employment of children at night, that the wages paid to children (sixty-five cents a day) were an insignificant contribution to family income, and that the recent introduction of machinery made the employment of children both unnecessary and more costly for the manufacturer. Starting in 1905, the NCLC fought for legislation against the glass manufacturers in New Jersey, Pennsylvania, and West Virginia, but it took a decade or more to get each of these state legislatures to prohibit night work in the glass industry for those under sixteen and to impose other restrictions on employment.[43]

The NCLC and other pressure groups, by their persistent campaign for child-labor legislation, for compulsory education, and for enforcement machinery, helped to bring child labor to an end in the United States. Through the efforts of these groups the number of factory inspectors was increased and a system was created for regulating the entrance of young

[43] Trattner, *Crusade for the Children*, pp. 78–79.

people into the labor market through the requirement of employment certificates. One of the most important legislative accomplishments of the NCLC was the development of the employment-certificate system in New York City between 1908 and 1915:

> While somewhat cumbersome, it represented the best thought of the day and was carefully designed to close as many loopholes as possible. When a New York City child wished to obtain working papers he first requested permission from his school principals who, after testing the child's ability to read and write, would send him to the appropriate borough office of the Department of Health. If the child had been born in New York City, he would be told to visit the Bureau of Records to obtain a birth certificate, and, if one was on file, the bureau would so certify. In the event no certificate could be found, the applicant was referred to the Employment Certificate Office (in the Board of Health) where Jeanie Minor (the agent) would counsel him about securing evidence of age. Once the child obtained acceptable proof of age he was sent back to the school principal who then issued a record of school attendance on an approved Department of Labor form. Accompanied by one of his parents, the child now returned to the Department of Health and made a formal application, countersigned by the parents. After 1912, every applicant for working papers was given a physical examination, a decided improvement over the old system where health officers had simply to state that in their opinion the child was "normally" developed for his age and could do the work he intended to do.

"Working papers," as the employment certificates were called, would be granted only to children who had completed at least six years of schooling and were fourteen years of age or, in the absence of six years of schooling, were sixteen years of age. From 1906 to 1917, between 20,000 and 47,000 employment certificates were issued each year in New York City to children between the ages of fourteen and sixteen.[44]

The NCLC campaigned to nationalize the child-labor laws. Before World War I they persuaded Congress to pass legislation overriding what they regarded as weak state laws, but the courts intervened in 1918 and 1922, declaring child labor a matter for state-government regulation. A child-labor amendment to the Constitution submitted in 1924 was never ratified. Minimum-wage standards were incorporated into the National Industrial Recovery Act (1933) and in 1938 a Fair Labor Standards Act was passed, which provided for a minimum age of fourteen for all employment during school hours in interstate commerce and eighteen for occupations classified as hazardous by the secretary of labor.

With the establishment of these state and federal laws advocates of controlling child labor then campaigned to raise the school leaving age

[44] Felt, *Hostages of Fortune*, pp. 103–104, 105.

from 14 to 16. As noted earlier, the then lieutenant governor, Herbert Lehman, who was a member of the New York City Child Labor Committee, argued that the 125,000 young people under the age of seventeen then holding jobs were displacing adults in the labor force. His efforts to raise the school-leaving age were opposed by the Catholic church, whose leaders charged that the bill was an invasion of parental rights, that it would create poverty by reducing family earnings, and that it would overcrowd parochial classrooms. The legislation was subsequently passed over the objections of the church. School attendance was required up to age sixteen in New York and in virtually all other states, and then extended in some states to age seventeen or to the completion of high school. In 1920, 62 percent of children in the fourteen-to-seventeen age group were in school. By 1930 the figure had risen to 73 percent, and by 1940 to 79 percent. In 1920, 17 percent of all youth completed high school; in 1930, 29 percent; and in 1940, 51 percent.[45]

The American experience with child labor and compulsory-education laws highlights the difficulties in a highly decentralized political system where labor laws were primarily matters for state governments and education was largely a local matter. The pressure from social-reform organizations, trade unions, and educators was directed primarily at state and local governments. Not until the 1930s with the New Deal did they have much success with limited national legislation. The principles asserted by these groups—that the state had the right to intervene on behalf of children and that children are better off if they remain in school and out of the labor market at least until they are sixteen, and preferably until they complete high school—became accepted throughout the country, but not without a long political struggle.

Japan

The role played by the Japanese state in the establishment of compulsory universal education is an effective refutation of the argument that state intervention is only possible after parents no longer need to send their children into the labor force and employers no longer require low-wage child workers. Japan was well on the way toward universal literacy by the end of the Tokugawa era, prior to Japan's opening to the West, prior to the Meiji restoration, and prior to Japan's industrialization. By 1868 the majority of town dwellers with a settled occupation and a good proportion

[45] David B. Tyack, *The One Best System: A History of American Urban Education* (Cambridge: Harvard University Press, 1974), p. 74.

of farmers of middling status were literate.[46] While Tokugawa Japan had no organized national educational system, there were thousands of small private schools. Some catered to samurai children and were financed by the governments of the fiefs, but most were unsubsidized, fee-charging private schools for the children of commoners (known as *terakoya* or parishioner schools). By 1870 perhaps half the male population of Japan could read and write simple Japanese, keep accounts, and read public documents and newspapers.

Samurai children attending fief-run schools were educated in the Confucian classics and studied both Chinese and Japanese. It was an elite education, "learning appropriate to the world of rulers," as one Japanese official said in the 1870s explaining why the system was no longer relevant.[47] A striking feature of the fief school was that the emphasis was on the training of men who would acquire administrative and technical skills and attitudes of loyalty that would make them useful to the fief. But both in the private, commoner schools and in the fief-run schools the emphasis was on moral education and on virtue, not usefulness, as the chief goal of study. Vocational education was important, but not to the neglect of moral education with its emphasis on the virtues of filial piety, loyalty, justice, courage, benevolence, bravery, and, of course, respect for teachers.

Tokugawa schools, like those of nineteenth-century England, sustained status divisions. Commoners were excluded from the fief-supported samurai schools, while the sons of the daimyos (feudal barons) were educated at home by private tutors. In time, the status divisions within the educational system were undermined as the principle of merit increasingly entered into the Japanese economic and administrative system. The Chinese emphasis on promotion to office by examinations (in contrast with the Japanese emphasis on hereditary rank) made inroads into the Tokugawa educational system as teachers awarded recognition to achievement in school. By the middle of the nineteenth century the principle of ascription was being undermined both in the bureaucracies of the fiefs and in the schools.

The most important educational developments in Tokugawa Japan were the sheer quantity of schools that were opened, the numbers of children who attended, and the extent to which literacy became so widespread. Tokugawa leaders believed that education would make the masses more moral and obedient. The Meiji leadership was even more enthusiastic about mass education, believing that education was essential

---

[46] R. P. Dore, *Education in Tokugawa Japan* (Berkeley: University of California Press, 1965), p. 3.

[47] R. P. Dore, "Japan," in Robert E. Ward and Dankwart A. Rustow, eds., *Political Modernization in Japan and Turkey* (Princeton: Princeton University Press, 1964), p. 179.

if Japan was to become a modern country with a strong military. "Henceforth, throughout the land," began a famous school regulation of 1872, "without distinctions of class and sex, in no village shall there be a house without learning, in no house an ignorant individual. Every guardian, acting in accordance with this, shall bring up his children with tender care, never failing to have them attend school."[48]

The promotion of mass education was thus a central objective of the Meiji regime. Between 1880 and 1900 the Japanese government increased the primary-school attendance from 41 percent of the six-to-thirteen age group to 82 percent. In 1910, 98 percent of the age group was attending school.[49] The Tokugawa emphasis on education suited to one's status was ended. What was retained was the Tokugawa concern for moral education, now redefined to emphasize loyalty to the emperor and to the nation rather than to the fief. The Imperial Rescript on Education, promulgated in 1890, emphasized the importance of inculcating in school the virtues of patriotism, respect for the laws, dedication to the emperor, and filial piety. Political indoctrination was a central objective of educational policy. An official ideology was developed that stressed the unique character of the "family-state" descended from a common ancestor. Filial piety was held up as a model for the relationship between the citizen and the state.[50] All elementary-school children were to take a morals course intended to foster a "national spirit" and to develop a love and reverence for the emperor, who embodied in his person the unity of the state and the people. Every school child was required to memorize and recite sections from the Imperial Rescript on Education.[51]

To ensure the inculcation of notions of national morality, the educational system was highly centralized. Prefectural schools were placed under the control of the Ministry of Education and textbooks for primary schools were prescribed by the ministry. The system proved to be efficient, both with respect to its capacity to inculcate political loyalty and submission and to create a remarkably educated population of workers and farmers.

[48] The last sentence of this much-cited statement is more subtly translated by Passin as follows: "While advanced education is left to the ability and means of the individual, a guardian who fails to send a young child, whether a boy or a girl, to primary school shall be deemed negligent of his duty," Herbert Passin, *Society and Education in Japan* (New York: Teachers College Press, Columbia University, 1965), p. 211.

[49] Dore, "Japan," p. 189.

[50] Herbert Passin, "Japan," in James S. Coleman, ed., *Education and Political Development* (Princeton: Princeton University Press, 1965), p. 307.

[51] William K. Cummings, *Education and Equality in Japan* (Princeton: Princeton University Press, 1980), p. 19. For a study that emphasizes the political and ideological conflicts in the development of Japanese education, see Teruhisa Horio, *Educational Thought and Ideology in Modern Japan: State Authority and Intellectual Freedom* (Tokyo: University of Tokyo Press), 1988.

Since the central government was not in a financial position to provide educational subsidies even for primary education, the central government ordered local governments to collect the revenues to support compulsory education. In the late 1880s the central government began to subsidize compulsory education, with the result that elementary-school enrollments soared, from 1.3 million in 1873 to 3.3 million in 1893 to 5 million in 1903.

With universal primary education and universal conscription, Japan developed both an educated army and an educated electorate. Universal manhood suffrage was established in 1925. Since the Japanese government emphasized state rather than private education at the primary-school level, Japanese children of all social classes shared the same kind of schooling for the first six years of school, reading the same textbooks, learning the same poems, acquiring the same values. The educational system also facilitated high rates of intergenerational social mobility, and thereby weakened class divisions. While social mobility would not have been possible had Japan not simultaneously experienced a high rate of economic growth, the high growth rate was itself made possible by the expansion of education, including the growth of technical and vocational education in the upper elementary schools.

There are some striking parallels between the Japanese experience with mass education and that of the countries of Europe. In Protestant Europe and in Japan the spread of mass education began prior to industrialization and in some countries, such as Sweden, even without formal schools. Countries like Japan, Germany, and Austria that initiated compulsory education early in their industrialization process had less of a child-labor problem than countries like England, which deferred making education compulsory until later.

Theology was an important force for compulsory education in many Protestant countries. In Japan theology was less important in the spread of mass education, but its equivalent—a concern for moral education as a means of preserving social order and political loyalty—played a significant role in shaping the state-run education system. So too did the recognition by the Japanese ruling elite of the need for mass education to build a modern state and a modern country capable of competing with the West.

Conclusions

In reviewing the circumstances that led countries to adopt compulsory education and child-labor laws one is struck by the diversity of the arguments, the diversity of the countries—industrial and preindustrial, democratic and authoritarian, parliamentary regimes and military dictatorships, centralized and decentralized—and the diversity of the political groups participating in the debates—churches, trade unions, educators, philanthropists, social activists, government officials, military officers, and political parties. The differences in the timing of state interventions are the result of these diversities.

First, Protestantism was the determining force for the early spread of education in central and northern Europe and in North America. In Austria, Germany, the United States, England, Scotland, the Netherlands, and the Scandinavian countries high rates of literacy (in some countries up to 80 percent) were achieved in the eighteenth century even before the establishment of compulsory education and state educational systems. In Catholic and Orthodox southern and eastern Europe less than 20 percent of the population could read. It was Protestantism that provided the moral fervor for compulsory education and the abolition of child labor and that shaped the moral content of elementary education.

Second, the notion of education as a duty was more speedily adopted as policy when it was taken up by those within the state apparatus rather than those outside. Germany, postrevolutionary France, Meiji Japan, and, as we shall see in the next chapter, the People's Republic of China, the Republic of China on Taiwan, and South Korea moved swiftly to make education compulsory because the dominant elites within the state (a party elite in some, the military in others, government officials in most), for whatever reasons, wanted education to be compulsory. England and the United States moved more slowly because the pressures for reform came largely from outside the state structure.

Third, while mass education spread in England and the United States early on, compulsory education was not introduced until relatively late, in both cases because of the high degree of decentralization, and in the English case also because of the concerns by the Anglican church and by the dissenting sects over the loss of control that might accompany a state-run educational system. More centralized systems, with state financing, standardized curricula, and centralized administration, are more able to create a national system of education based on compulsion than are decentralized systems, where educational financing is local (or private), where the curricula is unstandardized, and where the political ethos emphasizes voluntarism over state intervention.

Fourth, elite attitudes toward mass education in late-developing countries were motivated by considerations of national power, most notably in Japan and, as we shall see in the next chapter, among a number of currently developing countries. Among the European countries, a concern for military power was a contributing factor in Germany. In the main, however, neither considerations of economic development nor military prowess figured significantly in the spread of mass education in

Western Europe and the United States. Indeed, it is striking that in much of the early debate "human resource" considerations were of little importance, compared to a concern with the broader political, social, and religious benefits of education.

Fifth, forces outside the state structure pressing for compulsory education and for the abolition of child labor were extraordinarily varied, including church groups and religious leaders, trade unionists, school teachers and educational officials, philanthropists and social reformers, and many (though by no means all) party politicians. Generally opposed were businessmen and, often, those politicians of the Left or Right who sought the support of the working poor. Where the state was tardy, societal coalitions proved to be crucial in introducing and extending compulsory-education laws and banning the employment of children.

In all these countries there eventually developed the view that the family could no longer be relied upon as the institution for the transmission of those values, attitudes, skills, and knowledge that were essential in the modern world. Teachers appointed by and financially dependent upon the state were regarded as more effective than parents in promoting whatever notions (patriotism, discipline, obedience to authority, good citizenship, hard work) the state regarded as essential. The school emerged as a unique modern institution, indeed the only institution in which, with the introduction of compulsory education, everyone in the society was required to participate. As notions of equality, merit, mobility, citizenship, and nationality became societal and state goals, the school became a favorite institution for all political persuasions. The notion of child labor was replaced with the notion of schooling as the child's work. In a fundamental sense the school as an institution was linked to the emergence of modern civil society.

7

India and Other Developing Countries

AMONG developing countries there is considerable variation in the incidence of child labor and school attendance. As with European countries, the United States, and Japan in the eighteenth and nineteenth centuries, these variations cannot be explained by such economic variables as gross national product, average per capita income, the extent of poverty, or the level of industrialization. Nor can they be explained by whether a regime is democratic or authoritarian. Within India there are regional variations that are unrelated to economic or demographic variables. The critical factors are the belief systems of governing elites and the political coalitions toward the expansion of school education.

With Which Countries Should India be Compared?

India is the world's second most populous country. It is multiethnic and democratic. It is a low-income country, with a large portion of the population barely able to afford adequate food, clothing, and shelter. There is no country quite like it. China is populous, but not democratic. Sri Lanka is poor and democratic, but small. South Korea and Taiwan have had authoritarian governments. Nineteenth-century Prussia was autocratic. Scotland was tiny. Japan was ethnically homogeneous. France was centralized. The conditions for state action are never the same. Are the experiences of other countries relevant for India or does its size make it unique?[1]

[1] Commenting on India's education policies, Amrik Singh writes, "Not all economists are agreed as to what requires to be done. They look at various models around the world: European, American, Japanese, east Asia and whatnot and wonder where India fits into all this. The fact is that it does not fit in anywhere. India is different from all other models in that our population is so large that the various attempts at development, such as they are, get defeated by the sheer size of the population," Amrik Singh, "New Policy on Education: Two Years Later," *Economic and Political Weekly* (November 1989), p. 2484. For an analysis that explicitly compares Indian education with that of other developing countries, see the World Bank paper, *Achieving and Sustaining Universal Primary Education: A Study of International Experience Relevant to India*, India Population and Human Resources Development Division (Washington, D.C.: The World Bank, 1988). See also the several comparative studies published by the Harvard Institute for International Development and the Harvard Graduate School of Education, entitled BRIDGES or Basic Reseach and Implemen-

The comparative method does not depend upon finding cases that are alike except with respect to one variable.[2] Rather, we can use the comparative method to identify cases where the policies of states are the same though the cases are in every other respect different. Thus, by identifying countries that have different forms of government, different rates and levels of development, and different demographic patterns, but where similar policies have been pursued, we are in a position to suggest cause and effect by identifying any common elements that account for the adoption of these policies.

India is indeed unique, not because of its size or its political system, but because of its unique culture, the ethos or guiding beliefs that shape the way people think about the way in which their society is and should be organized. It is this unique cultural perspective that has guided Indians in their views on the relationship between the state and the children of the poor and that marks the differences between India and the countries analyzed here.

The Problems of Measurement

Effective comparison requires that there be some common measure of outcomes. How can we measure child labor? To start with, it must be noted that the data on the incidence of child labor are so unreliable (as we have noted, serious estimates in India range from 13.6 million to 44 million!) that a precise comparison between India and other developing countries is not possible. The director general of the International Labour Organization noted in his 1983 report that the number of children in the world under fifteen who were counted as being economically active in the early 1980s ranged from around 50 million to 75 or even 100 million.[3] Differences among countries in how child labor is conceptualized and measured—the nature of the work done; how "childhood" is

---

tation in Developing Education Systems, especially Mun C. Tsang, *Cost Analysis for Educational Policymaking: A Review of Cost Studies in Education in Developing Countries*, BRIDGES Research Report Series, no. 3 (October 1988); and Thomas Owen Eisemon, *The Consequences of Schooling: A Review of Research on the Outcomes of Primary Schooling in Developing Countries*, BRIDGES Education Development Discussion Papers, no. 3 (September 1988).

[2] The "method of difference" as developed by John Stuart Mill attempts to compare two or more countries whose "habits, usages, opinions, laws and institutions are the same in all respects," save one, but the standard is so demanding as to make comparative analysis virtually impossible. See John Stuart Mill, *Logic*, quoted by Denis Thompson, *John Stuart Mill and Representative Government* (Princeton: Princeton University Press, 1976), p. 22.

[3] *Report of the Director-General to the International Labour Conference*, 69th sess., Geneva, 1983, p. 7.

defined; whether children are working for parents, are self-employed, or are employed by an employer; how many hours children work, and whether they attend school or not—makes global comparisons problematic. What is certain is that virtually all the economically active children—close to 98 percent according to the director general—are found in developing countries.

School attendance is a surrogate measure for child labor. Children at school may be helping in the household or engaged in part-time productive labor. But school attendance imposes limits on the hours of work and on the character and conditions of employment. In country after country the establishment of universal schooling up to the age of fourteen has signaled the virtual end of child labor. But how do we measure primary-school enrollment and school attendance? How do we assess its effectiveness?

There are four measures for ascertaining the quantitative effectiveness of primary education. The first is the enrollment ratio for primary school; that is, what proportion of children of primary-school age are enrolled in school. A second is the survival rate to the final grade of primary education, usually the fifth or sixth grade. The third is the transition rate from primary to secondary education. And the fourth is the adult literacy rate.

Among these measures the most commonly used, but the least reliable, are enrollments. Enrollment does not necessarily mean attendance, and government educational statistics do not distinguish between the two, though school attendance is a more meaningful figure. Enrollment figures can be misleading. As we have noted previously, schools often report first-day enrollments, though many on the registers never actually attend school. If schools or local authorities are reimbursed on the basis of school enrollments, they have an incentive to overreport. Moreover, governments report enrollments as a ratio of children in school to children in the six-to-eleven age group, so that participation by children under six or over eleven overstates overall enrollments. Enrollments reported may exceed 100 percent, though many children are not in school.

Among the more useful and reliable measures of educational participation is how many children complete a given number of years of school, say five or six grades.[4] This measure is an indication of continuous schooling. It usually indicates how many children have remained out of the labor force until they reached eleven or twelve years of age. Children who have completed eight years of presecondary schooling have remained outside the full-time labor force up to age fourteen. The reten-

---

[4] Andre G. Komenan, *World Education Indicators: An Annex to "Improving the Efficiency of Education in Developing Countries"* (Washington, D.C.: Research Division, Education and Training Department, World Bank, 1987).

tion rate is also a useful measure of how effectively resources are being employed. If less than two-fifths of the children enrolled in first grade have completed four years of schooling, as is the case in India, then a considerable amount of educational resources have been wasted on children who are not in school long enough even to acquire literacy. Four or five years of schooling is what is generally needed to ensure life-long literacy. India's high rate of school dropouts thus has a double meaning—the wastage of human resources, and the wastage of educational resources.

Literacy rates among adults is another useful measure of primary-school participation rates. A rapid increase in primary-school enrollments and completion rates does not translate immediately into significantly higher literacy rates, but it is reflected in increased literacy rates within the decade.

Comparisons

The countries of South Asia, with the exception of Sri Lanka, have the distinction of having the lowest literacy rates in Asia. Only 40.8 percent of Indians over the age of fifteen are literate; in Pakistan, 25.6 percent; and in Bangladesh, 33.1 percent. This compares with 72.6 percent in China and even higher literacy rates for Indonesia, North and South Korea, Taiwan, Thailand, Vietnam, the Philippines, and, of course, Japan. Of fourteen countries in the world with more than 15 million people and per capita incomes below $500, India ranks ninth in literacy, behind (in rank order) Vietnam, Sri Lanka, Tanzania, China, Zaire, Burma, Kenya, and Uganda, and ahead only of Bangladesh, Pakistan, Sudan, Nepal, and Ethiopia. As noted earlier, India has a lower literacy rate than a large number of African countries—many of which have lower per capita incomes.

Nor is demography a critical determinant of variations in literacy rates among developing countries. As a result of population growth the number of illiterates in India has increased from 333 million in 1961 to 437 million in 1981 but in Indonesia (62 percent literate), with an equally high population growth rate, the number of illiterates has declined. The increase in India in the number of illiterates between ages fifteen and nineteen is even more revealing. From 1971 to 1981 the number of illiterates in this age group increased from 22.4 million to 31 million. In 1991 the number is expected to increase to 36.2 million. According to a UNESCO study, the numbers of illiterates in this age group are declining in many developing countries, including Nigeria, Brazil, Indonesia, and

Iran.[5] The countries other than India reporting an increase are Ethiopia, Afghanistan, Nepal, and Morocco. In 1970 India accounted for 37 percent of the world's illiterates (this UNESCO estimate, however, excludes China) in the fifteen-to-nineteen age group; by the year 2000 it is expected to rise to 54.8 percent.

These illiteracy figures are related to school-enrollment and retention rates. Though claimed enrollment figures for primary education in India are not significantly different from many other low-income countries, the differences in the percentages that remain in school to the fifth or sixth grade are striking (see table 7.1).

The very large difference between the school survival rate in India and that of other countries, many with lower per capita incomes, suggests that poverty alone is not an explanation and that elsewhere there are strong countervailing forces pressing parents to keep their children in school—the efforts of teachers and school administrators, pressure from local community and religious leaders and local officials.

A final point of comparison is the rate of educational change. The Indian government points to the increase in the average national literacy rate from 16.7 percent in 1951 to 36.2 percent in 1981 and to the impressive increase in primary-school enrollment from 19.2 million in 1950 to 81.1 million in 1983. (The percentage of the six-to-eleven age group enrolled in school, according to the most recent official claim, is 92 percent, compared with 43 percent in 1950.)[6] Putting aside the accuracy of the claim regarding enrollment, it should be noted that other large developing countries outside of South Asia have made significantly more progress in universalizing primary-school education, as measured by rising literacy rates. In Indonesia, for example, only 6.4 percent of the population was literate in 1930. By 1961, 40 percent of the population was able to read and write, and by the mid-1980s nearly three-quarters of the population was literate. By 1978, three quarters of all children attending primary school were completing their schooling. In China the literacy rate rose from 20 percent in 1949 to 72.6 percent in 1986, primary-school

[5] United Nations Educational, Scientific and Cultural Organization, *Literacy and Illiteracy*, Educational Studies and Documents, no. 42 (Paris: UNESCO 1982), p. 10. This UNESCO study notes a world-wide increase in adult (fifteen and over) illiteracy from 742 million in 1970 to 814 million in 1980 and an expected 883 million in 1990, though the world-wide percentage of illiterates has declined from 32.4 percent to 28.9 percent to an expected 25.7 percent over the same period (p. 7). (The figures do not include China, North Korea, and Vietnam.) For a critical look at the crash programs to achieve rapid literacy in the developing countries, see Philip H. Coombs, *The World Crisis in Education: The View from the Eighties* (New York: Oxford University Press, 1985).

[6] *India 1985* (New Delhi: Publications Division, Information and Broadcasting, Government of India, 1986), pp. 6–7.

TABLE 7.1

Primary-School Survival Rates in Low-Income Countries
(percent completing fifth or sixth grade)

India	38.0
Algeria	76.5
Bangladesh	20.4
Botswana	79.8
Burundi	94.3
China	70.0
Egypt	64.3
Ghana	74.7
Kenya	68.5
Malaysia	97.2
Mali	60.7
Morocco	79.9
Philippines	71.5
Senegal	85.9
Sri Lanka	90.8
Singapore	90.0
Tanzania	79.7
Uganda	57.6
Zambia	84.8

Source: United Nations Educational, Scientific, and Cultural Organization, Evolution of Wastage in Primary Education in the World between 1970 and 1980 (Paris: Division of Statistics on Education, Office of Statistics, October 1984). Figures are all for the latest year available, for fifth grade in some countries and sixth grade in others. The figure for China is from China: Socialist Economic Development, vol. 3: The Social Indicators, A World Bank Country Study (Washington, D. C.: World Bank, 1983).

enrollment increased from 25 percent in 1949 to 93 percent in 1979, and secondary-school enrollment increased from 2 percent to 46 percent.[7] South Korea's literacy increased from 55 percent in 1944 to 90 percent by 1987. Countries with varying political systems have moved more rapidly than India toward the universalization of primary-school education and the expansion of literacy.

The differences can be explained partially by differences in overall educational expenditures by governments. In the mid-1980s India was spending 3.6 percent of its gross national product on education, about average for low-income countries. Many low-income countries with higher levels of literacy spent equal or higher proportions of their GNP on education: Sri Lanka, with 86.1 percent literacy, spent 3.5 percent; Zaire (61.2

[7] World Bank, China: Socialist Economic Development, vol. 3: The Social Indicators (Washington, D.C.: World Bank, 1983).

percent literacy, 3.4 percent); Tanzania (85 percent literacy, 4.3 percent); Kenya (59.2 percent literacy, 6.7 percent); and Morocco (70.7 percent literacy, 7.9 percent).[8] However, a few countries with higher literacy rates than India and a higher proportion of school children completing primary school spent no more than 3 percent of their GNP on education: China, Burma, Uganda, Ghana, and Indonesia. If there is no clear relationship between public expenditures on education and literacy, it is because some countries spend a large portion of their educational budget on primary schools while others, like India, spend more on higher education. In South Asia, according to the World Bank, less than half of the public expenditures on education between 1965 and 1980 was spent on primary education, a proportion well below that of the countries of East Asia and of East Africa. India ranked second (after Egypt) among the twenty-one largest developing countries in the proportion of its young people going on for higher education, but ranked fifteenth in overall literacy and twelfth in the percentage attending primary school. In other words, India committed less of its national resources to the development of its primary schools than most other low-income countries with higher literacy rates and higher primary-school enrollments (see table 7.2).

What forces have propelled a higher commitment to primary-school education in many other developing countries? Are they the same or similar to those that affected western Europe and the United States? And in what way do they differ from the forces at work—or not at work—in India? An examination of four countries in Asia that have been successful in expanding primary-school education reveals the variety of forces at work, and the ways in which these countries differ from India in their approaches to child labor and education. A review of the Chinese experience enables us to consider the problems of expanding primary-school education in a country more populous than India. Taiwan provides us with an example of how primary education, initially expanded under colonial auspices, was used by the successor regime as the basis for the development of an educational system that helped to transform the island's economy and social structure. South Korea provides us with a contrasting example of an exceedingly poor country with a low level of literacy and school enrollments at the time of independence that succeeded in the course of a single generation in transforming mass education. Sri Lanka provides an example of a country within South Asia that, in spite

[8] *Financing Education in Developing Countries: An Exploration of Policy Options* (Washington, D.C.: World Bank, 1986). See also Aklilu Habte, George Psacharopoulos, and Stephen P. Heyneman, *Education and Development: Views from the World Bank* (Washington, D.C.: World Bank, 1983); World Bank, *Education: Sector Policy Paper* (Washington, D.C.: World Bank, 1983).

TABLE 7.2

Education in Low-Income Countries

	Per Capita Income (US$)[a]	Literates Over Age 15[b] (percent)	Public Expenditure on education (percent GNP)[b]	Percent of Age Group in School[c]		
				Primary School[d]	Secondary School	Higher Education
Bangladesh	160	33.1	2.1	60	15	4
India	300	40.8	3.6	79	30	9
Nepal	160	20.7	3.0	73	21	3
Pakistan	350	25.6	2.1	44	14	2
Sri Lanka	400	86.1	3.5	103	54	4
Algeria	2,680	44.7	6.1	93	36	5
China	290	72.6	2.7	110	35	1
Burma	200	78.5	1.6	84	20	1
Colombia	1,240	69.1	2.9	125	46	12
Egypt	680	44.9	5.5	78	54	15
Ethiopia	130	3.7	3.9	46	12	1
Ghana	390	53.2	2.6	76	34	1
Indonesia	450	74.1	2.0	120	33	4
Iran	3,830	61.8	3.8	97	40	4
Kenya	330	59.2	6.7	104	20	1
Malaysia	1,810	72.6	7.8	92	49	5
Morocco	610	70.7	7.9	80	28	6
Nigeria	370	42.4	1.8	98	16	3
North Korea	760	90.0	3.6	n.a.	n.a.	n.a.
Peru	1,470	87.0	2.9	114	59	21
Philippines	590	88.7	1.7	106	64	27
South Africa	1,890	79.3	3.8	n.a.	n.a.	n.a.
South Korea	2,690	90.0	4.5	100	59	25
Sudan	330	21.6	4.8	52	18	2
Thailand	850	88.8	3.9	96	29	22
Taiwan	3,160	91.2	3.6	n.a.	n.a.	n.a.
Tanzania	180	85.0	4.3	98	3	1
Turkey	1,210	65.6	2.1	102	39	6
Uganda	260	57.3	2.7	60	8	1
Vietnam	330	94.0	3.0	113	48	3
Zaire	150	61.2	3.4	90	23	1

[a] World Bank, *World Development Report 1989 (New York: Oxford University Press, 1988)*.

[b] *Brittanica Book of the Year 1990* (Chicago: Encyclopaedia Britannica, 1989).

[c] World Bank, *World Development Report 1985* (New York: Oxford University Press, 1984).

[d] Percentage sometimes exceeds 100 because children above or below age group are attending school.

of a level of poverty equal to that of India and other countries of South Asia, has achieved a high level of literacy and primary-school attendance. Finally, we shall examine the educational record of the Indian state of Kerala in an effort to understand why one Indian state has been able to achieve a literacy rate that is nearly twice that of the all-India average, with commensurate high levels of school enrollments, retention rates, and transition rates to secondary education.

People's Republic of China

The comparison with China is particularly striking. It is estimated that in 1949 only 20 percent of the Chinese population was literate and that only one-fourth of the children were in primary school. In 1982, 93 percent of all Chinese children attended primary school, and 70 percent completed sixth grade. Eighty-three percent of the urban and 79 percent of the rural primary-school graduates proceeded to junior secondary education. (In India, 79 percent of the children were enrolled, but only 40 percent completed the fifth grade. Of these, 74 percent continued in school.) In other words, for every 100 six-year-old Chinese children, fifty-two entered junior secondary school (the seventh grade in China) compared with only twenty-three children in India (the sixth grade in India). By 1982 China's adult literacy rate had risen to 68 percent.

China's success in achieving a high enrollment and high retention rate is linked to a strong commitment by the Communist Party Central Committee and State Council to the achievement of universal literacy.[9] The state emphasized the need for a system of education that was common to all, using simplified Chinese characters in all texts, with the Beijing pronunciation as the standard speech. Schooling was made compulsory, but the state relied upon local government institutions and the local party for enforcement.

Primary schools (*minban*, or "people-run schools") are financed largely by local governments, urban schools largely by the central government. Teacher training is conducted at the local level, but the primary curriculum and textbooks are under central government control. While a common-school approach is emphasized at the primary-school level (though there are curriculum differences between urban and rural schools), sharp differentiation occurs at the high-school level when children are streamed into a variety of different types, including specialized technical-vocational schools. According to Shirk, "although tracking assignments

---

[9] Characteristically, postrevolutionary Communist regimes launch mass national campaigns to reduce adult illiteracy. Those that have had the greatest impact have been associated with a significant expansion in primary-school education. See H. S. Bhola, *Campaigning for Literacy* (Paris: United Nations Educational, Scientific, and Cultural Organization, 1984), chaps. 4, and 6; Charles W. Hayford, "Literacy Movements in Modern China," and Ben Eklof, "Russian Literacy Campaigns, 1861–1939," in Robert F. Arnove and Harvey J. Graff, eds., *National Literacy Campaigns: Historical and Comparative Perspectives* (New York: Plenum Press, 1987); Valerie Miller, *Between Struggle and Hope: The Nicaraguan Literacy Crusade* (Boulder, Colo.: Westview Press, 1985). For an account of the expansion of literacy in prerevolutionary Russia, see Jeffrey Brooks, *When Russia Learned to Read: Literacy and Popular Literature, 1861–1917* (Princeton: Princeton University Press, 1985).

are based on meritocratic and not ascriptive characteristics, because of disparities in home environment and prior education, peasants are concentrated in *minban* schools, workers in technical-vocational schools and white-collar professional and political elites in key schools and universities."[10] As mass education expanded, educational qualifications for employment increased. Ordinary factory workers, who in the past had no educational qualifications, now must be junior-high-school graduates, while factory technicians, who in the past had only junior-high-school diplomas, must now have senior technical-vocational school diplomas.

A large number of primary schools were built in rural areas following the collectivization of land in the early and mid-1950s. But the major expansion of primary- and secondary-school enrollment took place during the Cultural Revolution, a period that damaged higher education. It was a period in which the state saw education as an instrument for creating a more ideologically committed population, when the emphasis was on "red" (i.e., the expansion of political consciousness, social equity, ideological conformity) rather than "expert" (i.e., skills leading to efficiency and productivity). Historically, Chinese governments have regarded education as serving state goals. China's nineteenth-century Qing rulers were concerned with ideological control.[11] The earliest modernizers believed that the strength of Western nations derived from their educational system, and pointed to Prussia, France, and Britain. By the end of the century Chinese reformers were persuaded that Japan's success was due to its emphasis upon education. While the rulers of imperial China regarded mass education as a political threat, the postimperial rulers regarded mass education as a step toward bridging differences between the elite and the masses and developing China as a military and industrial power.

The Communist government took still another step by regarding education as a duty. A clear distinction was made between universal and compulsory education. "The government," wrote one Chinese educator,

[10] Susan Shirk, "The Evolution of Chinese Education: Stratification and Meritocracy in the 1980s," in Norton Ginsburg and Bernard A. Labor, eds., *China: The 1980s Era* (Boulder, Colo.: Westview Press, 1984), p. 249. See also Susan L. Shirk, "Educational Reform and Political Backlash: Recent Changes in Chinese Educational Policy," *Comparative Education Review* 23, no. 2 (1979), pp. 183–217. For reviews of recent educational developments in China see World Bank, *China: Socialist Economic Development*, vol. 3: *The Social Indicators* (Washington, D.C.: World Bank, 1983); and Suzanne Pepper, "Chinese Education after Mao: Two Steps Forward, Two Steps Back and Begin Again?" *China Quarterly*, no. 81 (March 1980), pp. 1–65. For a study of external influences on Chinese education, see Ruth Hayhoe and Marianne Bastd, eds., *China's Education and the Industrialized World* (Armonk, N.Y.: M. E. Sharpe, 1987).

[11] Sally Borthwick, *Education and Social Change in China: The Beginnings of the Modern Era* (Stanford, Calif.: Hoover Instittion Press, 1988), p. 1.

"has an obligation to the people to provide necessary conditions for implementing compulsory education. The parents have an obligation to the state and society to send their children to schools where they are required to receive a certain number of years of education. When governments at all levels fail to provide the necessary conditions, or when the parents fail to send their children to schools, they will be charged with violating the law. However, with 'universal education,' there is no such strict law or regulation."[12]

Providing "the necessary conditions" was thus regarded by the regime as an essential element of its compulsory-education effort. The necessary conditions included the construction of an adequate number of local schools; provision of books, sports equipment, teaching aids, food, and clothing; training of teachers; and a major effort to ensure that girls were enrolled in school. Much of the school construction was done by communes and brigades. Contributions from communes and production brigades rose from 5 percent of expenditures on primary education in the 1950s to 24 percent in the late 1970s. The establishment of communes and the abolition of privately owned shops reduced parental need for child labor, but the subsequent creation of the responsibility system and provision for the establishment of private enterprises has increased the opportunity costs of schooling. "Time and again," said Jiang Yongjiu, division chief of the Elementary Education Department of the State Education Commission, "the state has come out against the use of child labor; and local governments have taken various measures to stop this practice. In Fujian Province, for example, enterprises hiring child laborers are deprived of raw and processed materials. Confiscating business licenses and imposing economic sanctions are additional measures. [Another] measure is to levy fines or economic penalties on those exploiting children." Jiang also noted that "some parents, for the sake of immediate profit, make their children work instead of allowing them to attend elementary school," a tendency that particularly affects girls.[13]

While education is compulsory, the national Compulsory Education Law allow flexibility to provinces, municipalities, and autonomous regions in setting their own pace. Large cities and economically developed regions have often implemented the nine-year compulsory law in one step, but most of the rural areas have made education compulsory for from three to six years, with the expectation that the required number of years will be gradually raised. Local governments have administrative power, but the central government supervises local governments to en-

---

[12] Wu Ming, "Differentiate Between Universal and Compulsory Education," *FBIS-China* (2 June 1989), p. 28. I am grateful to Susan Shirk for calling this article to my attention.

[13] "Primary School Education for Girls," in *Women of China* (March 1989), p. 6.

sure that each locality requires that its children receive a certain number of years of compulsory education; the central government also provides subsidies to localities with special financial difficulties.[14] The government has been particularly energetic in pressing for an expansion of female enrollment and retention in primary schools. While only 28 percent of primary-school students were females in 1951, it was up to 45.2 percent by 1975.

Taiwan

For much of its history Taiwan was a distant provincial outpost of China. It was a Japanese colony from 1895 until the end of World War II. The Japanese had a two-track educational policy in Japan: a lower-level system of primary education intended for the entire population; and an upper level consisting of a small number of secondary schools and an even smaller number of institutions of higher learning open for the 10 percent of the population that went beyond primary school. The Japanese government sought to replicate the lower-level system in Taiwan for the Taiwanese, reserving the upper levels for the Japanese population residing in Taiwan.

. In the early years of colonial rule the Japanese created a system of government-run common schools intended to compete with missionary and private Chinese schools. The emphasis was on teaching Japanese to the small number of middle- and upper-class Taiwanese interested in the education of their children. In 1906 only 5 percent of the Taiwanese school-age children were enrolled in the common schools, and of these only 65 percent were enrolled on an average day. In Japan, as we have seen, a massive attempt was under way during the last two decades of the nineteenth century to enroll all children of elementary-school age, a goal that was virtually achieved by 1910 for both boys and girls. The Japanese were similarly keen on achieving universal primary-school education for the entire Japanese population living in Taiwan. By 1910 Japanese enrollment in Taiwan was only 5 percent behind Japanese elementary-school enrollment in Japan.

The Japanese governors of Taiwan were eager to expand elementary-school education for the Taiwanese, but equally resistant to the idea that the Taiwanese should advance into higher positions through education. Emphasis in the school system was on acquiring the Japanese language, learning useful subjects (e.g., arithmetic and vocational skills), and timing school terms to be in harmony with the agricultural seasons, when

---

[14] Wu Ming, "Differentiate Between Universal and Compulsory Education," pp. 29–30.

planting, harvesting, and other tasks kept children from attending school. The Japanese were keen on breaking the traditional Chinese view that education was a way of winning freedom from physical labor. The Japanese rulers aspired to turn the Taiwanese into Japanese by teaching the Japanese language and ethics (including reverence for the emperor). Teachers were largely Japanese.

Between 1906 and 1918 the Japanese expanded and upgraded the common-school system in Taiwan, but resisted opening up secondary schools and higher education to the Taiwanese in order to provide opportunities for Japanese living in Taiwan and for Japanese in Japan who sought careers in administration and in the professions in their colony. Under pressure from the Taiwanese for more and better education, and in part influenced by the labor demands of the island's economy, the Japanese authorities revamped the educational system in 1919 into a single, coordinated system. Under this system all children were to attend a common school for six years, and thereafter tracked into a variety of schools: two-year vocational schools, industrial schools, commercial schools, agricultural and forestry schools, and various preparatory programs leading to normal school, medical school, and other professional schools. Existing private schools were allowed to continue, but new private schools could only be created for vocational studies or for the handicapped. The new system emphasized, in addition to the common educational experience for all children under the age of twelve, postprimary vocational training. Japanese was the medium of instruction and in time classical Chinese was dropped from the common schools. Assimilation was the goal. Separate schools, at all levels, were maintained for the Japanese residents on the island.

Enrollments grew. Only 21 percent of the school-age children were in elementary school in 1919. With the new system it rose to 25 percent in 1920, then creeped up a percent or two each year. It rose more rapidly in the late 1930s. By 1943, 65.7 percent of school-age children were attending elementary school. In 1943 the government introduced compulsory elementary-school education. At the same time the government closed down the handful of Chinese-medium private schools. The following year 71 percent of Taiwanese school-age children were in school—81 percent of the boys, 61 percent of the girls. Nearly 30 percent of the children under twelve remained out of school, a large proportion of whom were in the labor force.

When Taiwan was returned to China in 1945 the government revamped the educational system and replaced Japanese with Mandarin as the official language at all levels of the school system. Six years of education remained compulsory until 1968, when free compulsory education for nine years was introduced. The strong emphasis of the Japanese on vocational subjects for postprimary education and on medicine, pedagogy, applied science, and commerce for higher education continued. The Japanese legacy to the newly independent government was one of the most developed elementary-school systems to be found in former colonial countries. As Tsurumi wrote, "with the exception of the Americans in the Philippines, no other colonial power in Asia or elsewhere approached native education with anything like the seriousness of purpose of Japanese educators in Taiwan. The care that went into formulating and executing educational plans was outstanding."[15] It was not simply that the Japanese expended large sums on education, but that the bulk of the expenditures were for the lower level of the school system. Higher education was given lower priority than in some other colonial countries, though it is important to note that the Japanese did give priority to the training of teachers and physicians. Postelementary emphasis on vocational training eroded traditional Chinese contempt for manual work. The Japanese educational system in Taiwan was also highly egalitarian: a single school system was established for Taiwanese of all classes. What was inegalitarian was the existence of a separate school system for the Japanese in Taiwan, but that ended with independence in 1945.

With the movement of the Nationalist government from the mainland to Taiwan, the character of the island changed. Large numbers of Chinese migrated from the mainland. The United States became committed to the island's development and provided substantial resources. The new leadership regarded education as central to its concerns both for socioeconomic development and for creating a loyal population. It is difficult to ascertain the extent to which the diffusion of popular education that preceded Nationalist rule facilitated the extraordinary economic growth rate in Taiwan after 1950. A land-reform policy combined with incentives to farmers increased rural prosperity (between 1949 and 1960 agricultural productivity rose by 80 percent). An export-oriented industrial policy resulted in an increase in trade from a third of a billion dollars annually in the 1950s to $31 billion by 1979. Per capita income leaped from $40 in 1950 to $2,000 in 1980, seven and one-half times that of the mainland. (In 1986 Taiwan's per capita income was estimated at $5,000.) These developments were surely facilitated by the presence of a population with at least six years, and by the late 1960s nine years, of schooling. At the same time, the rapid growth in employment increased opportunities for social mobility and the demand for education. By 1980 all six-to-twelve year olds were in school, 90 percent of the twelve-to-fifteen age group

[15] P. Patricia Tsurumi, *Japanese Colonial Education in Taiwan, 1895–1945* (Cambridge: Harvard University Press, 1977), p. 224.

and 26 percent of the eighteen-to-twenty-two year olds.[16] For the first nine years (six years in elementary school and three years in junior high school) children share a common education. Thereafter, those who continue school enter a college-preparatory senior high school or a senior vocational school.

The decision to extend compulsory education from age twelve to age fifteen grew out of several considerations. By 1968 the country had become sufficiently industrialized so that there was a need for a more educated labor force. A second factor was the gap between the twelve-year-old compulsory-education minimum and the fourteen-year-old minimum (subsequently changed to fifteen) for entrance into factory employment. Primary school leavers had no place to go, especially since 40 percent of the primary-school leavers failed the entrance examinations to junior high school. The extension of compulsory education was thus essential if the child-labor laws were to be enforced. A third factor was an argument put forth by educators that because entrance into junior high school depended upon passing competitive examinations there was a "malign backwash," meaning that there was excessive preparation by primary-school children for these competitive exams. Once the decision was made to raise the compulsory-education age, the percentage of primary-school leavers that entered junior high schools leaped from 70 percent in 1968 to 96 percent by 1979. To accommodate the changing composition of the junior high schools, more emphasis was placed on optional vocational courses. One result was that more graduates of the junior high schools went on to vocational senior high schools than to general high schools. The government also spent more money on vocational than on general high schools.

Enforcement of compulsory education is in the hands of Compulsory Education committees established in each of the provinces and major cities, with representatives from the provincial governors, the city mayors, the education bureau, the bureau for domestic affairs, the financial bureau, the city planning department, the police, and the federal government. Similar committees are established for all secondary cities, towns, and districts, with representation from district departments and local governments. Each Compulsory Education Committee has the responsibility to introduce and carry out rules governing school attendance. A local residential records officer is required to prepare rolls of six year olds and submit them to the Division of Education, which in turn transmits these to the local authorities. Children who are not registered in school are visited by members of the local Compulsory Education Committee,

---

[16] R. Murray Thomas and T. Neville Postlethwaite, eds., *Schooling in East Asia* (Oxford: Pergamon Press, 1983), p. 106.

who advise parents to enroll their children, refer family problems to local governments and social-welfare organizations, and issue a formal warning letter if parents continue to keep their children out of school.[17]

One indication of the high value the Chinese place on the education of their children is the high status accorded members of the teaching profession. Surveys of occupational prestige report that university professors are among the highest in the prestige ranking, that secondary-school teachers rank on the same level as doctors and engineers, and that elementary-school teachers were ranked (still high) along with journalists and policemen.[18] A subsidized five-year training course for junior-high-school graduates is required for all elementary-school teachers, who then receive salaries that are higher than general government officials. In 1950 only 1.7 percent of the gross national product of Taiwan was expended on education. But by the 1980s it had risen to between 4 percent and 4.5 percent. Thirty-four percent of the 1980 public expenditures went to primary education, 21 percent for junior high school, 6 percent for senior high school, 6.3 percent for senior vocational schools, 15 percent for higher education, and 11 percent for administration. Starting from an already high literacy rate of 66 percent in the 1950s, Taiwan's literacy rate rose to 91 percent (96 percent of males, 87 percent of females) by the mid-1980s. Nearly half of the adult population (48 percent) had completed only primary education, 20 percent had completed secondary school, and 3 percent had completed higher education. Only 9 percent of the population, mainly older people, had no formal education.

South Korea

As in the case of Taiwan, the educational system prevalent in Korea when the Japanese took over in 1910 was directed primarily at preparing a small number of candidates for the government civil-service examinations.[19] The system was elitist, confined to males, and prestigious. In a population of nearly 20 million, only a handful of Koreans attended school (110,000 in 1910), and literacy levels were low. Education, not inherited wealth, military prowess, or membership in an ascriptive

[17] I am grateful to Professor Michael Hsiao of the Institute of Ethnology Academia Sinica in Taipei for providing me with a copy of the Compulsory School Attendance Regulations.

[18] Thomas and Postlethwaite, eds., *Schooling in East Asia*, p. 131.

[19] On educational developments in South Korea, see Thomas and Postlethwaite, eds., *Schooling in East Asia*; Ramon H. Myers and Mark R. Peattie, eds., *The Japanese Colonial Empire, 1895–1945* (Princeton: Princeton University Press, 1984), esp. E. Patricia Tsurumi, "Colonial Education in Korea and Taiwan," and Michael E. Robinson, "Colonial Publication Policy and the Korean Nationalist Movement."

group, was regarded as the vehicle for the achievement of political power. The Korean educational system was thus based on the principles of the Chinese Confucian system.

The Japanese did not eliminate the traditional Confucian schools, but instead created two new parallel systems of secular public education, one for Japanese immigrants to Korea, the other for Koreans. Japanese authorities imported Japanese teachers and introduced the Japanese language as the medium of instruction in place of Korean. Over a period of thirty years the Japanese expanded the school systems and increasingly enrolled Korean children. By 1941, 1.8 million children attended school. Still, only one out of every three Korean children attended government primary schools, although the government provided free textbooks and free lunches. Substantial numbers of Koreans sent their children to private primary schools, many of which were run by Protestant and Catholic missionaries. Many Korean parents regarded private schools as centers for creating a Korean national consciousness. The Japanese authorities sought to regulate private schools, including those run by Christian missionaries, and insisted that the Japanese language be taught, though Korean remained the medium of instruction. Nonetheless, Korean schools, both public and private, became centers of political hostility to the Japanese authorities, and even after the Japanese departed schools remained centers of political activity.

For several reasons, the Japanese were less successful in extending public elementary education in Korea than they had been in Taiwan: greater opposition in Korea than in Taiwan to the Japanese insistence upon assimilation to Japanese culture; the tendency of the Japanese to look down on Korean culture and on Koreans, in contrast with Japanese respect for Chinese civilization; the smaller number of people employed in the wage-labor force in Korea than in Taiwan and the greater employment opportunities that educated Taiwanese had than educated Koreans.

Korea was freed from Japanese rule in 1945. The country was partitioned, the northern portion under Soviet influence, the south under United States influence. The north, with 55 percent of the territory and most of the industry, had 9 million people; the south, 21 million, predominantly in farming and fishing. In both portions of the country the Korean governments emphasized education, as much for its political as for its economic benefits, since both regimes viewed education as an instrument for inculcating loyalty. Both countries were faced with a major teacher shortage after Japanese teachers returned to Japan. Both countries also suffered substantially from the Korean War of 1950–1953, which brought considerable destruction to school buildings. Both countries put substantial resources into expanding primary and secondary education, entirely by the state in the case of North Korea, more substantially by parents in the case of South Korea.

South Korea's remarkable economic growth that started in the early 1960s—6.6 percent annually from 1965 to 1985, with an increase in per capita income from $83 in 1961 to $2,150 in 1985—was accompanied by, and to a considerable extent facilitated by, an expanding educational system. The state moved in stages. From 1955 to 1970 the emphasis was on the quantitative expansion of primary schools; after 1965 greater attention was given to increasing the number of junior and senior secondary schools. By the end of the 1970s, 99 percent of all elementary-school-age children in South Korea were in school. The number of children in school leaped from 5 million in 1960 to 11 million by 1980. In the early 1980s one-fourth of the total population of South Korea was in school. Three percent of the GNP was expended on education in 1979 (19 percent of the government budget), a lower investment than in many other developing countries. However, tuition fees constitute a major source of educational investment in South Korea. It is estimated that parents pay 65 percent of the total educational costs, with the remaining 35 percent coming from government. Elementary education receives the lion's share of government funding, with only a small investment in higher education. Costs were kept down by a high student–teacher ratio—57 to 1 in 1971. Compulsory education, initially for six years in 1948, was extended to nine years of schooling. The educational system was directed at providing a minimal education to the entire population. Entrance examinations for high-school admission were eliminated and only maintained for admission into the university. The state put considerable resources into investment in normal schools for the training of primary- and secondary-school teachers and vocational instructors. Until 1961 primary-school teachers needed only a high-school level normal-school education; thereafter the normal schools were converted into two-year junior colleges. Students in these schools were exempt from fees, and males were exempt from military service if they agreed to teach for at least two years in public elementary schools after graduating.

From a literacy rate of 55 percent in 1944, South Korea's literacy rose to between 70 percent and 80 percent by 1966, and to 93 percent by 1981—97.5 percent for males, 88 percent for females. By 1981, 36 percent of the population had completed only primary school, another 17 percent completed secondary school, and 7 percent had a postsecondary education. Only 21 percent of the population over the age of twenty-five, mainly older people, had no formal education.

Sri Lanka

Among low-income countries Sri Lanka is often cited as an example of a country that provides considerable equity, including basic mass education. Sri Lanka's adult literacy rose from 58 percent in 1946 to 86 percent in 1984. Ninety percent of the primary-school-age population (five to eleven years) are in school, by 1981 about 70 percent of all children were completing five years of compulsory schooling, and at least three-quarters of these went on to lower secondary school. In the mid-1970s, 4.5 percent of the national income was devoted to education, about one-tenth of the government's budget, largely for primary and secondary schools rather than for universities. A study by the British Council of the Sri Lankan educational system in 1977 concluded by saying that "despite all shortcomings, the level of growth of the educational system is impressive, and the reforming of the secondary school system and curriculum a considerable achievement. Sri Lanka, after Japan, can claim to have one of the most developed systems in Asia."[20]

Sri Lanka's educational achievement is particularly striking because it is so markedly different from the other countries of South Asia, while its per capita income is not significantly higher. Under precolonial Buddhist rule, village and temple schools emphasized Buddhist teachings and, by all accounts, enrollments were limited. Under Portuguese and Dutch rule in the seventeenth and eighteenth centuries, Protestant and Presbyterian missions created schools intended to spread the faith. In the 1840s and 1850s English Evangelicals actively pressed for an expanding state role in education, but not until the 1870s, after educational reforms were introduced in England, was there a significant expansion of state expenditures on schooling. As a consequence of the heavy reliance upon missionary-run educational institutions, 65 percent of all children attending school in 1868 were Christian, only 27 percent were Buddhist.[21] By the end of the century Hindus, Buddhists, and to a lesser extent Muslims began to compete with Christian missionaries in the establishment of schools. Buddhist and Hindu opposition to the extension of the Christian

[20] The British Council, *Education Profile: Sri Lanka* (Colombo: The British Council, 1977), p. 29.

[21] C. R. de Silva, "Education," in K. M. de Silva, ed., *Sri Lanka: A Survey* (London: C. Hurst, 1977), p. 405. For other accounts of the history of educational development in preindependence Ceylon and in Sri Lanka, see Swarna Jayaweera, "Education and Socio-Economic Development in Sri Lanka," *Comparative Education Center Research Series 1975–76*, no. 3 (College Park, Md.: Comparative Education Center, College of Education, University of Maryland, 1976); *Education: A Centenary Volume*, 3 vols. (Colombo: Department of Education, Government of Sri Lanka, 1967); J. E. Jayasuriya, *Education in Ceylon before and after Independence, 1939–1968* (Colombo: Associated Educational Publishers, 1969); D. P. Wijegoonasekera, *External Resources for the Development of Education in Sri Lanka* (Paris: International Institute for Educational Planning, 1974); O. Engquist, L. Jiven, and K. Nystom, *Education and Training in Sri Lanka: A Sector Analysis: Educational and Psychological Interactions* (Malco, Sweden: School of Education, 1982); Swarna Jayaweera, "Education," in S. Fernando and Robert Kearney, eds., *Modern Sri Lanka in Transition* (Syracuse: Syracuse University Press, 1978).

missionary school system also played an important role in the growth of the state-supported schools. With the government's decision to enforce compulsory schooling in the 1920s and 1930s, enrollments in the state-supported system rose substantially.

As elsewhere in the subcontinent, there developed a small, privately financed but publicly assisted English-medium educational system parallel to the Sinhalese- and Tamil-medium schools. Those who completed the English-medium secondary schools were able to go on to the university and to the more lucrative careers in government and in the professions, while the schools in the *swabhasha* (national languages) provided a minimal education. With the establishment of universal suffrage, control over education was placed in the hands of local governments and an effort was made to develop an education relevant for rural youth, though with little success.

However, before independence only a bare majority of the schools was administered by the government. An ordinance passed in 1947 abolished fees in government-assisted schools and provided that grants would be paid only for students whose parents subscribed to the religion of the proprietor of the school, a policy intended to arrest the expansion of the missionary schools and to permit an expansion of state schools. Expand they did. The elections of 1956 brought to power the Sri Lanka Freedom party, committed to the strengthening of Buddhism, the Sinhalese language, and the position of the rural population against the urban, Westernized, English-speaking elite that had hitherto dominated the political scene. In 1960–1961, under pressure from Buddhist pressure groups, the government took over most of the privately run government-assisted schools. The system became highly centralized, run by the Ministry of Education through the regional departments, with limited local participation.

Elementary-school enrollments accelerated in the early 1950s, as did secondary-school enrollments in the late 1950s and university enrollments in the 1960s. The participation rate in primary education increased from 58 percent in 1946 to 74 percent in 1963, while secondary education increased from 11 percent in 1953 to 43 percent in 1963. The number of government elementary schools grew from 3,735 in 1956 to 8,409 a decade later, while the number of government-aided schools declined from 2,227 to 1,053. With the growth in cultural nationalism among the Sinhalese Buddhists, religion and language became the central issues in educational politics. Sinhalese became the primary language of administration, a decision that further stimulated the drive for government employment among young, rural Sinhalese. The earlier conflict between the English-speaking elite and those who used the national languages was replaced by an increasingly acute conflict between Tamils and Sinhalese.

To the Sinhalese, control over the educational system was essential both for the fulfillment of their cultural-nationalist ambitions and for equalizing their positions in government employment, in the professions, and in the modern sectors of the economy where Tamils had excelled.

Unlike South Korea and Taiwan, economic growth in Sri Lanka was exceedingly slow, with the result that graduates of the secondary schools were unable to find employment. There developed an inverse relationship between levels of education and unemployment, with the lowest unemployment rate among those with only a primary-school education and higher levels of unemployment among those with secondary-school diplomas and university degrees. Industrial growth had been too slow to absorb a significant portion of young people who sought entry into the work force. Educated and unemployed rural Sinhalese intellectuals became increasingly embittered at the small Westernized elite and at the economically more successful Sri Lankan Tamils. And as the Sinhalese gained control over the educational system and government employment, Tamil youth in turn became embittered. Thus, the transformative role played by education in Taiwan and South Korea, and earlier in Japan, the United States, and western Europe, was lacking in Sri Lanka, in spite of the extraordinary success achieved by the government in expanding the educational system. Nonetheless, primary- and secondary-school education remains in high demand as the vast proportion of young people defer entrance into the labor force.

Labor-force statistics indicate a sharp decrease in the number of children ages ten to fourteen in the labor force from 1946 to 1963, a result of increased school enrollment. The employment rate of this age group declined from 13 percent in 1946 to 6.2 percent in 1963. By 1971, with a further rise in school attendance, the number of children in the labor force declined to 5 percent.[22] However, significant numbers of children continue to remain out of the primary-school system, especially the children of Tamils working in the tea plantations. Studies conducted in the late 1970s found that 41 percent of six-to-nine year olds in the tea estate areas were not in school, with even higher rates of nonparticipation among girls. After 1977, however, when the government took responsibility for running the schools in the estates, enrollments reportedly increased significantly.

Along with other low-income countries, Sri Lanka continues to have severe educational problems—a poor quality primary-school system, persistence of primary-school dropouts, and substantial inequality among

[22] Swarna Jayaweera, "Educational Opportunity and the School Age Population in Sri Lanka," *Sri Lanka Journal of Social Sciences* (1979), p. 32, data drawn from the 1971 census of population.

schools. Compared with other low-income countries, however, Sri Lanka has achieved a remarkably high enrollment rate, high retention rate, and a corresponding decline in child labor.

Kerala

The government of India's National Sample Survey of 1971 reported that the work participation rate of children in Kerala was 1.9 percent, as against the all-India figure of 7.1 percent. In Kerala virtually all children in the six-to-eleven age group are in school. For the eleven-to-fourteen age group, 88 percent are in school in Kerala, compared with the all-India figure of 38 percent.[23] But perhaps the most impressive educational statistic is the primary-school retention rate. The National Council of Educational Research and Training reported in a 1975 survey that 82 percent of all children who entered primary school in Kerala completed the fifth grade, as compared with 26 percent for India. This high retention rate accounts for Kerala's high literacy rate—70.4 percent in 1981, nearly twice the national average.

Two other measures related to children distinguish Kerala from the rest of India. Kerala has half the infant mortality rate of the country as a whole, sixty-one per thousand. Kerala also has a lower fertility rate, 25.2 per thousand, compared with the all-India rate of 33.2 per thousand. Demographers have suggested that there is a causal relationship between a high level of educational achievement, especially of women, and these lower infant mortality and fertility rates.[24]

The Kerala government spends more on education than any other state government: sixty-four rupees per capita, as compared to thirty-three rupees for all states. As early as 1960–1961 Kerala was spending 3.6 percent of the state's GDP, or 35 percent of state revenues, on education, while West Bengal (with a higher GDP and higher per capita income) was spending only 2.1 percent and 19 percent respectively on education. Per capita expenditure on education in Kerala, then, was 11.5 rupees, while the all-India average was 7.8 rupees. In Bihar it was only 4.9 rupees, in

[23] Ministry of Education and Social Welfare, *Enrollment Trends in States, 1968–69, 1978–79* (New Delhi: Government of India, 1979), data for 1977–1978.

[24] Education of girls as a factor in Kerala's low fertility rate has received a great deal of attention. See P. R. Gopinathan Nair, "Decline in Birth Rate in Kerala," *Economic and Political Weekly*, Annual Number (February 1974), pp. 323–336; Moni Nag, "Fertility Differential in Kerala and West Bengal," *Economic and Political Weekly*, Annual Number (May 1983), pp. 877–896. For a review of the literature on the relationship between fertility and education, see S. Cochrane, *Fertility and Education: What Do We Really Know?* World Bank Staff Occasional Papers no. 26 (Baltimore: Johns Hopkins University Press, 1979).

Orissa 4.3 rupees, and in Uttar Pradesh 5.4 rupees. Many of the factors that affect school attendance—distance to school, number of teachers, availability of play facilities, and whether there are provisions for school lunches—are dependent upon the size of educational budgets for primary schools. In virtually all educational categories Kerala spends more: average annual salaries for primary-school teachers, annual expenditure per primary-school pupil, expenditure on primary education per head of population, and so on. There are also fewer one-teacher schools than elsewhere. Compared with other states Kerala has put more of its educational resources into mass education than colleges and universities. On only one major item has Kerala fallen behind other states: pupil-teacher ratio in primary schools. The reason for this is that in an effort to provide education for all children the state government adopted a double-shift system for teachers and only later reduced the extent of the shift system as funds became available. (It is noteworthy that South Korea also has a high pupil–teacher ratio.)

Kerala's educational growth can be traced to developments in the nineteenth century, the result of efforts by missionaries and by the governments of the princely states of Travancore and Cochin.[25] Foreign missionaries, mainly Catholic missionaries from Portugal and Anglican missionaries from Great Britain, created the first modern schools in Kerala early in the nineteenth century. Kerala attracted missionary interest because of the presence of the indigenous Syrian Christian community. Concern by members of the Nair caste that Christian missionaries were starting schools in Malayalum in order to convert the state to Christianity and use it as a base for the rest of India led them to create their own schools and colleges. The Travancore and Cochin rulers—the area was then under the control of Hindu maharajas—provided private schools with grants-in-aid. Along with the aid came supervision, inspection, approved syllabi, and common examinations. Modern mass education began in the 1860s (especially in Travancore under the divanship of T. Madhava Rao) and the government insisted that government-funded church schools be open to all. The Ezhavas, Kerala's low-caste community, who worked on the coir, tea, and coffee plantations, were incorporated into the schools and were themselves active in creating their own schools. In 1903 the Ezhavas organized a socioreligious reform organization called

---

[25] For accounts of the development of education in preindependence Kerala, see P. K. Michael Tharakan, *Socio-Economic Factors in Educational Development: The Case of Nineteenth Century Travancore*, Working Paper no. 190 (Trivandrum: Centre for Development Studies, 1984); P. R. Gopinathan Nair, *Educational Reforms in India: Universalisation of Primary Education in Kerala*, Working Paper no. 181 (Trivandrum: Centre for Development Studies, 1983).

the Sree Naryana Dharma Paripalana Yogam. Similarly, the Nairs formed the Nair Service Society in 1924 to coordinate their educational activities.

Competition in education grew not only between Christians and Hindus but among the Hindu castes as well. Educational qualifications were a key to entrance into positions in the state bureaucracy, white-collar jobs, and in the expanding educational system itself. Leaders of the Nair, Syrian Christian, and Ezhava communities were eager to break into what they regarded as a Brahman-dominated bureaucracy. In 1904 the government declared primary education free and committed itself to providing primary schools throughout the state. Today, there are both wholly government schools and government-aided private schools, including schools run by the Nair Service Society, the Muslim Educational Society, the Catholic Church, various Protestant organizations, and even by private businessmen. In 1978–1979 the private sector managed 59 percent of lower primary schools, 68 percent of upper primary schools, and 65 percent of high schools.[26] More than half the school children in the state attend government-aided or private independent schools.

The missionary schools gave particular attention to the education of women, the lower castes, and technical education. But in the main the educational demand in Kerala has been for academic schools rather than vocational training. Still, the educational system produces not only a large number of young people seeking white-collar jobs, but also carpenters, masons, electricians, and other skilled workers. Some are trained in the Junior Technical Schools, though many continue to be trained through apprenticeships outside the school system. Kerala produces a high-quality labor force. Unable to find employment in Kerala—industrial growth in the state is well below the national average—educated and skilled Malayalees seek employment elsewhere in India and abroad, especially in the Gulf states.

While child labor has been reduced in Kerala it has not totally disappeared. Since an estimated 18 percent of the children drop out of school after the fifth grade, children of twelve or thirteen do enter the labor force, many in automotive workshops, as apprentice electricians, and in other construction-related jobs. But even these children are usually literate, and the quality of jobs they obtain and the wages they receive are higher than in other parts of India. The Kerala government has made no special effort to end child labor. It is the expansion of the school system rather than the enforcement of labor legislation that has reduced the amount of child labor.

[26] T. J. Nossiter, *Communism in Kerala* (Berkeley: University of California Press, 1982), p. 33.

The Relevance for India

The comparison with other developing countries suggests how far behind India is in mass education by almost any measure—school attendance, retention rates, or adult literacy rates.

Both religion and political ideologies played a role in the expansion of primary education in the cases considered above. In Sri Lanka and Kerala Christian missionary activity was a significant element both in the growth of popular demand for mass education and in the response of the state. Elsewhere in India, Christian missions stimulated educational development in India's northeastern states of Nagaland and Mizoram and in the southwestern state of Goa, states with large Christian populations. Elsewhere in Asia, Christianity was important in educational development in the Philippines and to some extent in South Korea, Taiwan, Vietnam, and portions of mainland China.

In the Confucian societies described here—mainland China, Taiwan, and South Korea (along with Singapore)—governments have regarded primary and secondary schools as essential for the propagation of a set of values emphasizing an acceptance of state authority and national loyalty, as well as for national development.

School success rates are partly the result of efforts to stimulate parental demand for education, most notably by raising the quality of schools through the improvement of teacher training, and in part by holding schools accountable to local authorities. Making schools relevant has been important, though vocational training is typically not introduced until upper primary or secondary school. Improved access to education has been achieved by increasing the number of schools (often with financial and labor contributions from the local community), by abolishing fees, and by a variety of programs to relieve girls of the care of younger siblings so that they can attend school (e.g., crèches at places of employment and day-care facilities at schools for the younger siblings of female students).

Compulsory education, though not always effectively enforced, has been one of the stimulants of educational expansion in the four countries described above. A few other developing countries have made education compulsory (most notably Indonesia), while others have aggressively adopted and implemented policies intended to universalize primary-school education and to maintain high retention rates (notably Algeria, Kenya, Tanzania, Botswana, Zambia, Malaysia, Philippines, Thailand, and Turkey).

Finally, in all four countries, in Kerala, and in other countries that have achieved high levels of school enrollment and correspondingly low levels of child labor, substantial financial commitments have been made to primary-school education, sometimes with higher educational expenditures than in India, but often with a higher proportion of the educational budget devoted to primary-school education.

8

Values and Interests in Public Policy

The Idea of Education as a Duty

ALL advanced industrial countries and those contemporary developing countries that have made education compulsory regard education not as a right but as a duty. When education is made a duty, parents, irrespective of their economic circumstances and beliefs, are required by law to send their children to school; it is also the legal obligation of the state to provide an adequate number of schools, appropriately situated, and to ensure that no child fails to attend school.

As we have seen in the preceding chapter, one by one the countries of the West, and then several in Asia, introduced the notion of compulsion. In some countries the notion was so controversial and the political forces arraigned against it were so substantial that years, even centuries, passed between the first efforts and the final statutory actions. In 1524 Martin Luther informed German municipalities that it was the duty of parents to educate their children but it was not until 1817 that the Prussian state ordered parents to send their children to school. In 1642 the colony of Massachusetts passed a law requiring that parents see to it that their children were taught to read, and in 1647 all communities were obligated to build and finance schools, but it was not until 1873 that Massachusetts required all towns to appoint truant officers. At roughly the same time, other American states introduced legislation to make education compulsory, but it was not until 1918, when Mississippi finally acted, that education became compulsory throughout the country.

In spite of the eloquent arguments for compulsory education by John Stuart Mill and other distinguished and influential intellectuals (starting with Adam Smith), the British Parliament did not pass compulsory education legislation until 1870, and not until 1880 did Parliament pass legislation making education obligatory for all children. In Japan the Meiji leadership moved quickly with its decree in 1872 making education compulsory throughout the country. Under Japanese occupation, the imperial authorities made education compulsory in Taiwan in 1943. In 1948 South Korea, only a few years after it became independent of Japan, made education compulsory.

Postrevolutionary regimes have tended to act with great speed in adopting the idea of education as a duty. The new Soviet regime, faced with an illiteracy rate estimated at 70 percent, launched a literacy drive from 1917 to 1921, made education compulsory for members of the Red Army, expanded the number of primary schools in the 1920s, and in an official party decree declared four years of schooling compulsory for all children starting in 1931. Similarly, the People's Republic of China, governing a population with an illiteracy rate reported as high as 80 percent in 1949, launched one of the world's major campaigns against illiteracy, with compulsory education for children and a nonformal education program for adults. Other Communist and leftist regimes—North Vietnam beginning in 1945, Cuba in 1961, and Nicaragua in 1980—forced all children into schools and launched literacy campaigns for adults.[1]

Among countries with compulsory education there were differences in whether education was a state monopoly or private and church-run schools were permitted, how many hours of school children had to attend, the number of years of schooling that were obligatory, and whether the schools emphasized bookish learning, religious or moral instruction, civic or political education, or vocational skills. Once compulsion was introduced, then such issues as the hours of attendance, the years of schooling, and the content of education became a matter of public policy. So was the question of whether private schools could be permitted alongside state-run schools. Differences aside, what was common in these countries was that for part of the day children were required to attend school, though they were free the remainder of the day to help with chores at home, work in the fields, or even be employed part-time.

The shift from rights to duties is a profound one in the history of the relationship between children and the state. "Rights" implies access and choice. Education is free and widely available. Parents are free to choose or not to choose to send their children to school. The notion of duty denies parents the right to choose. Parents are told by the state that no matter how great is their need for the labor or income of their children they must nonetheless relinquish their child to school for a part of the day. The notion of duty also applies to the state. The state has a duty to make education obligatory, and in turn the central authority imposes this duty on local authorities as well as on parents and guardians of children.

How did it happen that states came to view education as a duty? One explanation, as we have seen, is the impact of religious ideas and institutions. In a great many countries religion provided an impetus for state intrusion. The conviction that every individual, starting at childhood, should be able to read the Scriptures was a powerful element in the diffusion of mass education in Protestant countries, so powerful an idea that

[1] H. S. Bhola, *Campaigning for Literacy* (Paris: United Nations Educational, Scientific, and Cultural Organization, 1984).

mass education became widespread even before state intervention. Protestant leaders often were unwilling to stand aside when parents failed to
provide their children with education. Governing elites and those who
had influence were inclined to force parents to perform their religious
duty. To be sure, the ideology of liberalism sometimes stood in the way
of state action, especially in England and the United States, where there
was a division between those who favored state intervention and those
who believed that the state had no business taking away private choices
from adults. In contrast with Protestantism, Catholicism was not a force
for state intervention. Catholic theology did not require that individuals
be able to read religious texts, only that they be able to recite through
rote when necessary. Other things being equal (which they rarely are!),
Protestant countries were quicker than Catholic countries to make education compulsory.

More indirectly, in Sri Lanka and Kerala religious institutions played
a role in the diffusion of mass education and in the growth of state intervention. As we have seen, in both instances competition with Christian
educational institutions was important in the response of indigenous religious groups—Buddhists in Sri Lanka, Hindus in Travancore and Cochin. Elsewhere in India, the higher-than-average literacy rates for Goa
(56.7 percent), Mizoram (59.9 percent), Nagaland (42.6 percent), and
Manipur (41.4 percent) can be related to the role of Christian missions
and government reactions to their educational presence. (The Christian
populations of these states are, respectively, 29 percent, 84 percent, 80
percent, and 30 percent. Nationally, Christians constitute 2.4 percent of
the Indian population.)

Religious institutions were not a force, or certainly not the major force,
for state-run education in postrevolutionary France, in nineteenth-century Japan, in the postrevolutionary Soviet Union, in mid-twentieth-cen-
tury China, in South Korea, or in Taiwan, though church missions were
active in creating educational institutions in several of these countries. In
these societies, however, ideologies rather than theologies were paramount. In France secularism and nationalism required a state-run education system to counter the influence of the Catholic church. In Japan
the Tokugawa rulers propagated Confucian notions of filial piety and obedience to authority. The successor Meiji regime then used the educational system as an instrument of political indoctrination, with emphasis
on obedience to the emperor rather than to feudal lords. In the Soviet
Union, the People's Republic of China, and other Communist countries,
the education of the masses was seen by the new rulers as central to the
goal of creating "new men," motivated not by material incentives but by
ideology. As Mao wrote, "the necessary condition for establishing a new

China is to sweep away illiteracy from the 80 percent portion of China's population."[2] Under Mao the preference for ideological purity over expertise was an explicit statement of the central ideological objective of the educational system. In Taiwan and South Korea "moral education," with its Confucian content, was an important driving force behind the spread of mass education. Both states regarded themselves as under siege from Communist neighbors, and their elites looked upon education in part as a form of political indoctrination and as a political weapon.

Theologians, with their vision of God-fearing, law-abiding, moral youth; educators, with their vision of schools transmitting the Enlightenment values of secularism, rationalism, cosmopolitanism, and individualism as against xenophobia, superstition, religiosity, fatalism, and passive obedience to authority; and revolutionaries, with their romantic vision of social transformation, provided much of the driving force behind the idea of compulsory mass education.

Primary-School Education and Development

Among contemporary development theorists the case for compulsory mass education has rested on four sets of findings. The first is the link between mass education and economic growth, the recognition that the skills, knowledge, beliefs, values, and attitudes acquired in the early years of schooling are valuable to those engaged in even relatively low-skilled occupations. The capacity of an entire population to acquire new knowledge, skills, values, and attitudes is now regarded by development theorists as fundamental to economic growth and material well-being. The evidence for this conclusion lies primarily in a variety of studies calculating rates of return from education.[3] These studies demonstrate that the returns from primary education are the highest among all educational levels. Of special interest are the findings that schooling correlates with increases in agricultural production, especially when the opportunity exists to introduce new technologies. In a survey of eighteen developing countries it was found that farmers with four or more years of primary education produced 13 percent more crops than uneducated farmers. A review of the various studies concluded that four years of schooling, usually of the male members of the family, is a threshold for productivity

[2] Ibid., p. 76.
[3] For a review, see G. Psacharopoulos and M. Woodhall, *Education for Development* (New York: Oxford University Press, 1985).

effects.[4] Each year of schooling is estimated to raise output by an additional 2 percent to 3 percent.[5]

But the relationship between education and productivity is not assured. The African experience demonstrates that increased education may coexist with declining agricultural productivity where governments are pursuing policies that are disincentives to growth. Education and increased literacy in themselves do not lead to agricultural growth in the absence of appropriate agricultural policies.

The second finding is the linkage between female education and fertility rates and the related linkage between education and public health. A reduction in fertility, morbidity, and mortality depends in large part upon having a population that is educated to understand causal relationships. A review of fertility studies by S. H. Cochrane at the World Bank, found that female education influences the number of children mothers have.[6] A review of studies on the impact of maternal education on child mortality by John Caldwell concluded that maternal education was the single most significant determinant of differences in child mortality.[7] A World Bank review found that "an additional year of schooling for a mother results in a reduction of 9 per 1,000 in the mortality of her offspring."[8] Schools may also contribute directly to the health of children when the schools provide free lunches, subsidized milk, immunizations and other health services. Moreover, schooling, by removing children from the physical drudgery and hazardous risks associated with child labor indirectly improves their physical well-being.

The third finding is the link between education and individual modernity. In a series of well-known cross-national surveys Alex Inkeles reported that schooling had a greater impact on the development of "modern" attitudes and behavior than factory experience, urbanization, or media exposure.[9] These and other studies have found that literacy enables individuals to make greater use of new technologies, prepares individuals to enter into new institutions (e.g., the factory) and establish new social networks, increases a sense of being able to control one's fu-

---

[4] M. E. Lockheed, D. T. Jamison, and L. J. Lau, "Farmer Education and Farm Efficiency," *Economic Development and Cultural Change* 29 (1980), pp. 37–76.

[5] D. T. Jamison and L. Lau, *Farmer Education and Farm Efficiency* (Baltimore: Johns Hopkins University Press, 1982).

[6] S. H. Cochrane, *Fertility and Education: What Do We Really Know?* World Bank Staff Occasional Paper no. 26 (Baltimore: Johns Hopkins University Press, 1979).

[7] J. C. Caldwell, "Education as a Factor in Mortality Decline: An Examination of Nigerian Data," *Population Studies* 33 (1979), p. 408.

[8] S. H. Cochrane, D. J. O'Hare, and J. Leslie, *The Effects of Education on Health*, World Bank Staff Working Paper no. 405 (Washington D.C.: World Bank, 1980), p. 92.

[9] Alex Inkeles and David Smith, *Becoming Modern* (Cambridge: Harvard University Press), 1974.

ture, and stimulates interest and participation in politics and civic affairs. These studies note that numeracy and literacy are essential for functioning in a modern society.[10]

The relationship between primary education, mass literacy, and political behavior is the fourth linkage, but the one in which the cause–effect relationships are the most problematic. Mass education has been variously described as a requisite for a democratic political system, a factor in the development of citizen efficacy and political participation, and a means of enhancing rationality, increasing norms of tolerance, reducing crime, and facilitating national integration. James S. Coleman, in his review of the studies, concluded that education can also perpetuate the gap between the elite and the masses and sharpen ethnic divisions, prepare individuals for political participation in either a radical or conservative direction, and reinforce as well as weaken prejudices. Nor does education ensure rationality in political behavior. Education can increase social mobility or can reinforce the existing system of social stratification, and when education expands significantly faster than employment the result can be the creation of a class of unemployed school dropouts, "whose political orientation toward the polity is marked by disaffection and alienation and whose behavorial disposition is basically anomic."[11]

The operative word in the literature on education and political development is "can." By providing some shared knowledge, values, and experiences among an entire population, schooling can enhance the sense of national identity. A common school education with equal educational facilities across regions and classes can facilitate social mobility. Education can break down ascriptive relations and strengthen achievement criteria. Primary-school education can contribute to political equality at the local level by reducing the power that those who are educated have had over the illiterate. Illiterates are all too often dependent and subordinate to those who are literate in dealing with laws and with officials. To exercise rights provided by the law, individuals must be able to read.

With this comparative perspective in mind, we can now review why it is that efforts to make education compulsory and to end child labor in India have been so desultory, public rhetoric and constitutional injunctions notwithstanding.

[10] For a review of these and other studies concerning the effects of schooling, see Thomas Owen Eisemon, *The Consequences of Schooling: A Review of Research on the Outcomes of Primary Schooling in Developing Countries*, Education Development Discussion Paper no. 3, Harvard University Basic Research and Implementation In Developing Education Systems Project (Cambridge: Harvard Institute for International Development, 1988).

[11] James S. Coleman, ed., *Education and Political Development* (Princeton: Princeton University Press, 1965), p. 29.

Indian Views Summarized

Indians of virtually all political persuasions oppose the notion that education should be imposed. The major objection, as we have seen, is that poverty forces children to drop out of school to find employment to augment the income of their families. It is an argument widely subscribed to by all political groups. The Communist government of West Bengal is no more committed to the enforcement of child-labor laws or compulsory-education laws than the Congress-dominated conservative state of Bihar next door. In the 1985–1986 debate over the government's proposed national policy on education, few critics called for compulsory education. No teachers' unions have demanded that education be made compulsory. No local authorities have invoked the state educational laws that permit them to make education compulsory. No religious groups have urged the government to make education compulsory. In the debate over the government's new policy toward child-labor laws, critics were distressed that the government accepted child labor as a "harsh reality," but virtually no one urged the government to remove children from employment in cottage industries and agriculture by forcing them to go to school, irrespective of their parent's wishes. In no states have trade unions launched a campaign for the enforcement of child-labor laws. And few, if any, voluntary organizations have actively pressed state labor departments to enforce child-labor legislation.

It is well-known that many poor parents bear children in order to enhance family income. As economists say, children are viewed as economic assets, not as economic liabilities. Indian policymakers accept as the basis for policy the fact that childbearing for low-income Indians is part of their strategy for family survival and well-being.

As we have documented, many other governments have not been deterred from making education compulsory by the presence of widespread poverty and by the argument that the poor need the income of their children. Government officials in other countries have reasoned that parents ought not to be allowed to use children to increase their own income. To permit otherwise is to view the child as the property of the parent, to be used as the parent sees fit, a conception that comes perilously close to notions of slavery. Such a policy, it has been noted by demographers, is also an inducement to a high fertility rate. By establishing policies that deny parents the income of their children, children cease to be regarded as economic assets and there is less incentive for increasing their numbers. In time, a social transformation takes place, with financial resources within the family flowing not from the very young to their parents, but rather downward from parents to children. Children then are no longer regarded by parents as financial assets contributing to the economic well-being of the family, but become, at least during the early years of their lives, financial liabilities that parents must bear. The attitudes of parents toward children is transformed. Parents are more likely to want fewer children as children become more costly, or "priceless." And they are likely to want their children to be better educated and healthier. It has been argued that structural changes in the economy—the introduction of technologies that require education or an increase in demand for labor as a result of rapid economic growth—will lead to a reevaluation of the relationship between education and employment for children and that only such structural changes can bring about a change in parental attitudes toward children. While there may well be instances where economic changes led to changes in parental attitudes, which in turn facilitated the introduction of compulsory education, the examples described here are more often ones in which policy changes preceded, and to a considerable extent shaped, parental attitudes.

The impact of child labor on the well-being of the poor is also seen differently in countries that have made education compulsory. While Indians believe that the poor gain when their children are employed, in other countries it has been argued that the poor are made worse off because the employment of children drives down the wages and employment of adults. Shopkeepers prefer to hire an eight year old than to employ an eighteen year old at a higher wage. The cattle owner prefers to employ a ten year old (who may be a bonded laborer) than hire someone older. In countries that have abolished child labor a powerful political argument—one made by trade unions—has been that the lot of the poor would improve since employers would then be forced to hire adults at higher wages rather than children.

Outside of India it is also reasoned that children would be better off with four or six years of schooling than with early employment. A literate young person is likely to be more productive and to earn more than someone who has had no education and whose health may have been damaged by early entrance into the labor force. From this perspective, child labor is not only a consequence of poverty, but also one of its causes. Its removal is likely to increase the well-being of the poor.

Indians challenge this view with the argument that the Indian educational system is defective because it does not prepare village children and the urban poor for living and working in their own environment. Instead, they say, schools inculcate in children a preference for white-collar jobs. Villagers want urban jobs, especially government employment, for their children because such jobs provide assured income, in contrast with the risk and uncertainty in agricultural employment. The school system increases the competition for white-collar jobs, leads to a growth in educated unemployment, and thereby threatens to create a semieducated lumpen proletariat that can be exploited by political groups that seek to destabilize the political system. A major concern of the middle class, therefore, and of middle-class officials, is that schools educate the poorer classes for jobs that the economy is not able to provide. By raising expectations, they say, education for the poor may create disruptive antisocial elements. From this perspective, a high dropout rate in the schools can be regarded as contributing to social stability. The high dropout rate also demonstrates, say many educators, that many parents do not regard the schools as useful. Why then make education compulsory?

In contrast with school education, childhood employment, it is said, teaches children of the poor to acquire the right attitudes and work habits at an early age. It is particularly valuable for the children of the poor to learn the skills of their parents. From this perspective, "work" should be regarded as apprenticeship or a form of education that enables children to acquire the skills and attitudes necessary for a life of working—commitment to manual work, diligence, acquiescence to managerial authority, pliability. Moreover, so the argument continues, the employment of children is productive for the economy. Nimble little fingers enable children to do work that adults cannot readily do, or do as well. Children can produce a greater number of knots in the weaving of carpets than can adults. They can roll bidis, pick leaves in the tea gardens, pack matches into boxes, and carry molten glass, tasks that need diligence, dexterity, and speed rather than physical strength. Without children in the labor force, it is said, these tasks would not be performed as well. And since children are paid less than adults they are able to produce goods at lower cost. Because of these lower costs some industries, such as carpet making, are better able to compete in world markets. Traditional handicrafts, a tie to India's ancient crafts, can also be preserved if children are employed. Without child labor, carpets and hand-loomed textiles might be replaced by machine-made products, bidis would give way to factory-made cigarettes, and matches and firecrackers would be made by multinational corporations. There is thus a conception of "children's work"—or, more precisely, poor children's work—as both a phase in the education of a child and a distinctive niche in the economy.

In this connection it should be noted that members of the Indian middle class conceptualize a distinction between the children of the poor and their own children. A distinction is made between children as "hands" and children as "minds"; that is, between the child who must be taught to "work" and the child who must be taught to "learn," the acquisition of manual skills as distinct from cognitive skills. Thus, traditional Hindu notions of social rank and hierarchy are subtly incorporated into the ways educated Indians distinguish between education for the children of those who do manual work and those who are in services. "There are various unconscious ways in which one social class in India prevents the rise of another through its control over education," Professor Surajit Sinha, one of India's leading anthropologists, told me. "You could call it pedagogic suppression." As examples, he pointed to the practice of upgrading requirements in English and in the sciences, which results in the failure of more children in the early grades and an increase in the school dropout rate, and the creation of a dual system of elementary education, which enables the middle class to send their children to separate private but government-aided schools while the lower classes send their children to underfinanced, underequipped municipal and village schools. A third example cited by Sinha is the creation of schools for India's tribal population, where Hindi or other regional languages rather than tribal languages are the medium of instruction, and where caste Hindu teachers regard the children as primitive and incapable of acquiring cognitive skills.

Ten percent of all children who enter the first grade are enrolled in private schools, some financially aided by the government, some not. The dropout rate in these schools is almost nil, while less than a third of the children in the public schools make it to the fifth grade (6.1 million compared with 19.1 million enrolled in grade 1). The result is that by the fifth grade 28 percent of India's children are in private schools. In the eighth grade, by which time even more of the children in the public schools have dropped out, a majority of India's children are attending private schools (2.8 million compared with 2.1 million attending schools managed directly by the government and local bodies (see table 8.1). In other words, for every 100 children in first grade there are twenty-three

TABLE 8.1
Public and Private School Enrollments, 1978 (millions)

Type of School	Grade							
	1	2	3	4	5	6	7	8
Government	7.5	5.1	4.2	3.4	2.7	2.7	1.9	1.5
Local body	11.6	8.4	6.5	5.1	3.4	1.6	1.3	.6
Private aided	1.9	1.7	1.6	1.4	2.1	2.5	2.4	2.5
Private unaided	0.6	0.4	0.4	0.3	0.3	0.3	0.3	0.3
Total	21.6	15.6	12.7	10.2	8.5	7.1	5.9	4.9

Source: Fourth All-India Educational Survey, 1978 (New Delhi: National Council of Educational Research and Training, 1982), pp. 838–839.

children in eighth grade of whom thirteen are in private (government-aided or unaided) and ten in public schools. India's entire middle class—the educators, social activists, government officials, politicians, and professionals who discuss, influence, make, or implement policies affecting public elementary education—send their children to private schools, not to the government-run municipal and village schools.

Even as educators publicly deplore the dropout rate from the public elementary schools and have introduced incentives (midday meals, free uniforms) to induce children to remain in school, privately many express the fear that too many children will want to go on to higher education pursuing certificates that will lead them to seek white-collar employment. To many educators, a reformed public elementary school system is one where the children of the poor (but not the middle class) will learn to work. Nonformal education for working children is desirable because, as a senior educator in Gujarat said to me children can be taught "topics like health and cleanliness. That is more important than the subjects taught in the regular school like language and arithmetic."

Educators and officials do not regard education as an equalizer, as an instrument for developing shared attitudes and social characteristics, but rather as a way of differentiating one class from another. Education is regarded as a way of escaping from physical labor. For this reason educators are content to see children leave school at an early age, or they would restructure education for the poor so as to persuade the poor to continue to engage in physical labor. Education in India is also regarded as a form of social superiority. Those who are educated dress and speak differently than those who are not educated. Those who are educated have power over those who are not. The educated can give commands to and shout at the uneducated and can expect deference and obedience.

While Indians rhetorically call for universal mass education, they can find innumerable reasons why it is legitimate that poor parents not send their children to school. A favorite argument against compulsory education, as we have seen, is that elementary schools in India are so defective that it is unreasonable to insist that parents send their children to school. Rote learning, crowded classes, inadequate equipment, inadequate vocational training, and poorly trained teachers are the norm, while one-teacher schools (with the teacher often absent) are commonplace. Not until the schools are improved and education made more useful, it is argued, should children be required to attend. The lack of attention by the government to remedying these defects and the low investment in primary education in India compared to many other developing countries are indications of the low priority that mass education is given in India. The experience of some countries also suggests that the educational system may improve after, not before, education has been made compulsory.

Indian Policies in Comparative Perspective

There are a great many variations in how governments set about making education compulsory and enforcing child-labor laws. Legislative approaches differ between centralized and decentralized educational systems. There are also a great many variations in how many years of schooling are required, at what ages young people can enter the labor force, the allocation of educational resources, the machinery used to enforce the various laws, and so on. Nonetheless, there are some elements that are widely shared, from which lessons can be extracted. What follows is an enumeration of some of these lessons.

1. Compulsory-education laws usually precede child-labor laws, and their enforcement substantially reduces or eliminates child labor. The reason for this is that the enforcement of school laws, though by no means easy, has proven to be less difficult than the enforcement of child-labor laws. Local officials know their community, know who is not attending school, and have clout over poor parents. In contrast, factory inspectors make infrequent rounds and cannot inspect thousands of small shops, and employers, properly warned, are able to take evasive action. Businessmen can readily bribe factory inspectors, while poor parents lack the resources to bribe truant officers.

2. The decision to make education compulsory rests everywhere on the belief in the efficacy of mass education on the part of those who make, influence, and implement education policy. The notion of efficacy rests on a diverse set of arguments, some of which may be empirically questionable (the notion that mass education will reduce juvenile crime) and morally reprehensible (education as an instrument of ideological control by an authoritarian state), while others may meet with our approval (mass education to facilitate equality of opportunity), but it is essential that some such belief in the value of mass education be firmly held by governing elites. Without such a conviction authorities will not commit the resources necessary to establish a national system of elementary education nor will they make education compulsory.

3. Elementary education is not usually made compulsory until a large proportion of children are already enrolled in schools. Compulsory education is possible when the task is to enroll the last 10 percent to 20 percent of the school-age population, and when the need is largely to deal with the problem of retention. Prior to the introduction of compulsion, governments have usually put in place a national network of schools that are readily accessible to most rural children. Teachers have been trained and blackboards, books, and other supplies have been provided. However, in many low-income countries education has been made compulsory even when school buildings are poorly constructed, teachers inadequately trained, and educational materials of indifferent quality.

4. With the introduction of compulsion into the educational system (and

often earlier) has come the establishment of a register of all children in the community. In some countries a system of birth registration preceded the introduction of compulsory schooling. Birth certificates are useful for the enforcement of all age-linked legislation, such as compulsory primary-school attendance, work permits for part-time employment, minimum-age requirements for full-time employment and marriage, and social-security benefits. For an effective system of enforcement, school authorities need to create registers with the names, birth dates, addresses, and the names of guardians of all children within the community, including those who have recently migrated into the community.

5. Compulsory education may be introduced into the entire country or selectively by state and local community. It is desirable, however, to introduce compulsory education for the entire country to facilitate enforcement and so that children who migrate from one community to another will not be handicapped. Politically, too, it is difficult to justify making education compulsory in some areas (usually urban centers) and not in others. Local authorities are also readily influenced by local businessmen, who prefer to keep education voluntary so that they can continue to recruit child labor. For these reasons, the decision to make education compulsory has generally been made either by state or central governments, not by local governments. When the authority to make education compulsory has been left to local governments, as was the case in England prior to 1880, the introduction of compulsory education has been a particularly prolonged process.

6. The successful enforcement of compulsory-education laws has required that attention be given to achieving universal enrollment of all school-age children and to ensuring that children are actually in attendance. Retention, not simply enrollment, has been essential. To prevent dropouts governments appoint attendance or truant officers to go to the homes of parents and guardians whose children fail to attend school. Attendance officers may be teachers, appointees of the local school board or the local government, or members of the local police department. They prepare enumeration registers, conduct house-to-house canvasses, check attendance records at schools, and visit the homes of children who have failed to attend class for several days or weeks. These officers employ persuasion to get truants to return to school, but they must be in a position to inform parents that the failure of their children to attend school for other than medical reasons is a violation of law and is subject to penalties. They should be able to go to judicial officers (a local magistrate or an administrative board) to issue notices against parents and guardians whose children have not attended school. When education is compulsory, parents who claim that their children should not be compelled to attend school because their assistance is needed at home, in the fields, or in the labor force are not accommodated.

7. It has been the widespread practice initially to introduce compulsory

education for children ages six to ten or twelve, and only later to extend in phases the minimum age at which children are permitted to leave school. Educational planners initially make education compulsory for the lower primary school, then extend it to the upper primary school, and finally to the high school. The phased extension of compulsory education provides school authorities with the necessary lead time to expand the schools to accommodate an increase in numbers. As authorities are faced with the need to expand the high schools, attention is then given to the issue of educational screening and vocationalization.

8. The legal minimum age for full-time employment is ordinarily matched to the minimum age at which children are permitted to leave school. The school-leaving age can be raised progressively at the same rate as the minimum age for admission to employment. If the school-leaving age is lower than the age of admission to employment, children are likely illegally to seek employment, and the enforcement of child-labor laws is rendered more difficult.

9. In many countries children who complete the minimum years of compulsory schooling are permitted to enter the work force only with a work permit. Proof of age and a medical certificate may also be required but are not sufficient. There are variations among countries as to which authorities can issue work permits—school boards, labor departments, local medical authorities, or the local police. All employers, including managers and owners of small businesses, restaurants, and cottage industries, are required to ask for a work permit from all young people they employ, and a register of such work permits may be made available to inspectors from the labor department. Failure to maintain such a register or to produce a copy of the work permit (or registration number) can subject employers to penalties.

10. While there are age and schooling requirements for entering any position in the labor force, there are often higher requirements for occupations that are considered physically or psychologically demanding or hazardous. The government may also permit children to engage in part-time paid employment in nonhazardous industries even before they have completed the compulsory years of schooling. But in such instances, work permits may be required and some form of registration by employers may be made mandatory, and punishable if ignored.

11. Inadequate ventilation, poor lighting, unsafe equipment, and toxic chemicals constitute a problem for all members of the labor force, irrespective of age or gender. But young people, by virtue of their inexperience, are often subject to greater risks, and there are some tasks for which they are physically and psychologically unprepared. For this reason, governments prohibit certain kinds of employment for young people or restrict the number of hours they can work, even for those who have completed the minimum years of schooling. But in a low-income country where conditions of employment are often primitive in many enterprises, it is exceedingly difficult for inspectors to impose

special requirements where young people are employed. For enforcement reasons, therefore, it is the age and work permit requirements that are the centerpiece of an effective child-labor law, rather than special rules regarding conditions under which young people may work.

12. When education is made compulsory, schooling is provided free by the state. School authorities may also make textbooks free, provide uniforms, and deliver midday meals. Inoculations and other health benefits may be provided as well. These measures are intended to improve the health and well-being of children and, by reducing or eliminating the costs for parents, make it less likely that parents will try to remove their children from school. But these benefits are not a substitute for compulsion. Parents are obligated to send their children to school even if these benefits are not provided. Nor do governments compensate parents for the loss of income that they would otherwise have obtained had their children been allowed to work, although some advanced industrial countries do have a system of providing financial payments to enable parents and guardians to adequately provide for their children.

13. Part-time education may be available, but only for those who are beyond the minimum age of compulsory education. Part-time education permits those who attended the minimum years of schooling but failed to complete the standard years of schooling to continue their education; it enables young people to continue their education while they work; and it can provide skills and training not available in the formal education system. But to permit children below the minimum age to substitute part-time education for full-time education is to nullify compulsory-education laws.

14. Finally, once education is made compulsory, school authorities may take steps to enable and to motivate poor parents to obey the law. Social workers may help working mothers make arrangements for the care of preschool children, and factories and construction sites may provide crèches at the place of employment so that older siblings who must care for younger children can attend school. Girls may be placed in separate classes or even separate schools to accommodate the concerns of socially conservative parents. Above all, school officials must ensure that teachers are present every day, that blackboards, books, and other teaching aids are available, and that children are in fact learning reading, writing, and arithmetic. Low-quality education increases repetition and induces parents to withdraw their children from school.

There are, no doubt, exceptions to one or another of the items enumerated above, but collectively they constitute a policy for removing children from the labor force and placing them in schools. The two key elements in this policy are *linkages* and *sequences*. The policy-pieces must fit together. Minimum-age laws and minimum-schooling laws must match. Age requirements and the content of nonformal part-time schooling must be linked to the formal educational system. Work permits issued by a labor department must be granted only after certification by the school to which the young person attended. Compulsory education laws must precede the enforcement of child-labor laws. The age requirement for entrance into the labor force must be raised only after the minimum years of schooling are increased. Minimum-schooling laws must be extended in phases.

The Politics of Doing Nothing

Since few people in India believe that education should be regarded as a duty, it is not surprising that there are no significant forces arrayed in favor of compulsory education. Some Indians have suggested that factory owners and other business proprietors constitute a "vested interest" that has stood in the way of enforcing child-labor laws, making education compulsory, agrarian reforms, irrigation, and rural development projects that would make it unnecessary for parents to send their children into the labor force. Of course, businessmen everywhere have often opposed the passage and enforcement of child-labor laws. Employers want low-wage, nonunion, pliable workers, whether they be children, uneducated women, or migrants. Actually, in India the proprietors of large businesses have not opposed child-labor laws, for in the main they do not employ child labor. Indeed, one of the complaints of managers of large firms is that their labor force is not sufficiently educated, that too many workers are unable to read manuals or follow the simple instructions written on machines. The chief beneficiaries of child labor are owners and managers of small businesses who either employ children directly or depend upon the low-cost products they can obtain by subcontracting to cottage industries that employ children. Owners of small businesses have considerable influence over legislators, and they invoke the Indian opposition to large companies and multinationals, and popular sympathy for the small "family-owned" cottage industries and small-scale firms, to oppose extension of child-labor laws. Indeed, as we have noted, some government officials do not regard the employment of children in cottage industries as child labor at all, for they do not consider the employment of children by parents or other relatives as "exploitation."

The opposition of parents is also cited in India as a reason for inaction. Again, the comparative evidence is that elsewhere many parents who send their children to work are opposed to compulsory-education laws that deprive them of the income of their children. Our historical survey and review of contemporary cases in the developing world suggest that state intervention depends not upon the attitudes of employers or parents, but rather upon the support provided by other groups in society and within the state. Outside of India, trade-union leaders, social work-ers, teachers, and religious leaders have been in the forefront of the movement toward protecting children from both employers and parents. Even more important, within the state apparatus itself there were offi-cials who insisted upon making education compulsory: the military, which wanted a more educated and physically sound conscript army; the education bureaucracy, professionally committed to universal education; and state leaders who envisioned mass education as essential to the prop-agation of a national ideology and political loyalty. There was also a new set of ideas about children: the belief that childhood as a time for school-ing and playing should be extended from the children of the well-off to the children of the poor; that children had rights independent of parents, and that parents had duties toward children; that education for children was an intrinsic, not merely instrumental, good; and that a major aim of education was *apprendre apprendre*, as the French say, teaching chil-dren to learn how to learn, a notion that represented a new modern sen-sibility.

Religious Groups

Hindu religious groups have not been a force promoting mass education in India, except when they feared Christian missionaries. Hinduism, a religion with a weak theology (it is essentially a religion of mythologies), gives no importance to the mastery of religious texts by ordinary people. Myths are passed by word of mouth and transmitted by songs, dances, plays, and the recitations of priests, sanyasis, and saddhus. Only Brah-mans and those of high caste are expected to have knowledge of the Ve-das and other texts. For the lower castes, it is considered sufficient that they be familiar with myths, sing religious songs in devotional assem-blies, and recite Puranas from memory when necessary. Indeed, many orthodox high-caste Hindus regard it as sacrilegious that members of the lower castes should read sacred texts, or that girls should learn to master writing. The notion that it is unnecessary (and even undesirable) for lower castes to acquire education is not easily shaken by schools teachers, many of whom regard lower-caste children as unfit for studies. The con-cern among educated Indians that bookish learning in the schools might lead the lower castes and classes to give up menial work and seek white-collar positions is not balanced by any religious belief in the intrinsic im-portance of reading sacred books.

Education Officials and Teachers

Elsewhere in the world, members of the educational establishment—educators, officials in education departments and ministries, teachers' unions, local school boards—have pressed for making education universal and compulsory. True enough, divisions among these groups are not uncommon and on many issues of educational reform the educational establishment, especially teachers, are often opponents of change. Nonetheless, the expansion of the educational system and the introduction of compulsory education often has had its strongest advocates from within the educational establishment. In India the role of educators is quite different. In describing that role, I can do no better than quote at length the late J. P. Naik, who, in a thoughtful essay, assessed the forces for educational reform.

J. P. Naik noted that the proportion of the five-year-plan allocations for education had declined from one plan to the next, that the allocations were never enough to meet the targets for universalizing education, and that the greater part of the education budget continued to be spent on secondary and higher education. Who, he asked, will be the agents of change in education?

> The assumption of the Education Commission (1966) was that the change agents for a new system of education are mainly teachers, students and education administrators, and if the State Government gave the lead and the financial support, the necessary transformation of education would be brought about by these three groups. . . . I find that in the last 12 years this assumption has not proved correct. I am not prepared to believe that teachers can be the change agents in education. . . . If you propose an education reform, it involves more work for teachers, and I have found, to my sorrow, that opposition comes from teachers rather than from others. . . . It is a glib assumption that teachers and students can be change agents in education or that education administrators can play this role.[12]

Naik described his unsuccessful efforts to persuade state governments to develop long-term educational plans for their states but concluded they were unwilling because it would have meant making financial commitments to education that they were not prepared to make. "Besides, as precedents show, it is the weakest and politically lightest person that is usually selected as the Education Minister whether it is in the State or in the Centre. Or, even if it is a member in the Planning Commission,

[12] J. P. Naik, "Educational Development in India during the Next Twenty Years: 1981–2000," *Indian Institute of Education Bulletin* (1982), p. 18.

the case is the same more often than not. . . . I have really given up hope of the Planning Commission ever preparing a long term perspective plan."[13]

Chitra Naik, writing on the question of why primary education has not been universalized, commented on the indifference of teachers.

> The majority of these children [children from tribal and poor, rural families] evade the compulsion laws simply by enrolling in a nearby primary school, with hardly any intention to attend. The teachers usually connive at this stratagem since it is convenient for them to show large enrollments on paper and actually have a small attendance in class. This enables them to send to the "higher authorities" good reports on the spread of primary education, while their routine teaching load remains light. Such an arrangement is mutually convenient for everyone concerned, i.e. the children, parents, teachers and even education offices where the "coverage" shown by enrollment statistics matters for the preparation of progress reports. The names of a few non-attending children are struck off the attendance register every now and then, thus satisfying the given regulation by token. The inadequate communication facilities in the tribal and rural areas prevent adequate personal supervision and lead to dependence on reports which cannot be easily verified.[14]

Having myself interviewed education officials in the central government and in a number of states (Tamil Nadu, Karnataka, Kerala, Andhra, West Bengal, Uttar Pradesh, Maharashtra, and Gujarat), and spoken to principals and teachers in many schools, I can strongly endorse the assessments of J. P. Naik and Chitra Naik. What remains unclear is why the educational establishment remains so conservative even on the issue of expanding primary education. True enough, a rational-choice explanation might lead one to expect teachers to oppose an expansion in school attendance because it would increase their burden. Then too, many teachers in urban areas earn private tuitions from students, and these would not increase by a rise in the enrollment of children who are exceedingly poor. Alternatively, by pressing for compulsory education and allying themselves with journalists and politicians, the educational estab-

---

[13] Ibid, pp. 19–20. The low regard with which Indians assess their public elementary-school system is reflected in the popularity of Ivan Illich's book, *Deschooling Society* (1971). Illich's view, publicized in a lecture tour in India, is that third-world countries should reject the educational model based upon the school but should instead develop nonschooling alternatives based on the principle of free choice. Rarely taken seriously by education departments around the world, Illich found an enthusiastic audience in India and may very well have influenced government thinking on nonformal education. His views are well-regarded for they are consistent with the Indian view that their own schools are defective and that parents should be free to choose not to send their children to school.

[14] Chitra Naik, "An Action-Research Project on Universal Primary Education," *Indian Institute of Education Bulletin* 2 (1981), pp. 137–158.

lishment might significantly expand the educational budget to the benefit of teachers, principals, and bureaucrats. In many countries the educational establishment has succeeded in doing precisely that.

But more to the point, the passive and even negative role of the educational establishment in India has to be seen in the larger context of the attitudes described here. With a few praiseworthy exceptions, the teachers I met in rural and in municipal schools were unconcerned about dropouts, regarded teaching as an unrewarding job, had little concern with whether the material they taught was understood by their pupils, regarded science as a set of materials to be taught and memorized rather than a way of thinking, and cared little for the individual children in their classes. Teachers in private schools were often quite different and it is these schools, with their financially better-off and higher-caste students, that have few dropouts and whose students go on for higher studies.

The low regard teachers have for teaching is reflected in studies of attitudes of teachers toward their own profession. Studies of primary-school teachers conducted by a team of investigators under the auspices of the Tata Institute of Social Sciences in Bombay in the late 1960s revealed that a majority of teachers viewed the status of their occupation as either equal to or lower than the occupation of their fathers. The studies also reported that a majority of male teachers and many of the female teachers intended to choose another occupation than teaching, and many continued to hope that they could switch to another occupation. As the author of one field study put it, "So it may be argued from the above data that half of our teachers engaged in imparting education to small children are not whole heartedly devoted to their present profession."[15]

One of the most interesting findings from these studies is that a majority of the headmasters of the schools surveyed (66 percent in the West Bengal study) said that "the students are incapable of independent thinking." Sixty-three percent of the headmasters also believed that there was a relationship between caste and educational performance, and 59 percent of the male teachers and 37 percent of the female teachers "were of the opinion that the upper castes do better than others."[16] A similar study conducted in Maharashtra reported that 46 percent of the teachers believed that students of the upper castes do better in their studies than students of lower castes, and 43 percent of the teachers described their students as "incapable of independent thought." Of special note is that these views were largely held by higher-caste teachers, while the small

[15] Ramakrishna Mukherjee, *Field Studies in the Sociology of Education: Report on Field Investigations in West Bengal* (Bombay: Tata Institute of Social Sciences, n.d.), p. 23.

[16] Ibid., pp. 34, 26.

number of teachers belonging to scheduled castes and other low castes had a better image of their students.[17]

Both the Maharashtra and West Bengal surveys reported that teachers overwhelmingly believed that the principle goal of education was to make a person "a good citizen or a cultured one." Both studies reported that teachers and headmasters did not believe these goals were achieved.[18] In neither survey did teachers or headmasters view an improvement in the economic circumstances of children as an educational goal.

The low regard that teachers (and headmasters) have for themselves, for the teaching enterprise, for their students (especially those of the lower castes) is reflected in the low regard by officials and politicians for the education departments and ministry. Secretaries of state education departments, the highest-ranking officials, have often been transferred from other ministries and have little expertise or interest in education. They regard the posting as a low one, transitional (they hope) to posting in the more prestigious departments such as finance. Those officials who have been in the departments for many years show no great interest in dealing with the serious problems faced by elementary schools. And the education minister, as J. P. Naik noted, is usually politically the "lightest person," neither capable of nor interested in educational reform and development. It is especially noteworthy that not a single central, state, district, or municipal education official I encountered advocated compulsory education. Officials repeatedly spoke of education as a right, not as a duty, and under questioning objected to the notion that the government should compel children to attend school over the objections of parents. Over and over again officials said that parents had the right to the labor of their children and government ought not to interfere.

Trade Unionists

Though some of India's trade-union leaders speak out against child labor, unions have not played any role in pressing state governments to enforce child-labor laws. In Tamil Nadu, for example, though there was much discussion in the press of the failure of the state government to enforce child-labor laws in the match industry in Sivakasi, no trade unions were engaged in the debate. As we noted earlier, elsewhere in the world trade unions were active in the movement against child labor. Union leaders and the rank and file believed that the employment of children was in-

[17] Y. B. Damle, *Field Studies in the Sociology of Education: Report on Field Investigations in Maharashtra* (Bombay: Tata Institute of Social Sciences, 1968), pp. 68, 48.

[18] Mukherjee, *Field Studies: West Bengal*, p. 36; and Damle, *Field Studies: Maharashtra*, p. 45.

jurious to the unions (since children were not unionized) and to the workers—for child labor depressed wages and displaced adult workers. There
were moral considerations, too, as trade-union leaders expressed outrage
at the treatment of children by owners of sweatshops.

Why have unions in India largely been indifferent to child labor? One
reason is that there are virtually no unions in the cottage industries and
small shops and businesses that employ children. But even in the few
industries that have both unions and child labor (e.g., plantations), union
leaders have not pressed for the enforcement of child-labor laws. In these
industries union leaders and their members approve the practice widely
pursued by employers of giving preferences in employment to the children of existing workers. Whether it be plantation workers, agricultural
laborers, or workers in small-scale and cottage industries, it is their own
children who are hired by their employers. Workers think of their jobs
as property: one owns it, shares it with one's children, passes it on. When
officials speak of "apprenticeship" in employment, they mean that children are hired and trained to do the same work as their parents. As one
official told me, "the parent would like the child to do the same work."
This notion that children should do what their parents do is widely held
by lower-income groups in India—a realistic notion for most low-income
people given the absence of economic opportunity—and it is a notion
that is widely held by trade-union leaders as well as by government officials. Indeed, one objection to compulsory education is that a few years
of schooling are of no particular help in getting a better job than the one
held by parents. Among tea-plantation workers and trade unionists it is
assumed that children of tea pickers can only hope to become tea pickers
and that they should begin work as soon as they are able. Union leaders
believe that if the children remain out of the labor force too long, plantation managers would hire others, and that "educated" children might
not be fit for plantation work. They have, therefore, not pressed for raising the minimum age (twelve) for working on plantations.

In short, trade-union leaders, like most parents, employers, teachers,
and education officials, presume a social order guided by the principles
of social reproduction. Children can best assume the same roles as their
parents by early entrance into the labor force. Education adds little toward social reproduction; indeed, it may arouse in children and their parents unrealistic expectations of alternative occupations and social status.

Social Activists

The term "social activist" is loosely used in India to refer to the many
social workers employed by nongovernmental organizations or who vol-

untarily engage in social work among the poor. Many of the social workers are informed by a Gandhian perspective; some are radicalized by the Left; some come out of Hindu social-reform movements; some are Christians. Since the Indian government and foreign donors provide some financial support for nongovernmental organizations, in recent years these have grown in numbers. Many college students, incensed at the rampant injustices in Indian society, have become activists, participating in efforts to organize victims in Bhopal, working with tribal peoples to prevent the cutting of trees by developers, organizing self-employed women. Social activists were almost alone in their opposition to the new government policies on child labor. Their moral outrage is usually directed against employers for the exploitation of children, against bureaucrats for collusion with employers, and against the social and economic order, which has produced an abject class of poor people. But the social activists are constrained from playing a leading role in pressing for compulsory education and the enforcement of child-labor laws by a host of conflicting values. They are strong supporters of small-scale and cottage industries for the employment they provide, though this sector is a major employer of children. They are fearful that the abolition of child labor in some industries (e.g., matches) would place these industries at risk in competition with multinationals. They accept the notion that the poor have the right to employ their children, though this "right" means that the state ought not to force children to attend school over the objections of parents. And some are so hostile to the schools for their failure to adequately educate the children of the poor that they are sympathetic to parents who remove their children from school even though it means that the children remain illiterate. Many of the social activists believe that child labor can be ended only when the government improves rural employment, the cottage and household sector grows, and the schools are improved and made more useful. Some of the social activists are radicals who do not believe that child labor can be abolished, or for that matter that any significant improvement can be brought about among India's poor, without "fundamental structural changes," that is, an undefined socialist revolution. In this respect they share Marx's view that child labor is inherent in the capitalist order and will remain so as long as private property and exploitation continue. Social activists are critics of the social order but with a few exceptions they lack a workable agenda for improving the position of the children of the poor.

The Research Community

Academic researchers have produced a great deal of empirically sound scholarship on child-labor in India. There are excellent studies of child labor conditions in specific industries—bidis, matches, bangles, brass-ware, glass. These studies document the impact that child labor has had on the health and well-being of children, their prospects for future employment, and the impact of child labor on their subsequent income as compared to school attendance. There are innumerable studies of school dropouts, who they are, why they leave, what they subsequently do. The research is as good as, and often considerably better than, what was produced at the time child labor was under public scrutiny in England and the United States. The Indian research appears in scholarly journals, or is published under international auspices, and in recent years some of the findings have appeared in the public press and received public attention. But the research findings have not been utilized by those seeking to bring about legislative change. Little, if any, of the research is conducted, financed, or utilized by trade unions, teachers' unions, religious institutions, or anti-child-labor organizations, as it was in the United States and England.

In India no major groups within or outside the government are concerned with enforcing child-labor laws or making education compulsory, for no particular group is moved by theological, ideological, moral, or even self-interest considerations. The result is that officials who prepare central and state budgets merely make incremental changes in yearly educational budgets, officials in state education and labor ministries show no interest in tightening legislation, administrators are not inclined to enforce existing laws, state and local governments pay little attention to elementary education, and teachers sit by idly as children drop out of their classes.

The political, economic, social, and demographic costs of doing nothing are not visible, with the result that few Indians regard the condition of India's children as a problem warranting government action. Since the issue is not raised by opposition parties or by any significant groups in the country, government officials feel no pressure to take action. Large numbers of adults are displaced from the labor market by child labor, but the poor see only the benefits of employing their children. So long as child labor persists, families have little incentive to have fewer children. Illiterate women are less likely than literate women to reduce their fertility. The lack of access to the written word by more than 450 million Indians has immeasurable consequences for the capacity of India's population to acquire new knowledge and new skills. Peasants cannot read agricultural extension materials; many workers cannot read safety instructions; illiterate women cannot read health-care booklets. The gulf between those who read and write and those who cannot reinforces India's inegalitarian, hierarchical social order. Illiterates are dependent upon others for dealing with the bureaucracy, the police, the courts. And those upon whom they depend do not regard illiteracy as a problem.

Indeed, those who are educated can control people better if they cannot read, for illiterates do not know their legal rights and nongovernment organizations are handicapped in their efforts to make the poor aware of their rights.

How, then, does one explain references to compulsory education and child labor in the Constitution and the many laws dealing with both? Why does one government commission after another recommit the government to universal compulsory education? Government documents on education ring with phrases that would lead one to believe that Indians are ardently committed to popular education—for these reports say that education is essential for "democratic values," "self-reliant and self-confident individuals," "social development," the "human resources" necessary for development, and for "national integration."

Puzzled by the plethora of unenforced legislation involving education and other social issues, Upendra Baxi, one of India's foremost legal scholars, noted that in India "for every problem there has to be a law." India's many laws regulating adulturation, factory safety, child labor, minimum wages, and bonded labor, he says, all give India the appearance of being a well-regulated society whose state is devoted to the protection of the disabled, the poor, and the powerless. In India, says Baxi, law has a symbolic value of setting norms, but there is little concern with law as a means of inducing compliance. Legislation and the arbitrary way in which laws are enforced or not enforced should be understood as a way in which bureaucrats engage in a form of harassment and augment their power and income. Thus, factory acts and other legislation intended to regulate business are not enforced unless a businessman has incurred the displeasure of officials, in which case the law can be used as an instrument of punishment. Baxi writes that

> legalism in the sense of a moral or ethical attitude prescribing that the legal rules ought to be followed because they are rules of conduct is not a dominant characteristic of Indian behavior and culture. It is not that the Indian people, as distinct from their governors, are unable to develop a strong commitment to legalism. It is rather that both the rulers and the ruled collectively feel that most legal rules do not set any genuine moral constraints to behavior motivated by strong personal or group interests. Rather, for the most part, rules are set to provide occasion for discretionary manipulation in a complex process of social interaction which is genuinely instrumental or result-oriented. Individual or group self-interest predominates over the value of following rules because they are rules, even if justified and justifiable ones.[19]

[19] Upendra Baxi, *The Crisis of the Indian Legal System* (New Delhi: Vikas Publishing, 1982), p. 5.

Baxi's brilliant analysis helps explain what appears to be a contradictory feature of India's legal system: a high rate of litigation while laws are not enforced or are enforced in an arbitrary fashion. Litigation is part of an adversarial process intended to weaken or destroy one's enemies, and selective enforcement is a weapon used by the bureaucracy to enhance its own power. Political power is best exercised through the administration of rules rather than in the process of rule making.

But social legislation in India, which is rarely enforced by the bureaucracy, serves still another purpose. Legislation involving untouchability, child labor, compulsory education, child marriage, dowries and the like are statements of intentions, and the words used in the legislation are a kind of modern talisman intended to bring results by the magical power of the words themselves. The legislation demonstrates that one is committed to all that is modern and progressive, and if the laws are not enforced the fault lies not with the legislators or bureaucrats but with a society that is not responsive to the law's injunction. Government officials are fully aware of the international embarrassment that comes with having the world's largest population of child laborers and adult illiterates, but they ascribe the failure to achieve universal education as a result of the country's poverty rather than the government's failure.

And so the legislative rhetoric continues, unrelated to considerations of enforcement. In an amusing vein an official in the Ministry of Labour explained to me that there had been a discussion among officials on a proposal to establish a uniform miminum age for employment in all sectors of the economy, replacing the different age limits incorporated into separate laws for each of several industries. "One state government minister," she explained, "said we should raise the age limit for all employment to fourteen or fifteen. But when I said that we don't even enforce the twelve-year-old limit, the minister said, 'never matter, so we won't enforce the fourteen- or fifteen-year-old limit!' "

Why Universal Schooling Will Not Come from Rising Incomes

It has been argued that with rising incomes parents will see the long-term financial benefits of sending their children to school. Parental attitudes will change as employment and income levels rise since parents could then afford not to send their children to work. With changes in technology employers will also need a more educated, more skilled labor force and therefore will no longer employ children. In time, even agriculture will need better-educated farmers and agricultural workers who can operate machines, use fertilizers and pesticides, and make the financial decisions required with commercialization.

There is evidence that individual demand for schooling is partially shaped by the character of the labor market. The emphasis is on the word "partially," for as we have seen religious motivations have led people to seek education irrespective of labor-market considerations. Moreover, governments, by requiring children to attend school, have thereby shaped the character of the labor market. It is useful to ask whether economic changes are taking place in India that will in time lead children to leave the labor force and enter school even if the government continues its policy of permitting children of any age to work rather than attend school.

There is little direct evidence to help us answer this question. Per capita incomes in India have been rising and school enrollments are going up as well. In 1981 the high-growth state of Punjab had a higher proportion of children in the five-to-fourteen age group in school than most other states, possibly the result of the increased prosperity and changing labor market associated with the green revolution. The census reported a literacy increase in the Punjab from 33.7 percent to 40.9 percent between 1971 and 1981, an increase commensurate with the all-India rise from 29.5 percent to 36.2 percent. The employment rate in the Punjab for males under fourteen dropped during the decade from 7.7 percent to 5.3 percent, and for females it increased from 0.12 percent to 0.25 percent. The all-India figures reported a decrease for males from 6.6 percent to 5.5 percent and a slight rise for females from 2.6 percent to 3 percent. If one takes these low numbers of child workers at face value, or at least the changes at face value, then the decrease in the Punjab is significant. However, it should be noted that between 1971 and 1981 the number of young people under fourteen rose by 17.7 percent, so that in absolute terms the decline in child labor in the Punjab was modest, the reported rise in school enrollments notwithstanding.

Many of the technological and labor-market changes that might lead to a decline in the employment of children are taking place very slowly in India, if at all. Employment in the nonformal sector is increasing more rapidly than in the modern, factory sector, and it is the former, not the latter, that employs children. Various government programs intended to provide income-generating schemes for the household, such as the provision of cattle to poor families, seem likely to increase the need of the family for labor. Indeed, government policies intended to promote cottage industries, hand-loom production, and small agro-industrial businesses could increase the demand for household labor, including children. It should also be noted that the 1986 Child Labour (Prohibition and Regulation) Act, even if it is enforced, will not reduce child labor since firms affected by the act can subcontract the processes enumerated in the act (regarded as hazardous) to so-called "family-owned" cottage industries, which are exempt from all regulations.

The annual increase in the number of schools built and the various programs to reduce school dropouts might conceivably make a difference in child labor, but demographic factors reduce the impact of such efforts. The number of children under fourteen increased by almost 40 million between 1971 and 1981, and the number is likely to increase by roughly the same magnitude between 1981 and 1991. Without a major increase in the amount of resources allocated for elementary schools, which no government has been prepared to make, a large proportion of the expansion in education will simply cover the increase in the number of school-age children. Considerable educational resources are also being utilized for expanding nonformal part-time education, a wholly voluntary system intended to enable children to remain in the full-time labor force. (Government targets are to add as many children each year to the nonformal schools as to the formal education system.)

One is left then with the pessimistic conclusion that barring a conceptual change in the thinking of those who make and implement policy, and a new direction in policy by the Indian government, the number of children in the labor force will not significantly decline, conditions for working children will not significantly improve, school retention rates will not significantly increase, and literacy rates will continue to grow at a slow pace and will leave a large part of the Indian population illiterate well into the middle of the twenty-first century. With illiteracy and child labor declining world wide at a faster rate than in India, India's global share of illiterates and child laborers will continue to increase.

Index

Tamil Nadu Institute of Labour Studies (Madras), 45
Tara, S. Nayana, 73
Tata Institute of Social Sciences, 199
tea plantations, 47, 50–53; Assam, 51; West Bengal, 51
teacher training, 67
Textile Labour Association (Ahmedabad), 58
Thornton, W. T., 122, 124
Tyabji, Nasir, 50–51

UNESCO, 87, 158n
UNICEF, 87, 90
United Nations Commission on Human Rights, 87
United States, 140–48; child labor in, 142–43, 145–48; common school movement in, 143–44; compulsory education in, 141–45
Uttar Pradesh, 73–74

vocational training, 105–6, 116
Voltaire, 115

William II of Prussia, 118
WIMCO, 26, 50
work permits: in Austria, 135; in New York City, 147
working conditions, 23–27, 77–78, 82–83; in carpet industry, 49, 53–54; in cottage industries, 49; in glass factories, 27–28; in match industry, 43; in pottery industry, 29
Working Group on Universalisation of Elementary Education (1977), report of, 99–100
World Health Organization, 87, 90

Zakir Hussain Committee Report, 61. *See also* Basic Education
Zelizer, Viviana, 110n

DATE DUE